KEVIN BROOKS

The Road of the Dead

Cornelsen

Kevin Brooks **The Road of the Dead**

Herausgegeben von: Inkeri Schumann
Verlagsredaktion: Neil Porter
Umschlaggestaltung: Cornelsen Schulverlage Design
Umschlagfoto: © Fotolia/ Vitaly Krivosheev
Layout und technische Umsetzung: Buchgestaltung + Berlin

www.cornelsen.de

1. Auflage, 2. Druck 2017

Alle Drucke dieser Auflage sind inhaltlich unverändert und können im Unterricht nebeneinander verwendet werden.

Druck: H. Heenemann, Berlin

ISBN 978-306-033861-0

PEFC/04-31-1156

PEFC zertifiziert
Dieses Produkt stammt aus nachhaltig bewirtschafteten Wäldern und kontrollierten Quellen.

www.pefc.de

Contents

For Ted Watson – still living in me!

Abbreviations and Annotations

adj	adjective	fml	formal
adv	adverb	infml	informal
BE	British English	n	noun
ca.	circa; about	sb.	somebody
derog	derogatory	sl	slang
e.g.	exempli gratia; for example	sth.	something
esp.	especially	usu.	usually
etc.	et cetera; and so on	v	verb

The annotations are arranged chronologically; the first time a word is used is where you will find it explained.

From Post Bridge starts the Lych Way, the Road of the Dead, along which corpses were conveyed to Lydford, the parish church, until, in 1260, Bishop Bronescombe gave licence to the inhabitants of Dartmoor, who lived nearer to Widdecombe than Lydford, to resort thither for baptisms and funerals.

A Book of Dartmoor, *S. Baring-Gould*

Fearsome almost beyond belief must have been that journey over the desolate and sinister land, with the sphinx-like grey rocks ranged like perpetual mourners beside the trail ... no sound save the raven's croak or the stumbling steps of the mourners 'as silent and slow they followed the dead', and before them mile after toilsome mile of rock and mire and flood ... This must often have necessitated setting forth by the light of a flying winter moon, or the even more eerie and less effectual beams of storm-lanterns flashing like will-o'-the-wisps along the way.

Devonshire, *D. St. Leger-Gordon*

The crack of doom is coming soon.
Let it come,
It doesn't matter.

Serbian Gypsy song

One

When the Dead Man got Rachel I was sitting in the back of a wrecked[1] Mercedes wondering if the rain was going to stop. I didn't *want* it to stop. I was just wondering.

It was late, almost midnight.

My brother, Cole, had brought the Mercedes into the yard[2] a few hours earlier and asked me to look it over while he went off to see someone about something. I'd spent an hour or so checking it out, seeing if it was worth stripping down[3], and then the rain had started – and that's when I'd got in the back.

I could have gone somewhere else, I suppose. I could have taken shelter in one of the old storage sheds[4], or I could have gone back to the house, but the sheds were dark and full of rats, and the rain was really pouring down, and the house was all the way across the other side of the yard ...

And and and.

I liked the rain.

I didn't want it to stop.

I liked the sound of it hammering down hard on the roof of the car. It made me feel safe and dry. I liked being alone in the yard at night. It made me feel happy. I liked the way the lights over the gates shone crystal-white in the dark, making everything look special. I liked seeing the raindrops as threaded jewels[5], the heaps of scrap metal[6] as mountains and hills, the tottering[7] piles[8] of broken-up cars as watchtowers.

I was happy with that.

1 wrecked: (here) so damaged that it cannot be driven **2** yard: area outside a building **3** strip sth. down: take away all valuable parts of sth. **4** storage shed: *Lagerschuppen* **5** threaded jewels: string of jewels **6** heaps of scrap metal: *Haufen Metallschrott* **7** tottering: unstable **8** pile: things stacked one on top of another

Then a gust of wind[1] caught the sign over the gates, and as it creaked on its rusty chains and I looked out through the shattered back windscreen[2] and read the familiar faded[3] words – ***Ford & Sons – Auto Spares***[4]*: Crashed Cars, Vans & HGVs*[5]*, MOT*[6] *Failures, Insurance Write-Offs*[7]*, Bought for Cash* – that's when I first felt Rachel in my heart.

I don't know how to describe these feelings I get. Cole once asked me what it was like to know everything there is to know, and not know anything about it. I told him that I didn't know. And that was the truth.

I *don't* know.

These feelings I get – the feelings that I'm *with* other people – I have no idea what they are, or where they come from, or why I get them. I don't even know if they're real or not. But I've long since stopped worrying about it. I get them, and that's all there is to it.

I don't get them all the time, and I don't get them from everybody. In fact, I very rarely get them from anyone outside my family. Mostly I get them from Cole. Sometimes I get them from Mum, and very occasionally from Dad, but the feelings are strongest when they come from my brother.

With my sister, though, it had always been different. Until that night, I'd never felt anything from Rachel. Nothing at all. Not even a flutter[8]. I don't know why. Perhaps it was because we'd always talked a lot anyway, so we'd never *needed* anything else. Or maybe it was just because she was my sister. I don't know. I'd just never got any feelings from her before, and that's why it was so strange to suddenly feel her that night – so strange and weird ...

So terrifying.

1 gust of wind: sudden heavy wind **2** shattered back windscreen: *zersplitterte Heckscheibe* **3** fade: become paler or less bright **4** spare: part of a car that can be used to replace a broken piece **5** HGV = heavy goods vehicle: lorry, truck **6** MOT: *TÜV* **7** Insurance Write-Offs: vehicles that are too damaged to be worth repairing **8** flutter: (here) tiny bit

One moment she was with me – sitting in the back of the Mercedes, looking around the yard – and then the moment suddenly cracked and I was with her, walking a storm-ravaged lane[1] in the middle of a desolate moor. We were cold and wet and tired and scared, and the world was black and empty, and I didn't know why.

I didn't know anything.

'What are you doing here, Rach?' I asked her. 'I thought you were coming home tonight.'

She didn't answer. She couldn't hear me. She was hundreds of miles away. She couldn't feel me. All she could feel was the cold and the rain and the wind and the darkness ...

And then suddenly she was feeling something else. A race of blood in her heart. A paralysing fear in her bones. A presence. There was something there ... something that shouldn't be there.

I felt it at the same time as her, and we were both too late.

The Dead Man came out of the dark and took her down, and everything went black for ever.

I don't know what happened after that. I stopped feeling. I passed out.

Some time later I awoke to the pain of a jagged knife[2] ripping open my heart, and I knew without doubt that Rachel was dead. Her last breath had just left her. I could see it stealing away on the wind. I watched it floating over a ring of stones and through the branches of a stunted thorn tree[3], and then the storm came down with a purple-black light that rolled the sky to the ground, and that was the last thing I saw.

1 storm-ravaged lane: small path destroyed by a storm **2** jagged knife: sharp knife with uneven edges **3** stunted thorn tree: *verkümmerter Dornenbaum*

Two

Three days later I was sitting in an air-conditioned office with Mum and Cole and a grey-faced man in a dark-blue suit. The office was on the top floor of Bow Green police station, and the man in the dark-blue suit was our Family Liaison Officer[1] – Detective Constable Robert Merton.

It was nine o'clock Friday morning.

This wasn't the first time we'd met DC Merton. On Wednesday morning, after the police had informed us of Rachel's death, he'd stayed at our house for a while and spent some time talking to Mum. Then, on Thursday, he'd come round again, and this time he'd talked to all of us. He'd told us what had happened to Rachel, and what was going to happen, and what might happen. He'd asked us questions. Told us how sorry he was. Tried to comfort us. Tried to help. He'd given us leaflets and brochures, talked to us about bereavement counselling[2] and victim support and hundreds of other things that none of us wanted to hear.

Talk talk talk.

That's all it was.

Just talk.

It didn't mean anything. It was just DC Merton doing his job. We knew that. But we also knew that his job didn't belong in our house, and neither did he. He was a policeman. He wore a suit. He talked too much. We didn't want any of that in our house. So when he'd phoned us on Thursday night to arrange another meeting, Mum had told him that this time we'd come to him.

'There's no need for that, Mary,' he'd said.

'We'll be there at nine,' Mum had told him.

1 Family Liaison Officer: police officer trained to assist families who have lost relatives due to crime **2** bereavement counselling: *Trauerberatung*

And now here we were, sitting at his cramped[1] little desk, waiting to see what else he had to say.

He looked tired. His shoulders were hunched[2] and his eyes were heavy, and I got the impression that he'd rather be somewhere else. As he removed a cardboard file[3] from a drawer and placed it on the desk, I could see him struggling to find the right face.

'So, Mary,' he said eventually, smiling sombrely[4] at Mum, 'how have you been coping?'

Mum just stared at him. 'My daughter's dead. How do you think I've been coping?'

'I'm sorry, I didn't mean ...' His smile tightened with embarrassment. 'I just meant with the media attention and everything.' He narrowed his eyes. 'I hear there was a spot of trouble yesterday.'

Mum shook her head.

'No?' Merton glanced at Cole, then turned back to Mum. 'A TV reporter claims he was assaulted[5].'

'He came into the yard.' Mum shrugged. 'Cole kicked him out.'

'I see.' Merton looked at Cole again. 'It's probably best to leave that kind of thing to us. I know you don't want people nosing around, but the media can be very useful at times. It's best not to alienate[6] them.'

Cole said nothing, just stared impassively at the floor.

Merton carried on looking at him. 'If anything becomes too intrusive[7], all you have to do is let me know.' He smiled. 'I can't promise miracles –'

'Just tell them to keep away from us,' Cole said quietly. 'If anyone else comes into the yard I'll kick the shit[8] out of them.'

Merton's smile faded. 'Look, I'll do my best to protect your family's privacy, Cole, but I'd strongly advise you not to take any further action –'

'Yeah, right.'

1 cramped: not having enough space **2** hunched: *hochgezogen* **3** cardboard file: *Aktenhefter* **4** sombre: grave, serious **5** assault sb.: attack sb. **6** alienate sb.: make sb. dislike or not support you **7** intrusive: affecting sb. in a way that makes him or her feel uncomfortable **8** kick the shit out of sb. (sl): beat sb. really badly

'I'm serious –'

'So am I.'

Merton looked at him, his face all flustered[1]. Cole stared back. Merton opened his mouth and started to say something, but when he saw the look in Cole's eyes he suddenly changed his mind.

I didn't blame him.

Since Rachel's death, Cole had sunk so far inside himself that it was hard to tell if he felt anything at all. There was just nothing there. No sadness, no grief, no hate, no anger. It was frightening.

'I'm worried about him,' Mum had said to me earlier that morning. 'Have you seen his eyes? They've got something missing. That's how your father used to look just before a fight, like he didn't care if he lived or died.'

I knew she was right. Merton knew it, too. That's why he was pretending to study the file on his desk – he was trying to forget the look in Cole's eyes. He wasn't having much luck, though. It's not the kind of look you can forget in a hurry.

'Yes, well,' he said after a while, looking up at Mum. 'It was very good of you to come all this way to see me, Mary, but you really shouldn't have put yourselves out. As I told you before, I'm perfectly happy to visit you at home whenever you want. That's what I'm here for. Any time you need anything, day or night –'

'We're fine,' Mum told him. 'We'd rather be left on our own, thank you.'

'Of course,' Merton smiled. 'But if you change your mind –'

'We won't.'

Merton looked at Mum for a moment, then nodded his head and continued. 'Right, well, I think I told you on the phone that your brother-in-law has now formally identified Rachel's body.' He paused for a moment, pretending to think about it. 'He drove down to Plymouth yesterday, I believe?'

'Wednesday,' Mum said.

'I'm sorry?'

1 flustered: upset

'Joe went down there on Wednesday night. He got back yesterday morning.'

'Have you spoken to him?'

Mum just nodded again.

Merton looked at her, waiting for her to say something else. When she didn't, he turned his attention to the file on his desk and started shuffling through pieces of paper. 'Yes, well,' he said, 'I just thought we'd go over one or two things again, if that's all right with you.' He looked up. 'I know it's difficult, but it's vital in these early stages to gather as much information as possible. We also think it's best to keep you informed about how the investigation[1] is proceeding.' He glanced at me. 'If Ruben here doesn't want to stay, I'm sure we can –'

'I'm all right,' I told him.

He gave me a patronising[2] smile. I stared back at him. He turned back to Mum with a questioning look, as if to say – what do *you* think?

'Ruben knows what happened,' she told him. 'He's already heard the worst of it. If there's anything else to know, he needs to know it as much as anyone else. He's fourteen. He's not a child.'

'Of course,' said Merton, lowering his eyes to the file. I could tell he wasn't happy, but there wasn't much he could do about it. He removed some papers from the file, studied them for a moment, then put on a pair of reading glasses and started going over the whole thing again.

We'd already heard it about a dozen times. The same questions, the same answers:

Yes, Rachel was nineteen years old.

Yes, she was unemployed.

Yes, she lived with her family at Ford & Sons Auto Spares, Canleigh Street, London E3.

No, she didn't have any enemies.

1 investigation: police examination **2** patronising: *gönnerhaft*

Yes, she was single.

No, she didn't have a boyfriend.

And then the same simple facts:

On Friday, 14 May, Rachel had taken a train to Plymouth to visit an old school friend called Abbie Gorman. Abbie lives with her husband in the small village of Lychcombe on Dartmoor. On the night of Tuesday, 18 May, Rachel set out from Lychcombe on her way back to London. She never arrived. Her body was found the following morning in a remote[1] moorland field about a mile from the village. She'd been raped[2] and battered[3] and strangled[4].

Simple.

Facts.

I glanced[5] at Mum. She wasn't crying – she'd done all her crying – but her face looked a thousand years old. She was exhausted. She hadn't slept in three days. Her skin was dry and pale. Her soft black hair had lost its shine. Her eyes were haunted[6] and still.

I took her hand.

Cole looked at me. His dark eyes were almost black. I didn't know what he was thinking.

Merton said, 'So far, the investigation is going as well as can be expected, but there's still a lot of work to be done. Forensics[7] are still very confident of finding something, and the investigation team are still working their way through dozens of witness[8] statements. We're doing everything possible to find out what happened to Rachel. But we have to follow procedures[9], and I'm afraid these things take time.'

'How much time?' Mum asked.

1 remote: isolated **2** rape sb.: force sb. to have sex against his/her will **3** batter sb.: beat sb. heavily and repeatedly **4** strangle sb.: squeeze sb.'s neck and cause death **5** glance at sb./sth.: take a brief look **6** haunted: (here) show much pain **7** forensics: *Gerichtsmedizin* **8** witness: person who saw a crime or knows sth. about it **9** procedure: official way of doing sth.

Merton pursed his lips[1]. 'That's difficult to say ...'

'Where is she now?'

'I'm sorry?'

'Rachel – where is she?'

Merton hesitated[2]. 'Her body ... your daughter's body is in the care of the Coroner's[3] Office in Plymouth.'

'She's in an *office?*'

'No, no ...' Merton shook his head. 'She'll be in a mortuary[4]. The Coroner's Office deals with the inquest[5] and the post-mortem[6] –'

'When can we get her back?'

'I'm sorry?'

Mum leaned forward in her chair. 'I want my daughter back, Mr Merton. She's been dead three days. I want to bring her back home and bury her. She shouldn't have to be on her own in a place she doesn't know. She's been through enough already. She doesn't deserve any more.'

Merton didn't know what to say for a moment. He looked at Mum, glanced at Cole, then turned back to Mum again. 'I understand your concerns, Mary, but I'm afraid it's not as simple as that.'

'Why not?'

'Well, there are all kinds of practical matters to consider.'

'Like what?'

'Forensic tests, for a start. Some of them are highly complex and time-consuming. I realise it's a distressing thing to think about, but we can learn a lot from Rachel's body. It can tell us a lot about what happened. And once we know what happened, we've got a far better chance of finding out who did it.'

The Dead Man did it, I thought. It was the Dead Man. You're never going to find him now.

1 purse your lips: *die Lippen spitzen* **2** hesitate: pause before saying sth.
3 coroner: *Untersuchungsrichter/in* **4** mortuary: room in which dead bodies are kept until they are buried **5** inquest: official investigation to find out the cause of sb.'s death **6** post-mortem: *Obduktion*

'To put it simply,' Merton continued, 'the Coroner will only release[1] your daughter's body when he's satisfied that it's no longer required[2] for examination. Unfortunately, this can take some time, especially if no one's been charged[3] with her murder. Once someone has been charged, their solicitors[4] are entitled to arrange a second and independent post-mortem. Once this has been done, the Coroner will usually release the body. However, if no one's been charged, but the police expect to charge someone in the foreseeable future, then the Coroner will retain the body in the expectation that a second post-mortem will be required.' Merton looked at Mum again. 'I'm sorry it's all so complicated, but I'm afraid it might be three or four months before your daughter's body can be released.'

'What if they find the killer?' asked Cole. 'How long will it take then?'

Merton looked at him. 'Again, it's hard to say ... but, yes, the sooner we find out who did it, the sooner we can release Rachel's body.'

Cole said nothing, just nodded.

Merton looked down at his papers for a while, then he took off his reading glasses and rubbed his eyes. 'I know this is a terrible time for all of you,' he said, 'but I can assure you that we'll do everything possible to help you cope with your loss.' He paused for a moment, then went on. 'If you have any problems in terms of your beliefs ...'

'Our what?' said Mum.

'Beliefs ... customs[5]...'

'What are you talking about?'

Merton looked down at his papers again. 'Your husband,' he said hesitantly, squinting[6] at the pages. 'Barry John ...?'

'Baby-John,' Mum corrected him. 'What about him?'

1 release sb/sth.: set sb./sth. free **2** require sth.: need sth. **3** charge sb. with sth.: officially accuse sb. of sth. (esp. a crime) **4** solicitor: *Rechtsanwalt/anwältin* **5** customs: traditions **6** squint: (here) look briefly

'He's a Traveller[1], I believe.' Merton looked embarrassed. 'Is that right – Traveller? Or is it Roma ... Romany?' He smiled awkwardly[2]. 'I'm sorry, I don't know what you people prefer –'

'He's a gypsy,' Mum said simply. 'What's that got to do with anything?'

'Well, I just thought ... I mean, I'm aware that certain cultures have certain beliefs regarding funeral[3] arrangements ...' His voice trailed off and he looked at Mum, hoping she'd help him out. But he was wasting his time. She just stared at him. He shrugged[4] uncomfortably. 'I'm sorry, I don't mean to cause any offence or anything. I'm just trying to understand why you want to bury your daughter so quickly.'

Mum stared at him. 'My husband's a gypsy – I'm not. He's in prison, as I'm sure you're aware – I'm not. I want to bury my daughter because she's dead, that's all. She's my daughter. She's dead. I want to bring her back home and put her to rest. Is that so hard to understand?'

'No, of course ... I'm sorry –'

'And if you're *that* concerned about my husband,' she added, 'why don't you let him out on compassionate leave[5]?'

'I'm afraid that's in the hands of the prison authorities. If they think he poses a risk –'

'John's no risk.'

Merton raised his eyebrows. 'He's serving a sentence for manslaughter[6], Mary.'

Cole suddenly stood up. 'Come on, Mum, let's go. We don't have to listen to this shit. I told you it was a waste of time.'

Merton couldn't help glaring[7] at him. 'We're doing our best, Cole. We're trying to find out who killed your sister.'

1 Traveller: *Roma* **2** awkward: (here) embarrassed **3** funeral: ceremony in which a dead person is buried **4** shrug: raise your shoulders slightly
5 compassionate leave: time when a prisoner is allowed out of prison for a family matter (esp. for a funeral) **6** serving a sentence for manslaughter: *Haftstrafe wegen Totschlag absitzen* **7** glare at sb./sth.: stare at sb./sth. in an angry way

Cole looked down at him and spoke quietly. 'You just don't get it, do you? We don't *care* who killed her. She's dead. It doesn't matter who did it or why they did it or how she died – she's dead. Dead is dead. Nothing can change that. Nothing. All we want to do is bury her. That's all we *can* do – bring her home and get on with our lives.'

Cole didn't say anything on the way back, and Mum was too tired and empty to talk. So, as we walked the familiar backstreets through the hazy[1] May sunshine, I just soaked up[2] the silence and let my mind wander around the things I knew and the things I didn't.

I knew the Dead Man had killed Rachel.

I didn't know who he was, or why he'd done it. But I knew he was dead.

I didn't know why he was dead.

And I didn't know what it meant.

I hadn't told any of this to Cole or Mum yet, and I didn't know when – or if – I was going to.

I didn't know what that meant, either.

But the biggest thing I didn't know was how I felt about Rachel. After that night in the back of the Mercedes, when all I'd felt was blackness and nothing, my head and heart had been invaded with all the feelings in the world, some of which I'd never felt before. I was sick and empty and full of lies. I wanted to hate someone, but I didn't know who. I was nowhere and everywhere. I was lost.

When we got home, Cole went straight up to his room without saying a word. I followed Mum into the kitchen and made us some tea, then we sat down together at the table and listened to the muffled[3] sounds coming from Cole's room. Measured footsteps, drawers opening, drawers closing ...

'He's going to Dartmoor, isn't he?' I said to Mum.

'Probably.'

'Do you think that's a good idea?'

1 hazy: *diesig* **2** soak sth. up: (here) enjoy **3** muffled: quiet

'I don't know, love. I'm not sure it matters what I think. You know what he's like when he sets his mind on something.'

'What do you think he's planning to do?'

'Find out who did it, I expect.' She looked at me. 'He wants to find out who killed Rachel so we can bring her back home.'

'Are you sure that's all he wants?'

'No.'

I looked around the kitchen. It's always been my favourite room. It's big and old and warm, and there are lots of things to look at. Old photographs and postcards, pictures we'd drawn when we were kids, china ducks[1], flowery plates, vases and jugs, trailing plants[2] in a large bay window[3] ...

I watched the sunlight streaming in.

I wished it wasn't.

'Do you want me to go with him?' I said to Mum.

'He won't want you to.'

'I know.'

She smiled at me. 'I'd feel better if you did.'

'What about you?' I asked her. 'Will you be all right here on your own?'

She nodded. 'Business is pretty quiet just now. Uncle Joe won't mind staying over for a couple of days to keep things ticking over.'

'I didn't mean the business.'

'I know.' She touched my arm. 'I'll be all right. It'll probably do me good to be on my own for a while.'

'Are you sure?'

She nodded again. 'Just keep in touch – OK? And keep your eye on Cole. Try not to let him do anything stupid.' She looked at me. 'He listens to you, Ruben. He trusts you. I know he doesn't show it, but he does.'

'I'll look after him.'

1 china duck: porcelain duck used for decoration **2** trailing plant: *Kletterpflanze* **3** bay window: *Erkerfenster*

'And see if you can get him to agree to you going. It'll make things a whole lot easier for both of you.'

I knew he wouldn't agree, but I gave it a shot[1] anyway.

When I went into his room he was sitting on his bed smoking a cigarette. He was dressed in a T-shirt and jeans, and his jacket was draped over a small leather rucksack on the floor.

'Hey,' I said.

He nodded at me.

I glanced at his rucksack. 'Going somewhere?'

'The answer's no,' he said.

'No what?'

'No, you can't come with me.'

I went over and sat down beside him. He tapped ash from his cigarette into an ashtray on the bedside table. I smiled at him.

'It's no good looking at me like that,' he said. 'I'm not going to change my mind.'

'I haven't even asked you anything yet.'

'D'you think you're the only one who can read people's minds?'

'You can't read minds,' I said. 'You can't even read a newspaper.'

He glanced at me, then went back to smoking his cigarette. I looked at his face. I like looking at his face. It's a good face to look at – seventeen years old, dark-eyed and steady and pure. It's the kind of face that does what it says. The face of a devil's angel.

'You need me,' I told him.

'What?'

'If you're going to Dartmoor, you need me to look after you.'

'Mum's the one who needs looking after.'

'So why are you going, then?'

'I'm going to get Rachel back. That's my way of looking after Mum. Your way is staying here.' He looked at me. 'I can't talk to her, Rube. I don't know what to say. I just need to *do* something.'

1 give sth. a shot (infml): try sth.

A flicker of emotion showed briefly in his face, and just for a moment I started to feel something, but before I could tell what it was he'd regained control of himself and blanked it out[1]. He was good at blanking things out. I watched him as he put out his cigarette and got up from the bed.

'How are you going to do it?' I said.

'Do what?'

'Find out what happened.'

'I don't know yet ... I'll think of something.'

'Where are you going to stay?'

He shrugged. 'I'll find somewhere.'

'How are you going to get there?'

'Train.'

'When are you going?'

'Whenever I'm ready. Any more questions?'

'Yeah – why don't you want me to come with you?'

'I've already told you –'

'I'm not stupid, Cole. I know when you're lying. You know as well as I do that Mum doesn't need anyone to stay with her. What's the *real* reason you don't want me to come?'

He went over to a table by the window, grabbed a couple of things, and shoved them into his rucksack. He fiddled around with the bag for a while – tying it, untying it, tying it again – then he stared at the floor, and then finally he turned round and looked at me. I don't know if he was going to say anything or not, but before he had a chance to speak, the phone rang downstairs.

We both turned to the door and listened hard. The ringing stopped and we heard the faint murmur of Mum's voice.

'Is that Dad she's talking to?' asked Cole.

'Sounds like it.'

'I need to speak to him before I go.'

He picked up his rucksack and headed out of the room.

'See you later,' I said.

1 blank sth. out: (here) suppress sth. (here: his emotion)

'Yeah.'

He walked out without looking back.

I wasn't worried. I knew what he was going to do.

While Cole was speaking to Dad on the phone, I checked out a few things on the Internet and quickly packed some clothes into a bag. Then I stood by the bedroom window and waited.

After a while, Cole came out of the house and headed across the yard towards a pile of old cars. He was wearing his jacket and carrying his rucksack. He took a key out of his pocket and opened up the boot[1] of a burned-out Volvo that was stacked at the bottom of the pile. After a quick look over his shoulder, he stooped down[2] and rummaged[3] around in the furthest corner of the boot. It didn't take him long to find what he was looking for. He put something in his bag, something else in his pocket, then he straightened up and shut the boot and walked out of the yard and away down the street.

I waited until he was out of sight, then I picked up my bag and went downstairs into the kitchen. Mum was waiting for me.

'Here,' she said, passing me about £200 from her purse. 'That's all the cash I've got at the moment. Is that going to be enough?'

'Cole's got plenty,' I told her.

'Good. Do you know what train he's catching?'

'He didn't say, but the next one to Plymouth leaves at eleven thirty-five, so I'm guessing he'll be on that.' I folded the cash into my pocket. 'How's Dad?'

'He's OK. He sends his love.' She looked at the clock. It was ten forty-five. She came over and gave me a hug[4]. 'You'd better get going.'

'Are you sure you're going to be all right?'

She ruffled my hair. 'Don't worry about me. Just try to keep Cole out of too much trouble. And make sure you both come back in one piece – OK?'

1 boot: *Kofferraum* **2** stoop down: bend forward **3** rummage: search about
4 give sb. a hug: squeeze sb. in your arms to show affection

'I'll do my best.'

The sun was still shining as I left the yard and headed down the street. I wondered what the weather would be like on Dartmoor. I wondered what *anything* would be like on Dartmoor.

A black cab was dropping someone off at the end of the road. I waited for the passenger to get out, then I got in the back and asked the driver to take me to Paddington station.

Three

The traffic around Paddington was all snarled up[1], and by the time I'd got out of the taxi and bought a ticket and scurried[2] around the concourse[3] trying to find the right platform, it was almost eleven thirty-five. I got on the train just as the guard was shutting all the doors. It was fairly busy, but not overcrowded. I waited while all the other passengers were sorting themselves out – looking for seats, stowing their luggage, aimlessly wandering around – and then, as the train pulled away from the platform, I started looking for Cole.

It was a long train and, as I made my way slowly through the carriages, I found myself thinking about Dad.

He'd told me once that the first thing he could remember was standing by a water trough watching a horse drink. That was it. That was his very first memory – standing on his own in a field of long grass, watching a horse take a drink from a trough. I've always liked that. I've always thought it must be a really nice thing to have in your head.

Dad used to love telling us stories about his childhood. I think it brought back good memories for him. He was born and raised in an aluminium caravan – or trailer, as he always called it – which he shared with his parents and two older brothers. 'It was the finest trailer on the site,' he'd tell us proudly. 'Fancy little mudguards[4] a three-ply[5] stable door, a chrome chimney with a cowl[6] on top ...' He'd start smiling then, remembering more details – the paraffin lamp fixed to the ceiling, the painted queen stove[7], the solid oak dining table, his mother's crystal ornaments ...

1 snarled up: jammed **2** scurry: rush, run quickly **3** concourse: large hall in a station or airport that people pass through **4** mudguard: *Kotflügel* **5** three-ply: made of three layers **6** cowl: *Schornsteinhaube* **7** queen stove: old-fashioned cooker

Sometimes he'd remember things that didn't make him smile, like the night a group of locals had set fire to the trailer while they were sleeping, or how his father would sometimes get drunk and beat him with a thick leather belt studded with rings. I often wondered if that was why Dad had become a bare-knuckle fighter[1] – to somehow get back at his father, or the locals, or anyone else who'd caused him pain when he was a kid. But I knew I was probably wrong. It was a lot simpler than that. As Dad always said: gypsy men are born to fight; it's in their blood.

I eventually found Cole in the very last carriage of the train. He was sitting alone at a table seat, staring blankly through the window. He didn't look at me as I moved along the carriage towards him, but I knew he was aware of my presence. I could feel him watching me inside his head. He carried on pretending to ignore me until I'd walked the length of the carriage and stopped right next to him, and even then he didn't say anything, he just turned his head and gave me a long slow look.

'All right?' I smiled.

He didn't say anything.

I nodded at the empty seat opposite him. 'Is anyone sitting there?'

His face remained blank, his eyes sullen[2] and hard, and I knew what he was feeling. He was feeling the same as he used to feel when we were little kids and I used to follow him around all over the place – forever getting in his way, getting on his nerves, never leaving him alone. He didn't want me hanging around then because most of the time he was up to no good and he didn't want me getting involved. He could never bring himself to say it, but he cared for me, and he was scared to death of seeing me hurt.

Now, as I sat down opposite him, I knew he was feeling exactly the same. He didn't want me with him because he knew he was heading for trouble, and the only thing that worried him about it was me.

1 bare-knuckle fighter: boxer who fights without gloves **2** sullen: bad-tempered

'Shit,' he said eventually.

I smiled at him again.

He shook his head and looked out of the window.

I shrugged and gazed around the carriage. It was about half full. The other passengers were all fairly quiet – reading books and magazines, talking in low voices, staring silently through the windows. I wondered where they were going, and what they were going to do when they got there ... and I wondered if they were wondering the same about me.

'We should be at Reading soon,' Cole said to me. 'You can get off there.'

'I'm not getting off.'

He looked at me. 'I'm not asking you, Rube, I'm telling you. You're getting off at Reading.'

'Yeah? And what are you going to do if I don't? Pick me up and carry me off? Throw me onto the platform?'

'If I have to.'

'I'll start screaming if you do. Everyone'll think you're abducting[1] me. The guards'll stop the train and call the police and you'll get arrested.' I smiled at him. 'You don't want that, do you?'

He breathed in heavily and sighed. 'Does Mum know you're here?'

'Of course she does. I wouldn't just leave her without saying anything, would I?'

'Did she tell you to follow me?'

'No.'

'But she didn't try to stop you.'

'She's worried about you. She knows what you're like.'

'Yeah? And what am I like?'

'You remind her of Dad.'

'What's that supposed to mean?'

'You *know* what it means. She doesn't want you ending up like him.'

'Yeah, well ...'

1 abduct sb.: kidnap sb.

'Come on, Cole,' I said brightly. 'It'll be all right. I can help you.'

'I don't need any help.'

'I'll keep you out of trouble.'

'There isn't going to *be* any trouble. All I'm going to do is take a look around and ask a few questions.'

'What kind of questions?'

He sighed again. 'I don't know yet.'

'I'm good at thinking up questions.'

He rolled his eyes. 'Tell me about it.'

'And when it comes to thinking,' I added, 'two heads are always better than one.' I grinned at him. 'Especially when one of them's yours.'

He looked at me, exasperated[1]. He'd had enough. I'd talked him into submission. He shook his head again and reached into his pocket for his cigarettes.

'You can't smoke in here,' I told him, pointing out the *No Smoking* sign on the window.

He looked at it, looked at me, then put the cigarettes back in his pocket.

'Shit,' he said.

After that, we let things ride for a while. Cole just sat there looking out through the window, and I just sat there sharing his silence. I was *with* him now, and I could feel the presence of Dad in his heart. It was a good feeling, good and strong, and it made me feel safe. But I could also feel the lack of feeling that Mum had mentioned earlier. The deadness[2]. The missing stuff. The stuff that neither Dad nor Cole seemed to have – the stuff that makes us care about ourselves and whether we live or die. I knew it was a necessary deadness, the kind of nerveless detachment[3] you sometimes need in order to get by in the world, but I also knew what could happen if the deadness took over, and it worried me to feel it in Cole.

1 exasperated: annoyed **2** deadness: lack of emotion **3** detachment: state of not being connected to the world

I could feel him thinking about Rachel, too. He wasn't aware that he was thinking about her, because he'd been thinking about nothing else for the last three days and his thoughts had become automatic. Like breathing. Like walking. Like living. When he thought about Rachel now, he thought with something that didn't belong to him. He thought with the core of his mind[1]. It thought *for* him. Searching the darkness, trying to find her, trying to picture her face – her eyes, her hair, the way she once smiled and lit up the world ...

But it was no good. It was all too far away. The pictures wouldn't come to him any more. The only thing he could see now was the naked corpse of a girl he didn't know.

He couldn't see Rachel any more.

I wondered if that's what was driving him.

As the train passed through Exeter and on towards Plymouth, the surrounding countryside began to change. The brown earth became red, brick[2] became granite, and the sunlight seemed to lose its brightness. Sad-looking hills loomed in the distance, casting cold grey shadows over the passing fields, making everything look mournful[3] and empty.

'It's a long way from Canleigh Street,' I said to Cole.

'It's not so different,' he murmured. 'It's just another place.'

'You reckon?'

He turned away from the window and stretched his neck. 'What time is it?'

I looked at my watch. 'Two thirty. We should be in Plymouth in about half an hour.'

Cole stretched again. 'I've been thinking ...'

'Yeah?'

He looked at me. 'About Rachel.' He rubbed his eyes. 'This girl she was staying with – Abbie Gorman. Do you know much about her?'

1 core of your mind: innermost part of your mind **2** brick: *Klinker, Backstein*
3 mournful: sad

'I thought *you* knew her. She was at school with Rachel. They were only a couple of years above you, weren't they?'

'I was never *at* school, was I? And even if I had been, you know what it's like at school – a couple of years is a lifetime. Rachel wouldn't have been seen dead talking to me. Come on, Rube – you must know something about Abbie. You were always talking to Rachel about her friends and stuff.'

I hesitated for a moment, waiting to see if he'd realise what he'd just said about Rachel not being seen dead ... but thankfully he didn't. So I told him what I knew about Abbie Gorman.

'She used to live on that big estate at Mile End. Rachel met her at junior school, then they went on to secondary school together. I don't think they were *best* friends or anything, but they used to hang around together a lot. Abbie came round to our place quite often. I think she even stayed over a couple of times.' I looked at Cole. 'Are you sure you don't remember her?'

He shook his head. 'What's she like?'

'I'm not sure, really. I only spoke to her once or twice. She seemed OK – friendly enough, pretty, a bit edgy[1] ...'

'What do you mean – *edgy?*'

'Like she could take care of herself if she had to. You know ... she had that look about her.'

'Like Rachel?'

'Yeah ... come to think of it, she looked like Rachel in lots of ways. Same height, same size, same kind of face. They could have been sisters.'

Cole ran his fingers through his hair. 'How did she end up living on Dartmoor?'

'Her mother lived there. Abbie was brought up by an aunt or something. I don't know why. A couple of years ago her mum got cancer and Abbie left London and moved down to Dartmoor to look after her. I think she must have been about sixteen or seventeen then. She met this local boy – I don't know his name – and when

1 edgy: irritable

her mum died, he moved in with her, and then a few months later they got married. Rachel went down for the wedding – remember?'

Cole shook his head again.

'Yeah, you do,' I said. 'She had that cream dress and the big hat and everything – you *must* remember. When she came back she showed us all the photographs and the video ...' I suddenly realised that Cole was upset with himself for not remembering, so I shut up about it and changed the subject. 'We're nearly there, look.' I pointed through the window at the approaches of a sprawling[1] grey town. Cole made a show of looking, but I knew he wasn't interested. His face had died. It wasn't that he cared about Rachel's cream dress or her big hat or the wedding photos or the video, he was just sad that he'd forgotten a moment when she was happy. He'd been there, and he'd missed it.

He'd lost it.

We got off the train and made our way out of the station to the taxi rank. There was a long queue and no taxis. I followed Cole to the end of the queue and watched him light a cigarette.

'You ought to give that up,' I said.

'I ought to do a lot of things,' he replied, breathing out smoke and giving me a look.

A taxi trundled past us and stopped at the front of the queue. A woman with a trolley full of suitcases loaded up and got in. The taxi pulled away and the queue shuffled forward.

'You're not sending me back then?' I said to Cole.

'I will if you don't stop yakking[2].'

It wasn't much of an invitation, but coming from Cole it was about the best I was going to get. He still didn't like it, but I think he'd realised that if I was determined to be with him, there wasn't much he could do about it. And besides, he liked being with me. He always

1 sprawling: that was spread out **2** yak (sl): talk non-stop

had. He'd never admit to it, but I could feel it – buried deep down inside him.

He was keeping a lot of other stuff buried, too – but most of it was buried so deep that neither of us knew what it was.

I didn't mind.

As long as we were together, that was enough for me.

I kept my mouth shut and my thoughts to myself.

Half an hour later we were sitting in the back of a black Metrocab and the driver was asking us where we were going. I looked at Cole, wondering if he'd given it any thought.

'Police station,' he told the driver.

'Which one?'

'What?'

'Which police station d'you want?'

Cole hesitated. He *hadn't* given it any thought.

'Breton Cross,' I told the driver.

He nodded at me and pulled away, and I settled back and looked out of the window. Cole didn't speak for about a minute.

Eventually he said, 'I suppose you think that proves something, do you?'

'What?' I said innocently.

'There's no need to look so pleased with yourself. I would have got there in the end. It just would have taken me a bit longer, that's all.'

'Right,' I said.

'How do you know which police station we want, anyway?'

'I looked it up on the Internet. Breton Cross is the main one. It's where the officer in charge of Rachel's investigation is based. That's who we want, isn't it?'

Cole looked at me. 'What's his name?'

'Pomeroy. He's a DCI[1].'

1 DCI: Detective Chief Inspector

Cole nodded. He almost said thanks, but then he remembered who he was and just nodded again instead. I looked out of the window and allowed myself a secret smile.

Breton Cross police station was a five-storey building that looked as if it had been dipped in shit. God knows what colour it was supposed to be. It was the kind of colour you get when you mix up all the colours in your paint box. A shitty colour, basically.

Cole paid the taxi driver and we went up some steps and through some doors into the reception area. There wasn't much going on. A ratty-haired drunk woman in a long nylon coat was sitting on a plastic chair staring at the floor, but apart from that the place was empty.

I followed Cole up to the glass-panelled reception desk. The reception clerk – a fat old man in a thin white shirt – was pretending to be busy. He was writing something really important in a really-important-looking ledger[1]. It was so important that he didn't even have time to acknowledge our existence. It didn't bother[2] me, but I knew Cole could only take it for so long, so I wasn't surprised when after thirty seconds or so he raised his hand and gave the glass panel a sudden hard slap.

The fat man jumped and looked up angrily. 'What the hell –?'

'Sorry,' said Cole. 'I thought you were dead.'

The fat man frowned[3].

'We want to see DCI Pomeroy,' Cole told him.

'You what?'

'DCI Pomeroy. We want to see him.'

'You can't just –'

'Is he here?'

'I don't know ...'

'Find out.'

1 ledger: book in which things are recorded **2** bother sb.: annoy sb **3** frown: *die Stirn runzeln*

The fat man's hand reached for the phone, but then he realised what he was doing – taking orders from a scruffy[1] kid he didn't even know – and he frowned again and stopped himself. He turned back to Cole and was about to say something, but Cole beat him to it.

'Tell him it's about Rachel Ford,' he said. 'Tell him her brothers are here.'

The fat man stared at Cole for a moment, then grudgingly picked up the phone.

Pomeroy's office smelled of Magic Tree[2] and Juicy Fruit[3]. It was a nondescript[4] kind of place – desk, chairs, filing cabinet, window. Nothing much at all, really. A bit like DCI Pomeroy himself. He was one of those men who don't seem to take up any space. Not big, not small, not anything. Just some kind of face, a haircut, a suit, some limbs[5], a voice.

'Sit down, please,' he said, indicating a couple of chairs on the other side of his desk.

We sat down.

Pomeroy smiled at us. It wasn't much of a smile. It looked like someone had cut into his face with a miniature penknife[6]. 'I'm afraid I'm going to have to ask you both for some identification,' he said. 'I know it sounds a bit paranoid, but you'd be amazed at the things people will do to get hold of information these days.'

Cole took out his wallet and passed over his driving licence. Pomeroy took it and looked it over. If he realised it was a forgery[7], he didn't show it. He nodded at Cole and passed it back, then looked at me.

'I left my driving licence at home,' I told him.

He smiled again but didn't say anything.

'I'm fourteen,' I said. 'The only thing I've got with my name on it is my Beano Club Membership card, and I think I've lost that. You

1 scruffy (infml): dirty and untidy **2** Magic Tree: *Wunder-Baum (Lufterfrischer für Autos)* **3** Juicy Fruit: *Art Kaugummi* **4** nondescript: having no interesting features **5** limbs: legs and arms **6** penknife: pocket knife **7** forgery: fake

could probably ring the Beano Club if you wanted to check. I think they're based in Dundee somewhere ...'

The look on his face told me to shut up.

'Give him your library card,' Cole told me.

I reached into my back pocket and passed over my library card. I don't know why I didn't do it in the first place. I just didn't feel like it, I suppose. Pomeroy glanced at the library card, then passed it back to me and leaned back in his chair.

'So,' he said, smiling at Cole, 'what can I do for you?'

Cole looked at him for a moment, wondering how to play it. I was wondering the same thing myself. Pomeroy hadn't said a word about Rachel yet. No commiserations[1], no heartfelt apologies, no platitudes. That was fine with me, and I'm sure it was OK with Cole, too – but it wasn't how it was supposed to be. And that was a little bit puzzling.

'We saw DC Merton this morning,' Cole said. 'He's our Family Liaison Officer –'

'I know who he is,' Pomeroy said.

'He's been keeping us informed about how the investigation is going.'

Pomeroy nodded. 'That's part of his job.'

'Right,' said Cole. I could feel his voice getting tighter. So could he. He looked down at the floor, took a couple of steadying breaths, then looked up at Pomeroy again. 'You're the Senior Investigating Officer, is that right?'

Pomeroy nodded.

'OK,' said Cole. 'What can you tell us?'

'What do you want to know?'

'I'll tell you what,' Cole said calmly. 'How about telling us why you're treating us like shit, for a start. Then maybe we can take it from there.'

1 commiseration: sympathy

Pomeroy didn't even blink[1]. 'I wasn't aware that I *was* treating you like shit. Of course, I apologise if that's how you feel, but I can assure you that wasn't my intention. I'm simply waiting for you to tell me what you want.' He smiled his nasty little smile again. 'I realise it's sometimes difficult to find the right words in these situations, but if it's a question of viewing the body –'

'We don't want to see the body,' Cole said.

'What then? If it's your sister's personal effects[2] you're after, I'm afraid we need to hold on to them for a while. You can probably have some of them back in a few days, but we'll need to keep her raincoat and clothes for evidence[3] –'

'We don't want any of Rachel's stuff.'

Pomeroy frowned. 'I'm sorry – I don't see what else I can do for you.'

'We want to bury her.'

'I beg your pardon?'

'We want to bury Rachel. We can't bury her until you get the man who killed her. We want to know when you're going to get him.'

'I see ...'

'Have you got him yet?'

Pomeroy rubbed his mouth. 'Well, I'm sure DC Merton has explained that we're following up a number of leads[4] –'

'What kind of leads?'

'I can't say at this moment.'

'Why not?'

'It might jeopardise[5] the investigation.'

'How?'

Pomeroy gave Cole a long hard look. 'This really isn't helping, you know. You're just going to have to trust us to do our job. We know what we're doing – believe me. There's nothing we're *not* doing to find your sister's killer and bring him to justice.'

'Do you know who did it?'

1 blink: *blinzeln* **2** effects (pl): belongings, personal things **3** evidence: proof
4 leads (n): clue **5** jeopardise sth.: endanger sth.

'I'm sorry, I really can't go into any more details. The best thing for you to do is just go home and wait. As soon as we have any news we'll contact DC Merton and he'll let you know.' Pomeroy stood up and looked down at us, waiting for us to leave. When we didn't move, he shook his head. 'Look,' he said, 'if you want me to sit here talking to you all day, that's fine. But if you want me to do my job, then I suggest you let me get on with it.'

Cole just sat there looking at him for a while, then eventually he got to his feet. I stood up, too. Pomeroy started leading us over to the door. I looked at Cole, wondering why he was giving up so easily, but when I saw the way he was staring at the back of Pomeroy's head, I realised he wasn't giving up anything. I should have known better, really. Cole doesn't do 'giving up'.

At the door, Pomeroy paused and put his hand on Cole's shoulder. 'Just one more thing before you go,' he said quietly. 'I'm not sure what your intentions are, but I hope you don't think your situation entitles you to any special treatment. I know you're a victim, and I know you're going through a terrible time, but that doesn't put you above the law. Do you understand?'

'No,' said Cole.

Pomeroy sighed. 'There aren't any secrets in a murder investigation, son. We have to look into everything – the victim, their friends, their family ...' He paused to let that sink in, then went on. 'I know all about you and your father ... and I don't just mean what's on file. Do you understand me now?'

Cole said nothing, just looked at him.

Pomeroy smiled. 'Just be careful – OK?'

Cole remained silent. If Pomeroy didn't take his hand off his shoulder soon, Cole was going to find it hard not to do something about it. I didn't think that would help things much, so I opened the door and took Cole's arm and gently pulled him away. His flesh felt like steel[1].

'Come on, Cole,' I said. 'Let's go.'

1 steel: *Stahl*

As Cole reluctantly gave in to me, Pomeroy gave him a final humiliating pat on the shoulder. I felt Cole's muscles tense.

'Just relax,' Pomeroy told him. 'Leave everything to us.' He looked at his watch. 'There's a train leaving for London in forty minutes. If you and your brother wait downstairs, I'll arrange for a car to take you to the station. How's that?'

Cole didn't answer, he just turned round and walked out of the door.

As I followed my brother along the corridor, I knew that this was just the beginning. There was a long way to go yet, but the fuse[1] was already burning.

1 fuse: *Zündschnur*

Four

Some people think I'm some kind of genius, but I'm not – I just feel things that other people don't feel, and I'm also really good at remembering stuff. I don't have a photographic memory exactly, but I can pretty much remember whatever I want. Facts, figures, information ... it doesn't matter what it is, as long as it means something to me, I can remember it. The only stuff I have trouble remembering is the stuff that *doesn't* mean anything to me, which is one of the reasons I always had trouble at school. But since I don't go to school any more – so I don't *have* to remember the stuff that doesn't mean anything to me – it's not really a problem.

It's not really important, either. I'm only mentioning it to let you know how I knew the way from the police station to the bus station. I knew because I'd looked at a map on the Internet that morning and remembered all the relevant details.

So when we left the police station, and I asked Cole where he wanted to go, and he told me he wanted to go to the bus station, I didn't have to think about it for long.

'It's just over there,' I told him. 'Down the street and through the subway.'

We headed for the subway.

Cole had already put Pomeroy to the back of his mind. He hadn't forgotten about him – he didn't forget about people like that – but for now he was content to put him to one side while he thought about what to do next.

'Where are we going?' I asked him.

'What?'

'Where are we going?'

'I just told you – the bus station.'

'Yeah, I know that. I mean, where are we going *from* the bus station?'

'Lychcombe.'

'Do you think that's a good idea?'

'Yeah.'

'You know Pomeroy's going to be keeping an eye on us?'

'Yeah.'

'He knows you've got a criminal record.'

'So? It's only for stealing cars. What's that got to do with anything?'

'What about the other stuff?'

Cole glanced at me. 'What other stuff?'

'Pomeroy said that he knew all about you and Dad, and he didn't just mean what's on file.'

'If it's not on file there's nothing to worry about, is there?'

'Yeah, but –'

'Forget it, Rube – all right? It's nothing. We're not doing anything wrong. We're just going to Lychcombe. There's no law against that.'

He was getting edgy again, so I decided to change the subject.

'Why don't we get a taxi?' I suggested. 'We might have to wait hours for a bus.'

'Rachel went by bus,' Cole said. 'Merton told us – remember? They found a return bus ticket from Plymouth to Lychcombe in her raincoat pocket.'

I looked at him. 'You want us to retrace her journey?'

'Something like that.'

'Do you think it'll help?'

He shrugged. 'I just want to know how it feels.'

We walked on in silence to the bus station. It was late afternoon now. The sky was clear and the sun was still fairly bright, but as we entered the bus station everything suddenly faded to a cold gloomy grey. It was a miserable place, dull[1] and ugly and airless. A world without smiles.

It was a bus station.

1 dull: (here) boring

I checked out the timetables. The next bus to Lychcombe was leaving in half an hour, which wasn't bad at all, considering the one before that had left five hours ago.

We went into the station café. Cole got me a couple of pies and a Coke, and a coffee for himself, and we took them over to a table by the window. We sat there in silence for a while – Cole sipping his coffee, me munching my way through mouthfuls of moist pastry[1] and gristle[2] – both of us staring idly[3] through the grease-smeared glass of the window. There wasn't much to look at. Concrete pillars[4]. Metal benches. Broken chocolate machines. Buses were lurching[5] and rumbling around the concourse, hissing[6] and juddering[7] into their parking bays, and lifeless people were shuffling around looking lost, or bored, or both.

It was a dead place.

Dead and cold.

I looked at Cole. His eyes were still, staring at nothing.

'I've been thinking about Rachel's raincoat,' I said to him.

'What?'

'Rachel's raincoat.'

He looked at me. 'What about it?'

'I'm not sure. It's just that Merton told us they'd found the bus ticket in her raincoat pocket, and Pomeroy said something about her raincoat as well.'

'So?'

'Rachel didn't have a raincoat.'

'What?'

'She didn't have a raincoat.'

'Are you sure?'

'Pretty sure.'

'How do you know she didn't have a raincoat?'

'I don't know ... I just *know*. I never saw her wearing one. The only coats she ever wore were those little zippy-up things. She wasn't the

1 pastry: *Blätterteig* **2** gristle: *Knorpel* **3** idle: lazy **4** pillar: *Pfeiler* **5** lurch: move unevenly **6** hiss: make a sound like a snake **7** judder: shake violently

raincoat type. Think about it, Cole. Can you see Rachel in a raincoat of any kind?'

He thought about it, closing his eyes, trying to picture her …

'Believe me,' I said, putting him out of his misery. 'She didn't have a raincoat.'

'Maybe she bought one,' he suggested. 'It was raining that night. Maybe she bought a raincoat –'

'Or borrowed one.'

I was looking out through the window as I spoke, my eyes suddenly transfixed. I was staring at Rachel's ghost. She was there. I could see her. She was right *there* – sitting on a bus station bench, surrounded by shopping bags, reading a glossy magazine.

I knew it wasn't a ghost, and I knew it wasn't Rachel, but for a fleeting moment my head was ablaze with delusion[1] – *it's a mistake … she's not dead … it was all a mistake … it was somebody else it was somebody else …*

'Ruben?'

It wasn't a mistake.

'Rube?'

I turned to Cole. 'Yeah …?'

'Did you hear what I just said?'

'What?'

He shook his head. 'I asked you who Rachel could have borrowed a raincoat from.'

'From *her*,' I said, nodding through the window at the girl who wasn't a ghost. 'From Abbie Gorman.'

We left the café and headed over to the bench where Abbie was sitting. She was wearing low-slung jeans and a tight black jumper, and her eyes were hidden behind sunglasses.

'Are you sure that's her?' Cole asked me.

'Yeah.'

1 delusion: false belief

Her resemblance to Rachel unsettled him. I could see the unease in his eyes, and I could feel him struggling with the pictures she stirred in the core of his mind.

The pictures of Rachel.

I could see them, too.

As we walked up to the bench and stopped in front of it, Abbie lowered her magazine and looked up at us over her sunglasses.

'Excuse me,' Cole said. 'I hope you don't mind –'

'What?' she said sharply. 'What do you want?'

'Are you Abbie Gorman?'

Her eyes flashed with fear. 'Why? Who are you? What do you want?'

'I'm Cole Ford, this is Ruben. We're Rachel's brothers.'

Abbie's mouth dropped open and she stared at us. The immediate fear had gone from her eyes, but there was something else there now, something deeper. I didn't know what it was, but it didn't feel good.

'You're *Cole?'* she said.

Cole nodded.

She looked at me, her eyes widening in recognition. 'Ruben? Christ ... look at you. Last time I saw you, you were just a little kid.' She shook her head in amazement. 'God, you scared me. I didn't know who you were. I thought you were after money or something.' She looked back at Cole again, beginning to smile. 'What are you doing here?' And then her face suddenly died. 'Oh God, Rachel ... God, I'm so sorry ...'

And she started crying.

Cole isn't very comfortable with tears. Me neither, come to that. We don't really know what to do with them. Especially when we're standing around in an unfamiliar bus station and people are beginning to stop and stare and wonder what's going on.

So we were both pretty relieved when the bus to Lychcombe pulled in and Abbie started pulling herself together.

'I'm sorry,' she said, wiping her eyes and collecting up her bags. 'I really have to go. This is the last bus back. I'd love to stay and talk to you –'

'We can talk on the bus,' said Cole.

'Sorry?'

'We're going to Lychcombe.'

Abbie froze. 'You're *what?*'

'We're going to Lychcombe,' Cole repeated. 'You don't mind if we join you on the bus, do you?'

'No,' she said, lying through her teeth. 'No, not at all.'

My dad used to travel all over the place before he married Mum. He spent most of his life on the road – working here, working there, doing this and that. He never cared what he did for money. Like most gypsies, he didn't live to work, he worked to live. He could turn his hand to just about anything – farm work, tarmacking[1], roofing, labouring. He even sold carpets for a while. Sometimes he'd go off somewhere and work on his own, but most of the time he travelled around with his family and a tight-knit[2] group of other families, often closely related. They'd set up camp on the edge of a town somewhere, work the land or the streets for a few months, then move on again and try somewhere new. During the summer they'd spend most of their time – and most of their money – at fairs and horse races all over the country: Appleby, Doncaster, Derby, Musselburgh. Dad used to fight at the races, too. Big fights, big crowds, big money.

His life was so bound up with being on the move that when he first started living at the breaker's yard with Mum, he was physically ill for a while. He just wasn't used to staying in one place. He tried to pretend that it wasn't a problem – 'Being a gypsy is a state of mind,' he used to say, 'not a state of action,' – but he never really got over it.

Anyway, I suppose what I'm trying to say is that although I'm half-gypsy, and although there's a big part of my dad in me, I haven't

1 tarmacking: asphalting roads **2** tight-knit: very close

really travelled at all. In my mind I've been around the world and back – in stories, in dreams, in thoughts – but in reality I've hardly been anywhere outside London. It's never really bothered me that much. I mean, I've never pined[1] for the open roads or anything. But as the bus rattled out of Plymouth that day and we headed up onto the moor, I began to realise that maybe I *had* been missing out on something after all.

After the bus had pulled out of the station and we'd all settled down in our seats, the three of us had spent the first five minutes of the journey just staring through the windows in awkward silence. None of us knew what to say. I was sitting on the long back seat behind Cole, and Abbie was sitting across from him. She'd piled all her shopping bags on the seat beside her, as if she didn't want either of us to get too close.

There wasn't much to see through the windows at first. Everything looked the same as everywhere else. Only greyer. And uglier. Same shops, same streets, same faces, same traffic. There weren't even any other passengers to look at. The bus was empty. Just us, the driver, and our awkward silence.

Gradually, though, as the grey of the town gave way to the rolling pastures[2] of the countryside, Cole and Abbie began to talk. It was all very hesitant at first – forced and wary[3], hard work for both of them – but at least they were talking. I listened for a while, but it was mostly nothing stuff – the kind of stuff you talk about before you start talking about the stuff you really want to talk about – so I just let them get on with it and turned my attention to the alien world passing by outside.

It was stunning.

I'd read books about Dartmoor, of course, especially over the last few days, but books are no substitute for the real thing – and the real thing was just incredible. I'd never seen such emptiness.

1 pine for sb./sth.: long for sb./sth. very much **2** pasture: field covered with grass for cattle **3** wary: careful

We'd left the lush green fields behind us now and were heading up into the heart of the moor. The road was narrowing, growing bleaker[1] and wilder as it stretched out in front of us over huge rolling slopes[2], and in the distance the landscape was darkening in the shadows of sinister[3] hills. The moorland skies were grey and endless, and the air was getting colder by the minute. Everything looked faded and dead: the bone-white grasses at the side of the road, the giant boulders[4] dotted over the slopes, the pale hills in the background. The emptiness went on for ever. There were no houses, no cars, no shops, no people, no nothing. Just a lonely grey road, leading to nowhere.

In the distance, dark forests loomed[5] against the horizon. On the high ground between the forests, towering outcrops of weirdly shaped rocks jutted out[6] from the ground, and in the slanting rays of the early-evening sun[7], the silhouettes of the weathered rocks formed nightmare faces against the sky: humans, dogs, giants, demons. Around the rocks there were strange stunted trees, their withered[8] branches sculpted by the wind.

The trees spoke to me of dying breaths.

My heart was cold.

'They're tors,' Abbie said, breaking into my thoughts.

'Sorry?'

'Those rocks in the distance – they're called tors.'

'Yeah,' I said, 'I know.'

She looked at me, and I immediately regretted the tone of my voice. I hadn't meant to sound rude, it'd just come out that way. I smiled at her, trying to make up for it.

'I remember reading something about them,' I said awkwardly. 'The tors, I mean. They're formed out of ancient granite that's been chemically eroded over millions of years ...'

1 bleak: (here) with less trees and vegetation **2** slope: *Hang* **3** sinister: evil **4** boulder: large rock or stone **5** loom: begin to appear **6** jut out: stick out **7** slanting rays of the ...sun: *tief stehende Sonnenstrahlen* **8** withered: dry and decaying

'Really?'

I nodded. She was staring at me now, and I should have shut up. But I was embarrassed, and when I'm embarrassed I *can't* shut up. My brain gets scrambled[1] and I start jabbering[2] like an idiot. 'Sorry,' I muttered, 'I expect you already knew that, didn't you? About the tors, I mean. Not that it matters … I mean, it doesn't matter if you knew it or not … I just meant, you know … I didn't *mean* anything …'

Abbie had turned to Cole now, looking at him with her eyebrows raised as if I was out of my head.

Cole just shrugged.

Abbie glanced back at me again. I looked at Cole. He gave me a meaningful look. I nodded at him, smiled at Abbie again, then went back to looking out of the window.

I wasn't sure what Cole's meaningful look was supposed to mean, but I guessed he wanted me to shut up and listen.

So that's what I did.

As the bus carried on rattling across the moor, and the landscape grew colder and greyer, I shut up and listened.

Cole and Abbie were talking seriously now – talking about the things they really wanted to talk about. I listened as Abbie asked Cole what we were doing here, and Cole carefully avoided telling her. I listened as she asked him how Mum was doing, and he replied with a few mumbled nothings. I listened as he asked her about Rachel, and she told him how devastated[3] she was, how sickened, how hurt. How heartbroken.

She wasn't lying. I could feel her pain. I could hear it in her voice and see it in her eyes. Her feelings for Rachel were genuine. No, she wasn't lying. But she wasn't telling the truth, either.

'Could you tell us what happened?' Cole asked her.

She looked at him. 'Didn't the police tell you?'

'Yeah, but you were here, weren't you? You know how it was.'

1 scrambled: confused and messy **2** jabber: talk nonsense **3** devastated: very shocked and upset

Her eyes blinked hesitantly.

Cole said, 'It'd really help us to hear it from you. I know it's difficult ...'

'I wasn't actually there,' she said. 'Not when it happened.'

'Where were you?'

'I was at my mother-in-law's house.' She paused, thinking about it, then she took a deep breath and began to explain. 'Earlier that evening, I'd walked down to the village with Rachel and we'd had a quick drink in the pub. She was getting the last bus back to Plymouth. It leaves at eight-thirty.'

'What time did you leave your house?' Cole asked her.

'About quarter to seven. The village isn't far away ... about twenty minutes' walk. Maybe half an hour. It was just starting to rain when we got there. I remember stopping outside the pub and looking up at the sky and seeing these huge black rain clouds rolling towards us across the moor. I tried telling Rach then that she should stay another night and go back in the morning, but she wouldn't listen. When I told her there was a really bad storm coming, she just shrugged and said "Let it come." '

I looked at Cole. He didn't show anything, but I knew what he was thinking. 'Let it come' is something that Dad often says. Whenever there's something bad on the horizon, he just shrugs his shoulders and says, 'Let it come. Just let it come.'

'Anyway,' Abbie continued, 'we went into the pub and had a couple of drinks, and while we were in there the storm started to break.' She shook her head. 'God, it was unbelievable. I've never seen anything like it. The skies just opened up and the rain came down in buckets. It was like a monsoon or something.' She looked out of the bus window. 'All this was flooded. The road, the moor, everything. Look ...' She pointed to the side of the road. 'You can still see all the stuff that got washed down from the moor.'

I looked out of the window. The edge of the road was littered with flood debris[1] – dried mud, leaves, twigs[2].

1 debris: remains of the flood and the storm **2** twig: small branch of a tree

Abbie shook her head again. 'I told Rachel she couldn't go back in the storm. I *told* her. I said I'd ring Vince and get him to pick us up before it got too bad, but she just wouldn't have it. She said she wanted to go home.' Abbie looked at Cole, then at me. 'She said she missed her family.'

Cole closed his eyes for a moment. I didn't close mine, because I knew if I did I'd start crying.

Cole said, 'Who's Vince?'

'My husband.'

Cole nodded. 'But Rachel wouldn't let you ring him?'

'No. She wouldn't even let me walk with her to the bus stop. "There's no point in both of us getting soaked[1], is there?" she said.'

'What time did she leave the pub?' Cole asked.

'About eight.'

'What did you do?'

'Nothing. I stayed in the pub for a while, then I went round to visit my mother-in-law. She lives in the street behind the pub.'

'And that was the last time you saw Rachel – when she left the pub?'

Abbie nodded. 'I found out later that the bus was about an hour late because of the storm, but she definitely got on it. The driver remembers her. But the bus never got to Plymouth. It had to stop ...' She leaned to one side and pointed through the windscreen at the road up ahead. 'It was just over there. See that steep little bank[2] at the end of the road?'

We both looked out of the window. About half a mile ahead, the road dipped down[3] and veered off[4] to the right under a steep bank of trees. As we got closer, we could see where the bank had collapsed. Piles of red earth and fallen trees had been bulldozed off the road.

'The road was blocked,' Abbie said. 'Nothing could get through. The bus had to turn around and come back. It was getting pretty late by then, and the road was getting really bad, so by the time the

1 soaked: completely wet **2** bank: *Böschung* **3** dip down: slope downwards
4 veer off: change direction

bus got back to Lychcombe it was gone eleven o'clock. The driver remembers Rachel getting off. He asked her if she was going to be all right. She told him not to worry, she had some friends in the village and she'd stay the night with them.'

'But she never showed up,' said Cole.

'No ... we just assumed she'd caught the train and gone home. We didn't know anything was wrong until the next day.'

'Why didn't she ring you?'

'The phone box by the bus stop was out of order.'

'She had her mobile.'

Abbie shook her head. 'You can't get a signal around here. The police think she probably tried calling us from the phone box, then when she couldn't get through she decided to walk to our house ...'

Her voice trailed off and she lowered her eyes, unwilling to go any further. But Cole didn't seem to notice. Either that, or he just didn't care.

'So that's when it happened,' he said. 'Somewhere between the bus stop and your place ... someone took her.'

Abbie nodded silently.

'Where were you then?' asked Cole.

Abbie looked up suddenly. 'What?'

'Where were you when Rachel was walking back to your place?'

'I just told you –'

'Were you still at your mother-in-law's?'

Her eyes were getting angry now. 'Why are you asking me –?'

'What time did you leave?'

She glared at Cole in disbelief. 'You don't have any right to *question* me.'

'Why not?'

'I was her *friend*, for God's sake. If you think –'

'I don't think anything,' Cole said calmly. 'I just want to know what happened to Rachel. The more you tell me the more I'll know.'

Abbie carried on staring at him for a while, but I could see her anger fading. 'Yeah, well ...' she muttered eventually. 'I can't tell you any more, can I? I don't *know* any more. I wish I did, but I don't.'

Cole was about to ask her something else, but before he could speak I tapped him on the shoulder and said, 'I think we're nearly there.'

He looked at me, then looked out of the window. Boundless[1] acres of empty moorland stretched out into the distance. 'Nearly where?' he said. 'There's nothing here.'

'We just passed a sign,' I told him.

'What sign?'

'Lychcombe.'

'He's right,' Abbie said, getting to her feet. 'It's the next stop. Just around the corner.'

As she walked off down to the front of the bus, Cole continued looking out of the window. His eyes took in the barren[2] slopes and the scattered[3] boulders and the lonely grey road winding its way into the fading hills, and I could feel him thinking to himself – *this is no place to die.*

We got off the bus and watched it pull away, and then we just stood there for a while, mesmerised[4] by the unworldly silence of the moor. I'd never heard anything like it before. It wasn't a soundless silence – there was the soft rush of wind in the grass, the lonely bleating of distant sheep, the call of crows in a nearby forest ... but somehow that made it all the more quiet. There were no *human* noises. No traffic. No voices.

It was the silence of another age.

Another time.

Another bus stop. Another day. Another night. I could feel it – the sky black with rain, Rachel getting off the bus, trying her mobile, then hurrying across the road to the telephone box, trying to call Abbie. But the phone's out of order. Broken, busted[5], jammed. No signal. No answer. She can't hear me. She's hundreds of miles away.

1 boundless: without limits **2** barren: (here) bare, without vegetation
3 scattered: spread around **4** mesmerised: fascinated **5** busted: ruined

She's all alone. She's cold and wet and it's dark and windy and there's something out there, something that shouldn't be there ...

'Don't think about it.'

Cole was standing beside me, his hand on my shoulder.

'I can't help it,' I told him.

'I know.'

He gave my shoulder a squeeze, then looked over at Abbie. She was waiting for us at the side of the road.

'Don't push her too hard,' I said quietly to Cole. 'She's frightened of something. If you try to force it out of her, she'll just clam up[1]. Go easy for a while – OK?'

Cole nodded. Still looking at Abbie, he said, 'Do you really think she looks like Rachel?'

'Sometimes,' I said. 'Other times I'm not so sure. Her face keeps shifting. Sometimes she looks like an *anti*-Rachel.'

Cole looked at me.

I shrugged.

We walked over to Abbie and she led us across the road to a V-shaped junction, where a hillside lane branched off[2] the main road and headed down into a valley.

'This is the road to Lychcombe,' she told us. 'The village is just down there.'

I looked down the narrow road and saw a scattering of dull grey buildings at the bottom of the valley. Apart from a lone twist of smoke coiling from a cottage chimney, there was no movement at all. The village lay mute and still in the early-evening light.

We set off towards it.

The road led steeply all the way down to a small granite bridge that crossed a shallow river into the village. We could see for miles all around us. On either side of the road, the open moor was broken up with jutting[3] stones and clumps of stricken[4] oak trees, and away to our right I could see fat little ponies standing motionless

1 clam up (infml): become silent suddenly **2** branch off: go in another direction
3 jutting: sticking out **4** stricken: (here) broken

in fields of dry grass. I could smell their horse-sweet breath in the air. I could smell other smells, too: earth, heather[1], gorse[2]. A faint breeze of petrol was wafting up from an old-fashioned filling station halfway down the hill, and on the right-hand side of the road, opposite the petrol station, wood smoke was drifting over a stretch of spindly[3] woods.

The road led down through it all – down the hill, over the bridge, into the village, and out the other side. A large stone house stood at the far end of the village, and it was here that the road turned sharply to the left before wandering up through the densely packed gloom[4] of a pine forest and away into the hills beyond.

I was lagging behind[5] Cole and Abbie now. They were about ten metres ahead of me, walking side by side. I could see they'd started talking again but I couldn't hear what they were saying. So I picked up my pace and caught up with them. As I walked up behind them, Abbie was just explaining something to Cole, pointing down at the village, and Cole was nodding his head.

'So where do you live, then?' he asked her.

'Just over there.' She moved her hand to the left, pointing beyond the village. 'You can't see it from here. It's about half a mile from the edge of the forest.'

Cole nodded again. 'Are you walking all the way back?'

She shook her head. 'Vince is coming to pick me up.' She looked at Cole. 'Do you want a lift[6] anywhere? He'll be happy to drive you –'

'No, that's all right. We'll walk, thanks.'

Abbie nodded. 'What are you going to do?'

He shrugged. 'Not much.'

'The last bus leaves at eight-thirty. You're not going to have much time. You could probably get a taxi back –'

'We might stay over.'

'What – here? In Lychcombe?'

1 heather: *Heidekraut* **2** gorse: *Ginsterbusch* **3** spindly: very long and thin
4 gloom: unpleasant darkness **5** lag behind: stay behind **6** want a lift: *mitgenommen werden wollen*

'Maybe. We'll see how it goes. Is there anywhere to stay? What about that pub you mentioned?'

Abbie looked at him. The fear in her eyes had resurfaced. 'The pub?'

'Yeah,' said Cole. 'Or a B & B, something like that.'

'I don't know,' she said hesitantly. 'I suppose the Bridge might have a room ...'

'The Bridge?'

'The Bridge Hotel. It's the village pub. It's not really a hotel any more –'

'We just need a room.'

Abbie seemed about to say something, but then she changed her mind and just shrugged, and we carried on walking in silence for a while.

The lane was bounded on either side by low stone walls topped with stunted shrubs[1]. The stones were encrusted with scabs[2] of lichen[3], and when I looked closer I could see little white stalks[4] with blood-red tips growing among the scabs – Devil's Matchsticks[5]. I left them alone and gazed down at the village. It was directly below us now, about 200 metres away. It still didn't look like much, but now that we weren't so far away I could see there was more to it than just a scattering of buildings. There was a main street, a couple of side streets ... cars and shops and people, bits of movement.

There was movement over at the petrol station, too. It was a run-down old place that looked as if it was closing down. The two ancient petrol pumps were sealed off[6] with tape, and the forecourt buildings were all boarded up[7]. It was far from deserted, though. A grubby[8] white petrol tanker was parked by the pumps, and across the forecourt a group of men were hanging around an old green Land Rover. In the background I could see a couple of motorbikes

1 shrub: small bush **2** scab: *Schorf* **3** lichen: *Flechte* **4** stalk: *Stiel* **5** Devil's Matchsticks: type of lichen **6** seal sth. off: (here) cover sth. with tape so that it cannot be used **7** board sth. up: cover sth. with wooden boards **8** grubby: dirty

and a Toyota pick-up truck. A man in blue overalls was lowering a heavy hose[1] from the petrol tanker into a fuel tank in front of the pumps, and the men at the Land Rover were watching him. At the back of the tanker, a generator was quietly chugging away[2].

'There's Vince,' said Abbie, looking over at the group of men.

I didn't know which one she meant, but I already knew I wasn't going to like him. They all looked as bad as each other.

'What are they doing here?' Cole said.

I thought he was asking Abbie about the men at the petrol station, but when I glanced over at him I realised he wasn't even looking at them. He was looking instead at a gathering of trailers in a wasteground field near the spindly woods on the other side of the road.

'They're gypsies,' said Abbie.

Cole glanced at her. 'I kind of guessed that.'

'Oh, right,' she said, slightly embarrassed, 'of course. Sorry.' She looked over at the camp. 'I don't really know anything about them. They've been living there for about six months now.'

Cole just nodded, staring at the camp. It was set back from the road, away to our right, at the end of a rutted track. There were eight trailers in all, parked in a ragged semicircle, and the rest of the field was dotted with cars and trucks – BMWs, Shoguns[3], pick-ups, vans. The camp was quietly busy. There was a little kid playing with a dog, a bonfire smoking in the wind, a piebald[4] pony tethered[5] by a trough[6]...

I liked it.

It made me feel good.

I heard a car starting up, and when I looked over at the petrol station I saw the Land Rover pulling out of the forecourt and heading up the road towards us. From the way Abbie was watching it,

1 hose: *Schlauch* **2** chug away: make the sound of a motor **3** Shogun: Mitsubishi car with four-wheel drive **4** piebald: black and white **5** tether sth.: tie sth. **6** trough: *Trog*

I guessed the driver was Vince. He was a big man. Heavy-headed, like a farmer. His face was ruddy[1] and his hair was thick and brown.

Abbie turned to Cole. 'Are you sure you don't want a lift?'

'No thanks.'

The Land Rover pulled up beside us. Vince wound down the window and slowly gave Cole a good looking over. When he was done with that, he turned his attention to me. He didn't seem too impressed.

'It's all right, Vince,' Abbie explained quickly as she walked towards the car. 'They're Rachel's brothers – Ruben and Cole.'

Vince looked at her.

She smiled tightly. 'It's OK. They're just …'

Her voice trailed off as she realised that she didn't actually know what we were doing here. Vince frowned at her for a moment – none too pleased – then he looked round and nodded gruffly at Cole. Cole held his gaze and nodded back. Vince glanced at me, this time trying to appear sympathetic, but it didn't work. The truth was still plain to see: he wanted to say the right thing about Rachel but he didn't know how to do it, and he wanted to know what we were doing here but he didn't want us to know it.

He looked back at Cole again. 'You staying in Plymouth?' His voice was deep, burred with a West Country accent.

Before Cole could answer him, Abbie opened the passenger-side door and climbed up into the Land Rover.

'They're thinking of staying the night at the Bridge,' she told Vince.

A flicker of surprise crossed his face as he looked at her. She looked away and fastened her seat belt.

Vince said to Cole, 'The Bridge ain't up to much.'

Cole shrugged. 'Neither are we.'

'I don't know if they'll have any rooms …' He glanced over his shoulder as a clanging sound rang out from the petrol station, followed by a lazy laugh. I looked down and saw the man in blue over-

1 ruddy: reddish

alls holding his hand as if he'd bashed it on something. The others were pointing and laughing at him. As Vince turned back and put the Land Rover in gear, his face seemed suddenly welcoming. 'Jump in the back if you want,' he said to us. 'I'll give you a lift down the Bridge. If they don't have any rooms you can come back to our place.'

Abbie's eyes widened.

'Thanks,' said Cole, 'but I think we'll just walk.'

'You sure?'

Cole nodded.

Vince reached into the glove compartment and pulled out a pencil and scrap of paper. 'I'll give you our number,' he said, scribbling on the paper. 'Just call us if you need anything – OK?' He passed the scrap of paper to Cole. 'There's plenty of room at our place if you change your mind. No one'll bother you.'

Cole slipped the paper in his pocket and thanked him again. Vince gave us a final nod, then glanced over his shoulder, reversed the Land Rover across the road, and sped off down the hill.

Five

The light was beginning to fade as we headed down the hill towards the village. There wasn't any real darkness to the sky, just a peculiar[1] absence of light. It felt as if the day was dying but the night had forgotten to come down.

In the valley below us, the village was still empty and dead. We'd watched the Land Rover passing through it and disappearing round the corner at the end of the main street, and once it had gone the world had seemed to stop moving again. The gypsy camp was lifeless. The petrol station was still. I wasn't even sure that *we* were moving. I knew we were – I could hear our footsteps. But even they were shrouded[2] in stillness.

Sound, silence, light, dark ... there was something about this place that deadened everything.

'What do you think?' Cole said eventually.

'About what?'

'Anything.'

'I don't know,' I told him. 'I think there's *some*thing weird going on, but I don't know what it is.'

'What about Abbie?' he asked.

'She's frightened. She doesn't like us being here. I think she feels guilty about something.'

'Rachel?'

'Maybe ... I don't know.'

'She didn't mention the raincoat.'

'No,' I agreed.

'What d'you think of her husband?'

'What do *you* think?'

Cole shrugged. 'I don't trust him. Don't like him, either ... not that it matters.'

1 peculiar: strange **2** shrouded: covered

He lit a cigarette and we carried on walking in silence.

As we approached the filling station, I looked over at the petrol tanker parked by the pumps. It was an old rigid-chassis Bedford[1] from the 1970s, similar to one that Dad used to keep at the yard – small and squat[2], four wheels at the back, two at the front, laddered steps leading up to the cab. The man in the blue overalls was still struggling with the fuel hose, but the group of men had stopped watching him now – they were watching us instead. There were four of them: a couple of metal-heads[3], a mad-eyed guy about eight feet tall, and a skinny little man in a ratty red suit.

'Keep walking,' Cole said to me.

'What?'

'Just keep walking and don't look at them.'

I did as he said, trying not to think about them, looking straight ahead – but I could still feel their eyes on us. They were the kind of eyes you can never get away from: redneck[4] eyes, hillbilly[5] eyes, Neanderthal eyes. Humanimal[6] eyes.

'What are they doing?' I asked Cole.

'Nothing ... just watching. Don't worry about it.' He touched my arm. 'What do you know about petrol tankers?'

'What?'

'I was just wondering what that old tanker's doing over there. It's not delivering ... the place is all closed up. It must be siphoning[7] the tanks, I suppose. What do you reckon?'

'I know what you're trying to do, Cole,' I said.

'I'm not trying to do anything –'

'Yeah, you are. You're trying to take my mind off those freaks at the petrol station.'

'Am I?'

1 Bedford: brand name of lorry **2** squat: *gedrungen* **3** metal-heads: fans of Heavy Metal music **4** redneck (usu. AE): white person with little education and prejudiced beliefs **5** hillbilly (usu. AE): person with a simple way of life living in the country who is considered slightly stupid by people living in the city
6 humanimal: (neologism) mixing human and animal **7** siphon sth.: draw liquid from sth.

'Yeah.'

'Is it working?'

'Not really.' I glanced up. 'You know they're coming over to us?'

'Yeah.'

'You're not going to do anything stupid, are you?'

'No.'

The four men were crossing the road now, heading straight for us – Red Suit in front, the other three in a line behind him. Cole touched my arm again and we both stopped walking. I knew I *shouldn't* stare – it was the worst thing I could possibly do – but I just couldn't help it. I'd never seen a skinny little man wearing a tatty[1] red suit in the middle of Dartmoor before.

How could I *not* stare at that?

Red Suit was smiling now – smiling at me. His close-cropped hair was almost as red as his suit. His teeth were sharp, and his eyes were wrong. I didn't know *how* they were wrong, but they were. Everything about him was wrong.

He stopped in front of us and put his hands in his pockets. The others stopped behind him.

'All right?' he said, staring at me.

I didn't answer. I knew if I said anything my voice would come out all shaky, so I just kept my mouth shut and waited for Cole to do his stuff. I didn't have to wait very long.

'You want something?' he said to Red Suit.

Red looked at him, still smiling. 'I'm sorry?'

'You heard me.'

Red's smile began to tighten. 'Just saying hello,' he shrugged. 'Saw you talking to Vince just now –'

'Is that it?'

Red looked confused.

Cole stepped towards him. 'Is that all you want?'

'What do you –?'

'You're in the way.'

1 tatty: shabby

The smile dropped from Red's face and his eyes went cold. Behind him, the big guy started blinking like a madman and shuffling forward. Cole ignored him and moved closer to Red, staring hard into his eyes.

'You're in the way,' he said again, very quietly. 'If you don't do something about it right now, you're going to get hurt.'

Before Red could say anything, the big guy pushed past him and reached out for Cole. Cole hardly moved. He just dropped his shoulder and slammed his fist into the big guy's throat. The big guy staggered back, his mad eyes bulging[1], and then Cole hit him again – a short right hook[2] to the head – and he dropped to the ground like a sack. As he went down, choking[3] and moaning and gasping for breath, Cole turned back to Red.

Red was already raising his hands and backing away, his shocked eyes flicking between the big guy and Cole. 'Shit, man,' he said, shaking his head, 'you didn't have to do that.'

'I don't *have* to do anything,' Cole muttered, flicking a look at the two metal-heads. They were just standing there, staring at the big guy on the ground. His face was turning a weird shade of blue. The metal-heads looked up at Cole, saw him watching them, and moved out of the way.

'Come on, Rube,' Cole said quietly, putting his hand on my shoulder.

As he led me past them, Red Suit and the metal-heads shuffled backwards to give us more room. Cole didn't look at them. I don't think he was even aware of them any more. I was, though. As we headed off down the hill, I could feel their eyes burning into the back of my neck.

'You promised you wouldn't do anything stupid,' I said to Cole.

'I didn't.'

'You could have *killed* him.'

'Yeah, but I didn't, did I?'

'Christ, Cole. Why do you always have to –?'

1 bulge: swell **2** hook: (here) kind of punch **3** choke: (here) partly breathing

I was interrupted by a sudden shout ringing out from behind us. 'Hey! HEY! You listening, breed[1]?' It was Red. We both ignored him and carried on walking. 'I'll see you later,' he called out. 'You hear me? Both of you – I'll see you later ...'

I looked at Cole. 'He called you *breed*.'

'What makes you think he meant me?'

'He said he'll see us both later.'

'I expect he will.'

As we moved on down the hill, I realised that we had another audience now. Over by the rutted track that led across to the gypsy camp, three figures were watching us quietly: a stocky[2] old man with a broken nose, a wide-eyed little girl of about twelve, and an older girl with a baby in her arms. Two dogs were sitting beside the girl with the baby – a lurcher[3] and a three-legged Jack Russell. The girl was about the same age as Cole. Pale green eyes, raven hair, silent and still and beautiful. I looked at Cole. He was staring intently at her, and I could feel something moving inside him. I wasn't sure what it was, but it didn't feel right to feel it, so I quickly left it alone and got out of his head.

As we approached the three gypsies, they carried on watching us. Their eyes were impossible to read.

'Did they see you hitting the big guy?' I asked Cole.

'Yeah.'

'Do you think they know who we are?'

'Probably.'

We were just about level with them now. I could hear the baby making quiet gurgling noises. I could see the shine of the girl's jet-black hair. I could feel her eyes studying Cole as he nodded his head almost imperceptibly[4] at the stocky old man. The old man didn't move for a second, then he too nodded his head.

And that was that.

1 breed (derog): person whose parents are from different races **2** stocky: short and strong **3** lurcher: type of mixed breed dog **4** imperceptible: almost unnoticeable

We passed them by without a word and carried on down to the village.

The way Cole said it, it sounded quite simple. 'We'll check into this Bridge Hotel, get something to eat, then first thing in the morning we'll start looking around the village.'

I thought about asking him what we were supposed to be looking around *for*, but I decided to keep my mouth shut. I was too tired and hungry to think about it now. All I wanted was to get some food inside me and go to bed.

Unfortunately, things didn't quite work out that way.

The trouble started on the narrow stone bridge that led into the village. We were about halfway across, and I was just telling Cole how the bridge was made from huge slabs[1] of granite, and how it had probably been here since the 14th century, and he was doing his best not to yawn[2], when suddenly we heard the sound of a car roaring up fast behind us. We both turned round and saw the Toyota pick-up racing towards us across the bridge. The big guy was slumped in the passenger seat and Red Suit was at the wheel, grinning like a lunatic[3] as he put his foot down and headed straight for us. My belly lurched and my legs turned to ice, and for a fleeting moment I thought we were dead. I really thought we'd had it. And the weird thing was, it didn't seem to bother me. I might have been petrified[4], but I wasn't scared. I wasn't anything, really. It wasn't until Cole grabbed my arm and yanked[5] me back onto one of the stone supports at the edge of the bridge, and the car flashed past us in a hail of laughter and shouting voices ... it wasn't until then that I started to feel anything at all. And even then I didn't know what it was.

It might have been fear, or shock, or sickness ...

Or it might have been some kind of love.

1 slab: thick slice **2** yawn: take a deep breath when tired or bored **3** lunatic: crazy person **4** petrified: extremely frightened **5** yank sb./sth.: pull

Cole had his arms around me, and we were balanced on the very edge of a narrow pillar of granite about ten metres above a fast-flowing river. The shallow waters looked cold and coppery[1]. Cole had his back to the river and was struggling to keep his balance. I went to step back onto the bridge, intending to give him some room, but he suddenly grabbed hold of me again and pulled me back.

'What –?' I started to say.

But then I heard it – the sound of motorbike engines – and I looked up to see the two metal-heads screaming their bikes down the hill towards us.

Cole started edging around[2] me, his eyes fixed coldly on the approaching bikes.

'What are you doing?' I said.

He didn't answer me, but it didn't matter. I knew what he was doing. He was trying to get back on the bridge. He was going after the bikes. I shuffled around to block his way. He shuffled back. I blocked him again. He stopped shuffling and looked at me, his eyes telling me to get out of the way.

'Don't be stupid, Cole,' I said. 'Stopping them's not going to help us, is it?'

The bikes were starting to cross the bridge now. Cole looked up at them. I watched his eyes as they roared towards us, swerved[3] half-heartedly, then straightened up and sped off into the village.

After a couple of long seconds, Cole turned back to me.

'It's all right,' he said. 'You can let go of me now.'

I hadn't even realised I was holding him.

Five minutes later we were standing outside the Bridge Hotel. It was a big old stone building about halfway up the main street. White paint was flaking off the walls, revealing large patches of dull grey granite underneath, and the windows were thick with dust. The sign over the door showed a faded picture of the bridge we'd just come

1 coppery: reddish-brown **2** edge around sb.: move around sb. little by little
3 swerve: turn away

across. *The Bridge Hotel,* it said, *Fine Wines & Beers, Family Dining, Accommodation Available.* A blackboard in the window advertised *Live Football!!,* and a sign on the door said *No Travellers.*

'Looks nice,' I said.

Cole grunted.

The streetlights were on now, but there wasn't much to see. The village was deserted. The streets and the pavements were empty. A lot of the houses had boarded-up windows and doors, and the only shop we'd seen so far was a closed-down newsagent's with a white-washed window.

'You ready?' Cole asked me.

I looked at him. 'Are you sure this is a good idea?'

'We need somewhere to stay,' he said simply.

'I know, but have you seen what's over there?'

He glanced over at the Toyota pick-up and the two motorbikes parked in front of the hotel.

'Don't worry about it,' he said.

'What about that?' I said, nodding at the *No Travellers* sign on the door.

Cole just shrugged. 'What about it?'

I looked at him.

'We're not Travellers, are we?' he said. 'We're half-breeds. It doesn't say anything about half-breeds, does it?'

'No,' I agreed.

'So what's the problem?'

'Nothing ... nothing at all.'

'Good – let's get going then.'

The main door of the hotel led us through into the stagnant air of a dimly lit corridor. A door on our right went through to the bar, and a pair of double doors on the left opened up to a dining room – or what used to be a dining room. There were still a few tables dotted around, and one or two dusty chairs, but apart from that, the room was as empty as everything else around here – the cigarette machine behind the door, the reception desk at the end of the corridor, the leaflet rack on the wall. All empty. Even the noise from the bar next door sounded empty – the loud voices, the chinking glasses, the drunken laughter. It was a noise filled with nothing, and I didn't like the sound of it at all. But when Cole opened the door and we both walked in, and everything suddenly went quiet, I liked that even less.

It was a narrow rectangular[1] room with a high white ceiling and a grimy[2] red carpet. A long wooden bar spanned the length of the wall to our left, and the rest of the room was taken up with a dozen or so tables and chairs. Sky Sports flickered on a widescreen TV fixed high on the wall at the back. The bar was packed, and most of the tables were full. There was no emptiness in here. Just a room full of staring faces, all of them staring at us. Old men, young men, old-looking young women – there were all sorts. All different, but all the same – sour and dead and unwelcoming.

I scanned the faces and spotted Red Suit almost immediately. He was sitting at a window table with a couple of hoods[3] in tight T-shirts and an older man with amber[4] eyes and a Quaker's beard[5]. Red was smiling at us. The bearded man looked as if he'd never cracked a smile in his life.

All in all, it was a pretty scary situation. The only good thing about it was the presence of a uniformed policeman sitting at the end of the bar. He didn't look like much of a policeman – his face was flushed, his eyes were glassy, he was smoking a cigarette and guzzling beer – but I guessed he was better than nothing.

I'd soon find out I was wrong.

The staring faces didn't bother Cole. He just stood there for a moment or two, casually looking around, then he unbuttoned his jacket and started moving across to the bar. I followed closely behind him. There wasn't a lot of room at the bar, and the people standing there didn't make any effort to get out of our way, but Cole

1 rectangular: *rechteckig* **2** grimy: greasy and dirty **3** hood (sl): *Ganove*
4 amber: *bernsteinfarben* **5** Quaker: member of a religious movement who traditionally had long beards but no moustaches

somehow managed to find his way through without having to push too hard. He even said 'excuse me' once. Behind the bar, a man in a white shirt was leaning against the till, drinking whisky and smoking a cigarette.

'We need a room,' Cole said to him.

'You what?' the man said.

'We need a room.'

Across the bar, someone laughed.

'Who's *we?'* the barman asked Cole.

'Me and my brother.'

The barman glanced at me, then back at Cole. 'Is that him?'

Cole nodded.

The barman shook his head. 'We don't take kids.'

'What do you mean?'

'What do you *think* I mean?'

'I don't know,' Cole said slowly. 'That's why I'm asking.'

The barman drained the whisky from his glass, took a drag on his cigarette, then stabbed it out in an ashtray. Along the bar, someone called out to him.

'When you're ready, Will – couple of pints.'

Will nodded and started filling a glass. As Cole stared at him, I realised that the bar was beginning to fill up with noise again. People were talking. People were drinking. People were laughing.

I moved up behind Cole and whispered in his ear. 'Come on,' I said, 'let's get out of here.'

He didn't move, just carried on staring at Will the barman. He watched him fill the beer glasses and pass them over. He watched him take the money and put it in the till. He watched him pass over the change.

Then he said, 'Hey, mister – I'm talking to you.'

As Will stopped and stared at him, the room went quiet again. The only thing I could hear was the sound of my thumping heart.

Will said to Cole, 'Listen, boy, I just told you – we don't take kids. You want a room, that's fine. But the squit[1] over there ain't staying here.'

He looked at me again, and for some strange reason I smiled at him. I don't know why … maybe it was because I'd never been called a squit before. I wasn't sure what it meant, but I kind of liked it.

'How old are you, kid?' Will said to me.

'What?'

'How *old* are you?'

'Forty-six,' I heard myself say. 'I know it's hard to believe, but I've got a very rare glandular condition[2] that makes me look perpetually[3] young. It's a genetic disorder – been in the family for years.'

He looked at me for a moment, then shook his head and turned back to Cole. 'Go on,' he said, jerking his head at the door. 'Out – both of you.'

'I want a drink,' Cole said.

'Try somewhere else.'

'I kind of like it in here. There's a nice atmosphere.' He pulled a £20 note from his pocket and dropped it on the counter. 'I'll have a pint of Stella.' He turned to me. 'What do you want, Rube?'

'A pint of Malibu.'

Cole turned back to Will. 'Pint of Stella and a pint of Malibu.' He pushed the £20 note across the bar. 'And have one yourself.'

Will didn't move. I saw his eyes flick to one side, and I looked over to see the uniformed policeman rolling along the bar towards us. He was bald[4] and fat – fat head, fat mouth, fat belly. His face was glowing with sweat, and he had a cigarette clamped in his mouth. As he stopped in front of us, I could smell the beer and smoke on his breath.

'All right, son,' he said to Cole, 'how about stepping outside for a minute?'

1 squit: *(hier) kleiner Stöpsel* **2** glandular condition: *Drüsenerkrankung*
3 perpetually: forever **4** bald: without any hair

Cole turned round and looked him up and down. 'Who the hell are you?'

The policeman put his hand on Cole's shoulder. Cole looked at it. The policeman said, 'You're not much of a one for listening, are you?'

'Get your hand off –'

'Shut up. What were you told this afternoon?'

'What?'

'What did Pomeroy tell you?'

'He didn't –'

'I'll tell you what he *didn't* tell you. He didn't tell you to come down here and start kicking the shit out of people, did he? He didn't tell you to come in here and start taking the piss[1], either. No, what he told you was to keep out of trouble and leave everything to us. *That's* what he told you. Remember?'

Cole said nothing.

The policeman smiled at him. 'Now, I know you're under a lot of strain[2] right now, what with your sister and everything, but you've already been warned against taking things into your own hands, haven't you?' Still staring at Cole, he took a long drag on his cigarette and blew the smoke from the side of his mouth. 'So, listen,' he said, 'here's what I want you to do. There's a phone box at the end of the High Street. You take your little brother down there and you call yourself a taxi. You wait at the phone box, you get in the taxi, you tell the driver to take you to Plymouth. When you get to the station, you get on the train and go back to London. You do all that for me and I'll forget about everything else – OK?'

Cole looked at him for a long time, weighing up all the options. I knew what he wanted to do – he wanted to beat the shit out of him, crack his fat head open, smash his smiling face to a pulp[3] – but Cole wasn't stupid. He knew there was a time and a place for everything. And this wasn't it.

1 take the piss out of sb./sth. (sl.): make a joke about sb./sth. **2** strain: emotional pressure **3** pulp: soft mass

He stared at the policeman for a little while longer, letting him see the truth, and then he just nodded.

'Good,' said the fat man, letting go of his shoulder. 'Off you go, then.'

As we walked out of the bar, I could feel the man with the Quaker beard watching Cole closely. Everyone was watching him closely – but the man with the beard was different. He knew what Cole was. He knew what he was bringing. He could already feel the storm coming down.

Outside the hotel, I watched in silence as Cole checked his mobile. From the way he stared at the display and snapped the phone shut, I guessed he didn't have a signal. He looked at me. I got my phone out of my bag, looked at it, and shook my head.

'Shit,' he said.

We started walking towards the phone box at the end of the street. It wasn't far. Nothing was far around here. You could walk the entire length of the village in about half a minute. The terraced cottages[1] on either side of the street were grey and cold and lifeless, and I counted three more that were boarded up. The large stone house at the end of the street wasn't boarded up, though. It wasn't that big, but it seemed to tower over everything else, glowering down at the rest of the village like a stern[2] grey sentinel[3] in the dark.

I followed along behind Cole, gazing around at the night. It had really come down now. I could almost feel it, draping itself over the world. It was a different kind of night to the nights I was used to – colder, darker, bigger. It invaded your senses. I could smell the drifting odours[4] of the surrounding moorland. I could hear the secret sounds of the hills. And when I looked up, all I could see was an ocean of stars in a pure black sky, like a million gleaming eyes. I'd never seen so many stars. I wanted to show Cole. I wanted to stand

1 terraced cottages: a row of small houses joined together along their side walls
2 stern: strict **3** sentinel: security guard **4** odour: smell

together with him and look up in silence, wondering at the meaning of it all ...

But I knew better than that. Cole doesn't hold with that kind of thing. Stars are just stars to him – they're there, and that's it. What's there to wonder about? And besides, even if he had wanted to look, he wasn't in the mood for stars right now. He was boiling up inside. I could tell by the way he was walking – his jaw[1] set tight, his eyes burning holes in the air. It was best not to disturb him. He'd controlled himself in the bar just now, but it wouldn't take much for him to turn round and go storming back in and rip the place apart.

So I watched the stars on my own.

When we got to the phone box, Cole reached into his pocket and pulled out the scrap of paper that Vince had given him earlier. As he unfolded the paper and stared at the phone number, I could feel his anger simmering down and a sense of resentment[2] stumbling up. He didn't want to have to do this. He didn't want to *ask* for anything. And I guessed if I hadn't been there, he probably wouldn't have bothered. If he'd been on his own, he would have just stolen a car and driven off somewhere and spent the night asleep in the back.

'Do you want me to do it?' I asked him.

He looked at me.

'Here,' I said, taking the scrap of paper from his hand. 'Have you got any change?'

He dug some coins from his pocket and passed them over. I went into the phone box and dialled the number. Vince answered the phone. He sounded really abrupt at first, but as soon as I'd told him who I was and what had happened at the hotel, his tone quickly changed and he suddenly became really friendly.

'Where are you now?' he asked.

'In the phone box at the village.'

'All right – just wait there. I'll come and pick you up. I'll be about five minutes – OK?'

'Yeah, thanks ... that's really kind –'

1 jaw: *Kiefer* **2** resentment: *Groll*

He put the phone down before I could finish.

I looked out at Cole. He was just standing there, smoking a cigarette, looking at nothing. I put some more money in the slot and called home. Mum answered almost immediately.

'How's it going?' she asked. 'Is everything OK?'

'Yeah, it's fine. We're staying at Abbie Gorman's place tonight. We met her in Plymouth.'

'How's Cole?'

'He's all right.'

'Any trouble?'

'No –'

'Don't lie to me, Ruben.'

'I'm not – honestly. Everything's fine. He's being really good.'

I heard her sigh. She knew him better than that.

'How are you?' I asked her.

'I'm OK.'

'Is Uncle Joe there?'

'Yeah, he's staying over for a couple of days. When do you think you'll get back?'

'I'm not sure,' I said. 'I think we're going to have a look around tomorrow, see if we can find anything –'

'Do you think you will?'

'I don't know, Mum. It's not much of a place. If there's anything here, it shouldn't take long to find it. Couple of days, maybe.'

'Well, just you be careful – OK?'

We spent the next few minutes talking about nothing – the yard, the business, what was happening, what wasn't – and then I heard a car pulling up outside the phone box. It was Vince in his Land Rover.

'I have to go, Mum,' I said. 'I'll ring you sometime tomorrow.'

We said goodbye and I put the phone down and went outside. Cole was standing by the Land Rover talking to Vince. I went over and joined them.

'Who were you talking to?' Cole asked me.

'Mum.'

'Is she all right?'

'Yeah.'

I looked up at Vince. He was sitting in the driver's seat with his hands resting lightly on the steering wheel, watching us intently. For a brief moment I saw him as a thick-headed spider, waiting in his web, waiting to paralyse us and wrap us in silk and drag us back to his lair[1] ...

'You can put your bags in the back,' he said.

I looked at Cole. He nodded. We threw our bags in the back of the Land Rover, then got inside and headed off into the darkness.

1 lair: (here) home

Six

It didn't take long to get from the village to Vince and Abbie's place. A winding road led us up through a pine forest to a plateau of moorland, and then we were just racing along through an absolute darkness that could have been anything – sky, space, land, sea. It was impossible to tell. For all I knew it could have been nothing.

'Everything all right?' Vince asked me.

'Yeah,' I murmured, looking around. 'It's pretty empty, isn't it?'

'You get used to it.'

After a minute or two he slowed down and changed gear and swung the Land Rover around a corner and down a steeply banked lane. The lane was barely any wider than the Land Rover, and as we swept along through the blurring darkness, the beam of the headlights lit up the banks either side of us like the walls of a speeding tunnel.

I closed my eyes and held on tight.

After a while I felt the car slowing again, and when I opened my eyes we were turning off the lane into some kind of yard. Across the yard, pale lights were glowing in the windows of a small white farmhouse, and off to one side I could see the vague outlines of some larger buildings. Farm buildings, I guessed – barns[1], outhouses, cattle sheds. Beyond the yard, on the other side of the house, I could just make out a patchwork of granite-flecked fields in the dark.

Vince rolled the Land Rover across the yard and parked outside the house.

'Here we are,' he said, cutting the engine and looking at Cole. 'You must be hungry.'

Cole shrugged.

Vince looked at me.

I smiled at him. 'We don't want to put you to any trouble –'

1 barn: *Scheune*

'No trouble,' he said. 'I'll get Abbie to fix you something.'

We got out of the Land Rover, grabbed our bags from the back, and followed Vince into the house.

I'd never been in a farmhouse before, so I didn't know if it was a typical farmhouse or not, but I guessed it probably was. Wooden beams[1], wooden floors, logs[2] crackling on an open fire. An Aga[3] cooker in the kitchen. A larder[4] out the back.

Abbie took us upstairs and showed us into the smaller of two large bedrooms. It had a double bed and a folding sofa bed and lots of pine furniture.

'The bathroom's just along the landing,' she explained. 'There's plenty of hot water if you want a shower or anything. The food'll be ready in about ten minutes.'

'Thanks,' I told her.

As she stood in the doorway, looking slightly uncomfortable, I could feel a sadness weighing her down. I could feel other stuff, too, but I wasn't quite sure what it was. Some kind of longing, maybe ... a desire to be somewhere else. I thought I could sense a hopelessness, too. Whatever it was she was longing for, she didn't think she was going to get it.

'Is this the room where Rachel stayed?' I asked her.

She nodded. 'She left a few things behind – a couple of T-shirts, some hair grips ... I was going to send them down to you, but the police wouldn't let me.'

I looked at the double bed. 'Is that where she slept?'

Abbie nodded again. I carried on looking at the bed for a while, trying to think of something to say – but there wasn't anything. It wasn't a moment for words. I looked over at Cole. He was just standing there, like he does – letting things be what they are.

I smiled at Abbie.

1 beam: long, straight piece of wood, used in ceilings **2** log: thick piece of wood
3 Aga: old-fashioned gas cooker **4** larder: room in which food is stored

She smiled back. 'Well,' she said, 'I'll see you downstairs then ...' And she turned round and walked out.

We listened to her footsteps clonking down the wooden stairs, then Cole shut the door and dumped his bag on the sofa bed and went over to the window.

'Are you all right?' I asked him.

'Yeah.'

'Do you think we can do this?'

'What?'

'I don't know ... whatever it is we're doing.'

He turned from the window and looked at me. 'We're already doing it. We're here, aren't we? We're right in the middle of it. You probably know that better than I do.'

'Yeah, I suppose ...'

'So why are you asking?'

'I'm insecure,' I said, smiling at him. 'I need to know what you're thinking sometimes.'

'You *know* what I'm thinking.'

'I need to hear it.'

He looked at me, his head perfectly still. His eyes were as dark as the night.

'You want to know what I'm thinking?' he said softly.

'Yeah.'

He paused for a moment, then moved off towards the door. 'I need to go to the bathroom,' he said. '*That's* what I'm thinking.'

'I knew that,' I told him.

'I thought you might.'

'I knew that, too.'

He opened the door and went out without looking at me.

While he was gone I went over and lay face down on the bed. It was freshly made – the sheets and duvet recently washed, the pillows firm and plump. There was no physical trace of Rachel left, but I could still feel her presence. As I closed my eyes and buried my face in the pillow, I could smell her sleeping skin. I could smell her dreams. I could see her face in the darkness. Her eyes were closed. Her breath was sweet. Her shining black hair lay soft on the white of the pillow.

Her lips fluttered.

Go home, Ruben, she said. Let the dead bury the dead. Go home.

When we went downstairs, the food was ready on the kitchen table. There was ham, chicken, salad, bread. Bottled water, beer, wine. Abbie opened the wine and started to pour some for Cole.

'Not for me, thanks,' he told her.

'You sure?'

He nodded.

'Ruben?' she said, offering the wine bottle to me.

I shook my head. 'Could I have some water, please?'

As she poured me a glass of water, Vince cracked open a couple of beers and passed one to Cole before he could say no.

'Cheers,' said Vince, taking a long drink.

His speech was slightly slurred, so I guessed this wasn't his first beer of the evening. Cole raised his can to him, but didn't drink from it. I clinked glasses with Abbie. She took a big slurp of wine, and then we all got stuck into the food.

'So,' said Vince, chewing on a chicken leg, 'they wouldn't let you stay at the Bridge then?'

I looked at Cole. His face said – *you tell him.* I already *had* told him, on the phone earlier on, but I guessed this was just a way to get the conversation going, so I played along and told him what had happened all over again. I didn't go into any details, and I didn't mention anything about the policeman, but I got the feeling he already knew about that.

'Yeah, well,' he said when I'd finished, 'you're probably better off here anyway. The Bridge is a bit of a shit-hole, to be honest.'

'Is it closing down?' Cole asked him.

Vince stopped chewing for a moment. His eyes blinked a couple of times. Then he started chewing again. 'Who told you that?' he asked Cole.

'No one. It just looked like it was closing down. The dining room –'

'Oh right, yeah ... it's being refurbished[1].'

'What about the rest of the village?' said Cole. 'The houses, the shops, the petrol station – are they all being refurbished, too?'

A hint of annoyance darkened Vince's face. He wiped his mouth with a napkin and reached for his can of beer. 'There's a lot of redevelopment work going on,' he said, 'a lot of reinvestment. It's happening all over the moor. We were hit really hard by the foot-and-mouth thing[2] a few years ago ... the whole moor was closed off for months.' He looked at Abbie. 'Things were pretty rough for a while, weren't they?'

Abbie nodded. 'I'd only been here a few months. Mum was ill, the farm was shut down ... it was really tough. A lot of places went under – farms, pubs, restaurants –'

'How did you manage?'

Abbie glanced at Vince, then back at Cole. 'Well, it was a struggle ...'

'But you survived?'

She just looked at him for a moment, then started eating again. Cole opened a bottle of water and poured some into a glass.

'Not drinking your beer?' said Vince.

'Not right now.'

Vince shrugged and bit off a chunk of bread. 'I hear there was a bit of trouble up at the petrol station earlier?'

Cole shrugged. 'It was nothing – just a scuffle[3].'

'Yeah? It must have been some scuffle. Big Davy's still in hospital.'

'Big Davy?'

'Yeah, the guy you hit – Big Davy Franks. I'd watch out for him if I were you. He's not going to forget what you did to him.'

'He's not supposed to. Who's the slink[4] in the red suit?'

'What?'

1 refurbish sth.: make sth. look new again **2** foot-and-mouth thing: foot-and-mouth disease, which broke out in England in 2001 affecting many farm animals, which then had to be killed **3** scuffle: small fight **4** slink: *Schleicher*

'The skinny little guy with the red hair – the one you were talking to at the petrol station. What's his name?'

'Redman,' Vince replied cautiously. 'Sean Redman. Everyone calls him Red. Why do you –?'

'What does he do?'

'What?'

Cole had stopped eating now. He was just sitting there staring at Vince, burning questions into his eyes. I could tell that Vince was starting to get annoyed with it. Not that I cared – I was still trying to come to terms with the fact that Red Suit was actually called Red.

'This Redman,' Cole repeated. 'What does he do?'

Vince frowned. 'He doesn't *do* anything. He just ... I don't know. He does a few odd jobs now and then. A bit of farm work, a bit of building ... whatever comes along. Why do you want to know?'

'Just curious,' said Cole. 'I was wondering how he knew who we were, that's all.'

Vince shrugged. 'You know what it's like in a place like this – nothing ever happens ... everyone knows each other. News soon gets around.'

Cole's eyes darkened. 'I wouldn't say that *nothing* ever happens.'

'Sorry,' Vince stuttered, suddenly realising what he'd just said. 'I didn't mean ... I just meant –'

'I know what you meant.' Cole turned away from him as if he didn't exist and started talking to Abbie. 'You said that Rachel left some stuff behind – T-shirts or something?'

She nodded. 'The police took it all away when they searched her room.'

'Local police?'

'We don't have any local police.'

'What about the one in the Bridge?'

'Sorry?'

'There was a policeman in the bar at the Bridge – fat, bald, drunk.'

'Sounds like Ron Bowerman,' Abbie said cautiously. She glanced at Vince. 'Ron drinks in the Bridge sometimes, doesn't he?'

'You could say that,' muttered Vince.

Abbie turned back to Cole. 'Ron's the Rural Community Officer for this area. He's based in Yelverton but he covers all the local villages.'

'Is he involved with Rachel's case?'

'Well, not exactly ...'

'What does that mean?'

She hesitated, looking over at Vince again, but his face was empty of help. She swallowed quietly and turned back to Cole. 'Ron was the first one to arrive at the scene.'

'He *found* her?'

Abbie shook her head. 'No, a forestry worker[1] was the first one to find her. He called it in on his radio[2], and the forestry people called Ron. Ron went out there and sealed off the area until the detectives arrived from Plymouth. They took over after that. I don't think Ron had anything else to do with it.'

As she was telling us this, I was thinking of what Bowerman must have seen. He must have seen Rachel's body, all naked and battered and ruined. He must have *seen* her. He was there. He was *with* her. And now, less than a week later, he was humiliating her brother and hounding[3] him out of a bar ...

I looked at Cole. The hate in his heart was killing him. He was keeping it under control for now, but I knew it couldn't stay that way for long. When the time came – and I didn't doubt that it would – Ron Bowerman was going to wish he'd never been born.

'Where was her body found?' Cole asked Abbie.

'About a mile from here,' she told him, turning to point through the window. 'Up that way. There's a wide track of moorland that runs through the forest up towards Lakern Tor–'

'Can we go there?' Cole asked her.

'When?'

'Now.'

1 forestry worker: person who works in the forest **2** radio: *Funkgerät* **3** hound sb.: drive sb. away

Abbie quickly shook her head. 'No … not now. You can't see anything out there this time of night. We'd never find it.'

'Never find our way back, either,' Vince added.

'Maybe tomorrow,' Abbie said.

Cole nodded quietly and gazed out of the window. The darkness was impenetrable. There was nothing to see – no lights, no movement, no life – but Cole carried on looking anyway.

Abbie muttered something to Vince, then she started clearing away the plates and things. Vince went over to the fridge and got himself another beer. He was beginning to look quite drunk now. His face was more flushed than usual, his eyes were loose, and when he sat back down at the table he had to put out a hand to steady himself.

'All right?' he said to me, popping open the beer.

I nodded and turned to Cole. He was still looking out of the window, still staring into the darkness.

'Cole?' I said.

He blinked and looked at me.

'Are you OK?' I asked quietly.

He didn't reply, he just blinked again and looked over at the sink where Abbie was drying her hands on a tea towel. 'What time did you get back that night?' he asked her.

'Sorry?'

'The night Rachel died … you said you were at your mother-in-law's.'

'We've already been through all this –'

'I know. I'm sorry. I just want to get things straight.'

'All right,' she sighed. 'Yes, I was at my mother-in-law's.'

'What time did you get back here?'

Abbie glanced at Vince. He just stared at her. She turned back to Cole, still drying her hands on the tea towel. 'I don't remember exactly … it was late.' She looked at Vince again. 'It was about one o'clock, wasn't it?'

'Something like that.' He drank some beer. 'I was going to pick her up,' he told Cole, 'but I couldn't get the car to start. She had to walk back.'

Cole looked at Abbie. 'You walked back?'

She nodded. 'I got soaked –'

'You walked back from the village to here?'

She nodded again, more slowly this time, staring at the twisted tea towel in her hands. Cole just stared at her. I did, too. We were both thinking the same thing: if she'd walked back home from the village that night, she would have gone the same way as Rachel. Same night, same journey.

Same night.

Same journey.

When Abbie finally looked up, her face was pale and her eyes were laden with sadness and guilt.

'I'm sorry,' she said. 'I was going to tell you – honestly. I just feel so bad about it. I didn't know how to –'

'Did you see her?' Cole asked quietly. 'Did you see Rachel?'

Abbie shook her head. 'I was probably about ten minutes behind her ... maybe less.' She wiped a tear from her eye. 'God, if only I'd left a few minutes earlier –'

'It wasn't your fault,' Vince told her.

She flashed a look at him then, and for a brief moment I saw something else behind her tears. I saw disgust and anger. I saw hatred. It passed as quickly as it had appeared, but I knew I wasn't mistaken. I could see the mark it had left on Vince – he looked like a man who'd just had his face slapped. Cole could see it, too.

'What was wrong with your car?' he asked Vince.

'What?'

'Your car. You said it wouldn't start. What was the matter with it?'

'Carburettor[1].' Vince shrugged. 'I thought it was just the rain at first, you know ... it was pouring down. I thought the engine was

1 carburettor: *Vergaser*

wet. But even after I'd got everything dry, it still wouldn't start. I had to get a new carb[1] fitted the next day.' He shrugged again. 'It was just bad luck.'

'Why's that?' asked Cole.

'Well, you know ...'

Cole just stared at him.

Vince said, 'I just mean we might have seen something, that's all. You know, if the car hadn't broken down and I'd picked up Abbie –'

'You might have seen Rachel?'

'Yeah.'

'But you didn't?'

'No.'

Cole turned to Abbie. 'And you didn't see anything when you were walking back, either?'

She shook her head.

Cole went quiet again.

Everything went quiet.

I was beginning to get a bit lost now. There was too much going on that I didn't understand. There were too many feelings. Too many directions. Too many lines and colours in my head. Too many shades.

'I think we'd better go to bed,' I said into the silence.

Cole looked at me. *Not yet,* his eyes said, *I haven't finished.*

'I'm tired,' I said, kicking him under the table.

He carried on staring at me for a moment, then nodded. 'Yeah, well,' he said, 'it's been a long day, I suppose. Maybe you're right.' He rubbed the back of his neck and turned to Abbie. 'Do you mind if we get off to bed now?'

'Of course not.'

He smiled at her then, which took me by surprise. I knew it was only a fake smile, but it was still nice to see it. Cole doesn't smile much at the best of times, and since Rachel's death he hadn't even come close.

1 carb: carburettor

He carried on smiling as we said goodnight and left them to it, but as soon as we were out of the kitchen his face went cold and the smile disappeared like the light of a clouded sun.

As far as I could remember, I'd never spent the night in the same room as Cole before. I'd never had to. Unlike Cole – who was born in a trailer – I was born and raised in the house at the breaker's yard. As houses go, it's not the most stylish place in the world, but what it lacks in style it more than makes up for in rooms. If there's one thing our house has got, it's rooms. It's got *loads* of them – sitting rooms, dining rooms, bathrooms, bedrooms. It's got so many bedrooms I used to sleep in a different one every week. Sometimes I wouldn't even be on the same *floor* as Cole, never mind in the same room.

So this was a new experience for me – sharing a sleeping place with my brother. And I kind of liked it.

Not that we did much sleeping.

For the first hour or so we just sat on the bed and talked in whispers. Cole kept asking me what I felt about things – about Abbie and Vince, about Red, about Pomeroy and Bowerman. And I was happy enough to tell him. But after a while I realised that he wasn't giving anything back. The information was all one-way, and I wasn't getting anything out of it. So when Cole paused for a moment to light a cigarette, I took the opportunity to ask him what *he* thought about everything.

He didn't answer me at first. He lit his cigarette, went over and opened the window to let the smoke out, and then he just stood there for a while, looking down at the yard below.

'Cole?' I said.

'Hmm?'

'What do you *think?*'

'What do I think about what?'

'Everything ... anything. All those questions you were asking Abbie and Vince. The stuff about the car, where Rachel was found –'

'Keep your voice down,' he reminded me. 'They'll hear us.'

'I'll start shouting if you don't answer me.'

He breathed smoke out of the window, then turned and looked at me. 'What do you want to know?' he said softly.

'*Any*thing,' I sighed. 'I just want to know what's going on.'

'I'm not sure yet.'

'But you've got an idea?'

'Not really ... just a feeling.' He came over and sat down beside me on the bed. 'I need time to think things through. I'm not like you, Rube. I'm slow. It takes me a while to get hold of things.'

'You weren't very slow tonight,' I told him. 'You were shooting questions at them like a machine gun.'

'Yeah, but I didn't really know what I was doing. I was just asking whatever came into my head. I don't know what any of it means yet.'

'But you think it means something?'

'Yeah, it has to. I mean, Vince doesn't like us, does he?'

'No.'

'So why was he so keen for us to stay here?'

'He wants to know what we're doing. He wants to know where we are. He wants to keep an eye on us.'

'Right. And he's in with this Redman guy, and Bowerman, and they both want us out of here –'

'Everyone wants us out of here.'

'Exactly. And you know what that means, don't you?'

'What?'

'Either they've all got something to hide, or they're all *scared* of someone who's got something to hide.'

We carried on talking for a while – about feelings and raincoats and cars and coincidences[1] – and although we didn't come to any conclusions, we knew we were getting close to something. It was just a matter of finding out what it was.

1 coincidence: accidental happening

At some point in the early hours of the morning we heard Abbie and Vince coming up to bed. We stopped talking and listened, but there wasn't much to hear – footsteps and mumbles, bathroom sounds, doors opening and closing. Eventually, a door along the landing[1] clicked shut and the farmhouse went quiet again.

Cole got up and went over to the window. It was still open. The night air was still quiet. But as Cole stood there looking out, his figure silhouetted against the blue-black sky, I could hear the faint whisper of a rising wind coming down from the hills and creeping over the moor. It sounded cold and lonely, like a final breath, and when I closed my eyes and opened my mind, I could see it all again – the ring of stones, the stunted thorn tree, Rachel's last breath stealing away on the wind ...

'What's that?' said Cole.

I opened my eyes and looked at him. He'd turned away from the window and was staring hard at the bedroom door.

'Listen,' he said.

I couldn't hear anything at first, just the quiet moan of the wind outside and the deathly silence of the farmhouse, but then – just as I was about to say something to Cole – I heard the unmistakable sound of someone crying. The sobs were muffled and indistinct, so it was hard to tell where they were coming from, but we both knew it could only be Abbie. She was in her bedroom, crying her eyes out, trying desperately not to make any noise. I imagined her clutching a pillow to her face, trying to smother the sound of her sobbing. I imagined her shoulders heaving, her stomach lurching, her breath coming out in uncontrollable gulps ...

I couldn't imagine what Vince was doing.

I looked at Cole. It was hard to tell what he was feeling, but I doubted it was sympathy. He lit another cigarette and stared at me without expression.

'What do you think?' I asked him.

He didn't say anything, just shrugged.

1 landing: area at the top of the stairs

The sound of the sobbing was fading now. The silence was returning. I looked at the door, thinking of Abbie and Vince in their room, and I wondered what they meant to each other.

I said to Cole, 'They're not very happy, are they?'

He shrugged again. 'Who is?'

I looked at him. 'I think Rachel was pretty happy most of the time.'

'Yeah ...'

We both sat in silence for a while, alone together with our thoughts. Mine were mostly good ones: Rachel smiling, Rachel laughing, Rachel singing to herself when she thought she was alone in the house. I was right – she *had* been pretty happy most of the time.

'It's not fair, is it?' I said to Cole.

'No.'

'How come all the crap people don't die?'

'It's a crap world.'

We finally got to sleep around three. Cole let me have the bed, and he stretched out on the unmade sofa bed. It didn't look very comfortable, but he didn't seem to care. He hadn't even bothered getting undressed.

'Why don't you cover yourself up?' I suggested. 'There's probably some blankets in one of the cupboards.'

'I'm all right,' he said.

'You'll freeze like that. Let me get you a blanket –'

'Ruben?'

'What?'

'Shut up and go to sleep.'

I shut up and went to sleep.

It didn't last long.

I'm underground. I'm cold. It's dark. A poisonous stink thickens the air and clings to my skin like fog. For a tick of a moment I think I'm awake, and the stink is just a sleep fart, but I know in my heart that I'm wrong. This is no sleep fart – this is something foul.

This is *inhuman.*

This is the Dead Man.

I can feel him. His skin – stiff with muck[1]. His hands – purpled with blood. His smell – the gaseous reek[2] of decay. This is the death of his body: the peeling scraps of skin, the loose teeth, the blowflies[3] crawling in his mouth and his eyes, flesh flies, maggots[4], bacteria. I can feel it all. I can feel his innards[5] bursting, liquefying[6], fermenting. I can feel the insects feeding on the liquid stink ...

And now, worse than anything, I can feel him dreaming of me in his death – telling me what he did to Rachel, showing me, telling me, showing me, telling me ... showing me the mortal fear on her face. Making me see it. Making me feel it. And I'm crying like I've never cried before. I'm begging him to stop. I'm tearing at myself. I'm raging and sobbing and screaming like a crazy man – no, oh no no no no *NO!* nothing should ever be like this ... *NOTHING!* nothing nothing *NOTHING* oh God oh God *OH GOD* ...

'Ruben!'

Now he's got me ...

'Ruben!'

Now he's shaking me ...

'RUBEN!'

My eyes snapped open and the Dead Man died. I was sitting up in bed, staring into Cole's dark eyes. He was holding me gently, his hands on my shoulders. My eyes were bulging and I was shaking like a leaf.

'It's all right,' he said calmly. 'It's only me ... you were dreaming.'

Cold sweat was pouring from my skin and my heart was pounding like a hammer. I could feel the dream-screams lodged in my throat, choking the breath from my lungs.

1 muck: filth, rubbish **2** reek: strong smell **3** blowfly: fly that leaves its eggs in decaying meat **4** maggot: *Made* **5** innards (pl; infml): organs inside a person **6** liquefy: become liquid

'I c-can't breathe,' I gasped.

'Yes, you can,' Cole said. 'Just take it easy. Breathe slowly. Not too much ... nice and steady, just take a little breath and then let it out again.'

I breathed in, then coughed and retched[1] into my hand. I could still smell him – the Dead Man. His stink of death was still inside me. I could feel it under my skin, poisoning my blood, crawling into my heart. It was sickening. Terrifying. I didn't *want* to breathe that smell.

'Come on, Rube,' Cole said, tightening his grip on my shoulders. 'Just breathe ... get some air into your lungs. You'll be OK.'

'I don't want to die,' I told him.

He froze for a moment, then said, 'What are you talking about? You're not going to *die*.'

'I don't want to be with him.'

'Who?'

'The Dead Man.'

I was crying now. Not just for myself, but for Rachel too. It wasn't right, what we were doing. We were taking her down there ... taking her back to the Dead Man. It wasn't *right*. We were taking her home to put her in a box and lower her down into the ground with him. Down into the dead of dark, down into the underground cold, down with the insects ...

'Ruben?' said Cole. 'Who's the –?'

'It's not right,' I said.

'What?'

'It's not *right*.'

'Ruben – look at me.'

'We shouldn't be –'

I stopped suddenly as he took my head in his hands. His fingers felt cool and calm and strong. 'All right,' he said firmly. 'Just look at me, now – OK? Look at me.'

1 retch: nearly vomit

I looked into his eyes through a veil[1] of tears. He didn't say anything. He just cradled my head in his hands and let the tears flow over his fingers until the river was dry. All the time, his eyes never wavered. They held me in the darkness like a distant light on a winter's night. I don't know how long we sat there for, but eventually I realised that I wasn't trembling any more and my breathing was back to normal again. Cole had taken his hands from my face, but I could still feel the touch of his fingers cooling my skin.

Best of all, he was smiling at me.

'All right?' he asked. 'Feeling better now?'

I nodded.

'Good,' he said. 'It was just a dream, Rube. You know that, don't you? Dreams don't mean anything.'

'This one did.'

His eyes never moved from mine. 'Do you want to talk about it?'

'It's not just that … it's not just the dream.'

'I don't understand.'

'I was going to tell you …'

'Tell me *what?*'

I lowered my eyes, unable to look at him. When I spoke, my voice was barely audible. 'I saw him do it, Cole. I was there. I saw him get Rachel.'

'Who?'

'The Dead Man.'

I told him everything I could. I told him about my night in the Mercedes. I told him about being with Rachel on the moor. I told him about the Dead Man. I even told him about the ring of stones and the stunted thorn tree. He didn't say anything when I'd finished, he just went over to the open window and stood there gazing out at the pre-dawn[2] sky. As I sat in bed watching him, waiting for him to say something, a gentle breeze drifted in through the window, scenting

1 veil: *Schleier* **2** pre-dawn: time of day just before the light of the sun starts to appear

the air with something sweet. The room seemed to glow in a lazy blue-black light.

After a while, Cole came back over and sat down next to me again.

'Why didn't you tell me before?' he said.

There was no anger or bitterness in his voice. He wasn't annoyed with me for not telling him about the Dead Man – he just wanted to know why I hadn't.

'I don't know,' I said honestly.

'Did you think I wouldn't believe you?'

'No.'

'What, then?'

'I don't know. Maybe I was just waiting to see if it meant anything.'

'Why shouldn't it mean anything?'

'Because up until now it didn't matter who killed Rachel, did it? You said it yourself when we were talking to Pomeroy – it doesn't matter who did it or why they did it or how she died. She's dead. Dead is dead. Nothing can change that – reasons, revenge, punishment, justice. Nothing can change what's already done.' I looked at him. 'Right?'

'Right.'

'So, up until now, the Dead Man didn't mean anything. It didn't matter who he was. It didn't change anything.'

'Up until now.'

'Yeah – but things are different now. Now he means something. If we can find him and prove he killed Rachel, we can bring her home and put her to rest. That's what Mum wants, isn't it?'

'Yeah.'

'That's what we're doing here.'

'Right.'

'And that's all that matters.'

Cole lit a cigarette and smoked it thoughtfully for a while, digesting[1] what I'd just told him. I watched the smoke drifting in the breeze, and I wondered idly if what I'd just told him was true. I guessed that most of it was. And even if it wasn't, I was pretty sure that Cole hadn't been telling me everything he knew, either.

But that was OK.

'All right,' he said quietly. 'Tell me about this dead man.'

'There's nothing else to tell,' I said. 'I've told you everything I know about him.'

'No, you haven't – why do you call him the dead man?'

'Because he's dead.'

'But you called him that *before* he killed Rachel. He couldn't have been dead then, could he?'

'Yeah, he was –'

'Come on, Rube. You can't kill someone if you're already dead.'

'He wasn't dead *physically*.'

'What do you mean?' Cole frowned. 'What other kinds of dead *are* there?'

'He was as good as dead,' I tried to explain. 'It was already decided. I don't think it even mattered whether he killed Rachel or not. He was going to die whatever he did.'

'Someone had already decided to kill him?'

'Yeah.'

'Who?'

'I don't know. All I know is that there was nothing he could do about it. Once it had been decided, that was it. He was dead from then on.'

'And he's definitely dead now?'

'Dead and buried.'

'Where?'

'I don't know. I think it's probably around here somewhere, but I'm not sure.'

'Are you sure about the rest of it?'

1 digest sth.: think about and try to understand sth.

'No.'

'But you felt it?'

'I think so.'

'You *think* so?'

'Yeah,' I said, 'I think so.'

I hesitated for a moment, wondering if I could tell him what I wanted to tell him. We'd never really talked about the weird stuff I feel before. I knew he knew about it, and I knew he believed in it, but I'd never tried explaining it to him. I'd never been sure that he wanted me to. And I wasn't sure now, either. But I knew if I didn't do it now, I probably never would. So, before I could change my mind, I just opened my mouth and started talking.

'It's hard to explain,' I told him, 'but when I get these feelings, I don't have any control over them. They just come to me. I can't *do* anything with them. They're not facts or thoughts or sensations, they're not anything I can describe. They're not even feelings, really. I only think of them as feelings because that's the closest I can get.'

I looked at Cole to see how he was taking it so far. His face was blank, but his eyes were waiting for me to go on.

'I don't *know* what they are,' I went on, 'and a lot of the time I don't even know what they mean. Sometimes it's simple. Most of the stuff I get from you is pretty simple.' I smiled at him. He didn't smile back. 'I don't get everything,' I said, trying to reassure him. 'I only get what I'm given.'

'Who gives it to you?' he said.

'I don't know.'

He nodded. 'What about the stuff that isn't simple?'

'I don't know … it's like it doesn't come to me fully formed. It comes in pieces – fragments, notes, layers, shades … weird kinds of pieces. And when that happens, I have to guess what's missing – or feel what's missing – and then I have to try to work out what's supposed to be there. That's why I'm not sure about stuff sometimes. I know it's supposed to be there, but I don't know what I'm looking for. I don't even know what I'm looking *at* half the time. It's like trying to solve a multidimensional crossword puzzle with most of the clues missing, and the clues that *aren't* missing are written in a language I don't understand.'

Cole nodded again. He ran his fingers through his hair and looked at me. 'Pretty weird stuff,' he said thoughtfully.

'Yeah.'

'But it's real?'

'As real as anything else. It doesn't lie.'

'But that doesn't mean you're sure about everything.'

'No.'

'Are you sure about Rachel?'

'Absolutely.'

'What about the Dead Man?'

'Yeah, I'm sure about him. I just don't know any details.'

'What about the stuff in your dream? Was that real?'

'I think some of it was ... but some of it was just a dream.' I closed my eyes, feeling the fear of the dream again – the coldness, the darkness, the death. I looked at Cole. 'You don't feel anything when you're dead, do you?'

'No,' he said simply. 'That's what death *is* – feeling nothing.'

'And if there's nothing to feel, there's nothing to fear, is there?'

'Nothing at all.'

We finally drifted off to sleep again just as the first light of dawn was beginning to colour the sky. My last waking thought was of Rachel. I could see her quite clearly: her sleeping skin, her shining black hair, her face on the pillow beside me.

Go home, Ruben, she whispered again. Let the dead bury the dead.

Go home.

Seven

I'm not used to silence in the morning. I'm used to the clatter and grind[1] of the breaker's yard, the groan of car crushers and scrap magnets, the drone of traffic on the east London streets. So when I woke up that morning and everything was quiet, it took me a while to realise where I was. When I finally did realise where I was – Dartmoor, farmhouse, bedroom – I also realised how tired I was. I'd only had about an hour's sleep all night. My eyes were thick, my body ached[2], my head was all tight and buzzy[3].

I closed my eyes and tried to go back to sleep, but I knew that I wouldn't. Sunlight was streaming in through the window, birds were singing ... everything was *too* quiet. I could hear too much: Abbie and Vince in the kitchen downstairs, Cole in the bathroom, a dog barking somewhere in the distance. And now the smell of breakfast was beginning to drift up the stairs – bacon and eggs, toast, coffee ...

It was all very nice – but I wished I wasn't there. I wished I was at home – in *my* house, in *my* room, in *my* bed, smelling *my* breakfast.

After a minute or two, the bedroom door opened and Cole came in.

'Come on, Rube,' he said, 'it's time to get up. We've got a lot to do today.'

I didn't move.

I could feel him looking at me, then I heard him crossing the room, and then I heard myself swearing at him as he yanked the duvet off my bed and threw it on the floor. I was only wearing a pair of boxers, and the sudden blast of fresh air on my skin was shocking.

'Shit, Cole,' I snapped, sitting up straight. 'I might have been *naked*.'

1 grind: crushing noise **2** ache: hurt a little bit **3** buzzy: (here) with many things swirling around in his head

He didn't even look at me. He just turned away and went over to get something from his bag. I watched him, remembering when he'd left the house yesterday morning and removed something from the boot of the smashed-up Volvo in the yard. I tried to see what he was doing now, but he had his back to me and was keeping the bag out of sight. I knew what he was doing, though. I made a mental note to bring it up with him later, then I got out of bed and started getting dressed.

'What's the plan?' I said.

'I want to go into the village and poke around[1] for a while, see what I can find. See if anyone's got anything to say. Then I might go up to the gypsy camp.' He retied his bag and turned round to face me. 'I don't understand what they're doing here.'

'The gypsies?'

'Yeah – I mean, there's nothing here for them, is there? No work, nowhere to sell anything. Are there any fairs around?'

'Not that I know of.'

He shook his head. 'It's not even much of a site.'

'Maybe there's some work around that we don't know about. There's plenty of farms ...'

'It's all sheep and cattle. Gypsies don't work with sheep and cattle.'

'Maybe they're stealing them?'

'No one steals sheep any more. It's not worth the effort. Do you know how much you get for a sheep these days?'

'Well, maybe they're here to look after us?'

'What?'

'Like angels.'

'Angels?'

I grinned at him. 'Guardian angels.'

He didn't even bother telling me I was an idiot, he just shook his head and started putting his shoes on. 'Anyway,' he said, 'I might go up and talk to them later if I've got time.'

1 poke around sth.: look around for sth.

'Do you think they'll want to talk to us? You know what some of them think of Dad.'

'They can think what they like.' He looked at me. 'You won't be there, anyway.'

'Why not?'

'You're staying here.'

'What?'

'I want you to stay here –'

'No way,' I said. 'I'm coming with you. I'm not letting you –'

'Listen to me,' he said, holding up his hand. 'Just listen a minute.' He looked over at the door, then spoke quietly. 'There's something going on here, isn't there?'

'Yeah, but –'

'We need to find out what it is.' He looked at me. 'Right?'

'Yeah, I suppose ...'

'There's no suppose about it, Rube. We need to know what's going on. One of us has to stay here.'

'All right – but why does it have to be me?'

'Because if you go into the village and meet up with Red and Big Davy and whoever else is there, they'll scare the shit out of you.' He paused, looking me in the eye. 'And if you stay here you can take a look at the place where Rachel's body was found.'

I knew what he meant, and I knew he was right. It made sense for him to go to the village, and it made sense for me to stay here. I still didn't like it, but then we weren't here to *like* things, were we?

'OK?' said Cole.

'Yeah, OK. I'll ask Abbie to tell me where Rachel was found. She can draw me a map or something –'

'No, get her to take you there. Don't go on your own. If Abbie doesn't want to take you, or if she's out all day or something, wait for me to get back and we'll go together.'

'Why?'

'Because I said so.'

I looked at him. His face said – *don't argue*. So I didn't.

'All right,' I said. 'Is there anything else you want me to do?'

'Like what?'

'I don't know ... I mean, how am I supposed to find out what's going on? What should I do?'

'Nothing – just hang around, see how it feels.' He almost smiled. 'See if anything comes to you.'

Not much happened at the breakfast table. Vince was quiet, concentrating on his food, and Abbie didn't even sit down. She just pottered around making coffee and toast and keeping out of the way. Her eyes looked a bit red from crying, but then I expect mine probably did, too.

Outside, the sky looked clear and bright, and a pale white sun was beginning to warm the air.

When Vince had finished eating, he wiped his plate with a slice of bread, popped the bread in his mouth, then washed it all down with a big slurp of tea. 'You need a lift anywhere?' he said to Cole. 'I'm heading off to Plymouth in a minute.'

'Could you drop me off in the village?'

'No trouble.' He drained the tea from his mug. 'Going anywhere in particular?'

'Not really.' Cole looked at him. 'Anywhere in particular you'd recommend[1]?'

'Not really.' Vince put his mug down and stood up. 'I'll be ready in about five minutes – OK?'

Cole nodded. As Vince left the room and went upstairs, Abbie came over and started clearing the table.

'Are you going anywhere today?' I asked her.

She shrugged. 'I shouldn't think so.'

'Do you mind if I stay here with you?'

She paused for a moment. 'Aren't you going with Cole?'

'I'm a bit tired,' I said. 'I thought I'd just hang around here ... if that's OK with you?'

1 recommend sth.: suggest sth. because you think it is good

'Yeah, fine,' she said indifferently, taking the plates over to the sink. 'I'm not going anywhere.'

Five minutes later I heard Vince starting up the Land Rover. I went out into the hallway and saw Cole coming down the stairs with his rucksack slung over his shoulder.

'How long do you think you'll be?' I asked him.

'I don't know ... as long as it takes. If I'm going to be late I'll give you a ring.'

'Don't forget –'

'There's no mobile signal. Yeah, I know. I'll use a phone box and ring you here.' He started towards the door. 'I'll see you later.'

'Cole?' I said, as he opened the door.

He turned around. 'What?'

I nodded at the bag on his shoulder. 'Do you really need that?'

His eyes blinked hesitantly. 'What do you mean?'

'You know what I mean.'

He didn't know what to say. He studied my eyes, trying to work out if I knew what he had in the bag, or if I was just guessing. I let him look. It didn't make any difference to me – I didn't know whether I was guessing or not myself.

While I was waiting for him to say something, a car horn sounded from the yard. Cole leaned out of the door and waved his hand at Vince, then he turned back to me.

'I'd better go,' he said. 'I'll see you later – OK?'

Before I could say anything else, he'd walked out and shut the door.

I went upstairs and used the bathroom, then I wandered back down and joined Abbie in the kitchen. She was doing the washing up. As I sat down at the kitchen table, she flashed a quick smile at me.

'All right?' she said.

'Yeah.'

'Looks like we've been left behind.'

'Yeah.'

She smiled again and went back to the dishes. I knew I should have made more of an effort to talk to her, but I couldn't stop thinking about Cole. I was worried about him. I was worried about who he might meet in the village – Red, Davy, Bowerman, the creepy[1] guy with the beard. He was bound to meet up with some of them sooner or later. In fact, knowing Cole, he was probably going to be looking for them. And when he found them?

That's what I was worried about. I just hoped he'd get through the day without killing anyone.

'Do you want a cup of coffee?' Abbie said.

'Sorry?'

'Coffee,' she repeated, waggling a cup at me.

'Oh, right ... yeah, please.' I smiled at her. 'Sorry, I was miles away.'

'Yeah, well,' she said, 'I don't suppose you're sleeping that well at the moment.'

I didn't know what to say to that – she'd probably heard me crying in the night, and she probably knew that I'd heard *her* crying too – so I just shrugged and smiled at her again. She smiled back at me and started making the coffee.

'Do you know what Cole's doing in the village?' she asked casually.

'Just looking around, I think.'

She nodded. 'What does he think he's going to find?'

'I don't know. Maybe something about Rachel ...'

Abbie didn't say anything. She carried on making the coffee – filling the cups, getting the milk out of the fridge, looking for a teaspoon. I thought I saw the glint of a tear in her eye, but I could have been mistaken.

'What did you do when she was here?' I asked her.

'What do you mean?'

'You and Rachel – what did you do?'

She shrugged. 'Nothing much. We just hung around, mostly ... you know – talking, eating, going out for a walk now and then.' She

1 creepy: scary, weird

smiled sadly. 'It was really nice. There's not much to do around here any more, and Vince is away a lot of the time, so it gets a bit lonely. It was nice to have some company for a change.'

'What about the farm?' I said. 'Doesn't that keep you busy?'

'What farm?'

'All this,' I said, looking vaguely out of the window. 'All these fields and buildings and everything ... isn't it a farm?'

'It used to be. Most of it doesn't belong to us any more. My mother sold a lot of the land when she was ill. Me and Vince tried to keep things going for a while after she died, but it didn't work out. We've had to sell what was left of the land.' She looked out of the window. 'The farm buildings are still ours, not that they're any use to us any more. And we still own the house ... but that's about it.' She looked over at me. 'Do you want milk and sugar?'

'Yes, please. Four sugars.'

'Four?'

'I like sugar.'

She fiddled around with the milk and sugar for a while, then brought the coffees over to the table and sat down beside me. 'I knew Rachel for a long time, you know. We used to be really close.'

'I know – I remember you used to come round to our place after school sometimes.'

She smiled again. 'That was a lifetime ago.'

'Do you ever think of going back?'

'To London?' She shook her head. 'I still miss it sometimes, but I could never go back. I couldn't leave this house. It was my mum's. She was born here, she died here. It means too much to me. And, besides, Vince could never live in London.' She laughed to herself. 'He couldn't cope[1]. It'd drive him mad.'

'Does he come from around here?'

She nodded, sipping her coffee. 'He was born here – in the village. He's never lived anywhere else.'

'What did he think of Rachel?'

1 cope: manage

Abbie froze, her coffee cup paused in mid-air, and her eyes went cold. I knew I'd said the wrong thing – I knew it as soon as I'd said it. It was a question too far. Too close. Too pushy. I looked innocently at Abbie, hoping she'd let me get away with it, but I knew I was wasting my time. All I could do was watch and wait as she slowly lowered her cup to the table, stared at it for a moment, then raised her eyes and fixed me with a hateful stare.

'You just can't leave it alone, can you?' she said icily.

'I didn't mean anything –'

'Yeah, you did. You and your brother have been niggling away[1] at me ever since you got here. *Where were you when Rachel died? What were you doing? What did you see? What did you do?* I mean, *Christ* ...' she shook her head angrily, '... I've already *told* you everything I know about Rachel. I've *told* you what happened. I've *told* you where I was. I've *told* you I'm sorry. What more do you want from me? And now this ... interrogating[2] me about Vince, like *he* had something to do with it –'

'I didn't say that. I was only asking –'

'Don't *lie* to me,' she snapped. 'God, you're worse than your brother. At least he's got the guts[3] to be honest about it. At least he doesn't *pretend* to give a shit about anyone else.'

I couldn't really argue with her. I didn't *want* to argue with her. And even if I did, I wouldn't have known what to say. So I didn't say anything. I just sat there, trying not to look guilty, but probably not succeeding.

Abbie carried on staring at me for a while, then she shook her head again and got up from the table and walked out without saying a word.

I waited until she'd stomped[4] up the stairs and slammed her bedroom door, then I closed my eyes and rewound the tape recorder

1 niggle away at sb.: (here) ask sb. questions all the time **2** interrogate sb.: question sb. **3** have the guts (infml): have the courage **4** stomp: make a noise as you walk

inside my head and played back the last fifteen minutes. It was interesting stuff. I wasn't sure what any of it meant, but it gave me a lot to think about.

When I'd finished thinking about it, I drained the last dregs of my cold sugary coffee, then went outside to get some fresh air.

The farmyard seemed a lot smaller in the daylight. When we'd arrived last night, I'd somehow got the impression that it was a big old rambling[1] place with acres of wasteground[2] and dozens of tumbledown[3] buildings. But now, as I shut the front door and stepped out into the sunlight, I could see it for what it really was – and it wasn't very much at all. Just a medium-sized patch of rutted dirt, a ramshackle[4] barn, and a couple of mouldering[5] outhouses.

That was it.

I started walking towards the barn. Although the sun was out and the air was warm, the ground was mostly slick with mud. It wasn't thick mud – it was easily walkable – but it squelched[6] under my feet and it didn't smell good. With every squelching step, it gave off a faintly gaseous smell. It was the smell of dead things, rotting things, and it reminded me of my dream. It also reminded me of the rainstorm – Rachel's rainstorm – and I couldn't help wondering if the moisture[7] under my feet had come from the clouds that had rained on my sister.

I didn't know what to think about that.

So I didn't.

I emptied my head and carried on towards the barn. The edges of the yard were littered with agricultural rubbish – bins and boxes, empty sacks, rolls of wire-mesh[8], sheets of corrugated iron[9], a trough, a scythe blade[10], coil springs[11] and drive wheels and cogs[12] and chains. In the breaker's yard at home, these things would have

1 rambling: stretching in various directions **2** wasteground: empty piece of land **3** tumbledown: in a very bad condition **4** ramshackle: nearly falling to pieces **5** mouldering: slowly decaying **6** squelch: crush **7** moisture: dampness **8** wire-mesh: *Maschendraht* **9** corrugated iron: *Wellblech* **10** scythe blade: *Sense* **11** coil springs (pl): *Spiralfedern* **12** cog: *Zahnrad*

seemed exotic, like remnants[1] of another world, but here they just seemed sad and abandoned. Dead things in a dead place.

I stopped outside the barn and looked around. The yard didn't have any clear-cut boundaries – no walls or fences or hedges[2] – it just merged[3] uneasily into the surrounding landscape of the moor. And the moor was massive. Everything seemed to go on for ever – the sky, the fields, the hills, the colours. Everywhere I looked, in every direction, all I could see was miles of emptiness.

It was endless and enormous, and it made me feel really small.

'You *are* really small,' I reminded myself.

I entered the barn, smiling stupidly to myself, and looked around. It was a big old wooden building, about twice as high as the farm-house, with a dirt floor and no windows and big double doors at the front. Sunlight filtered in through the cracks in the timbers[4], lighting up clouds of straw-dust, and the air was calmed with a cool interior silence. It was the kind of silence you can almost smell. The whole place was painted black, inside and out. Apart from some more farmyard rubbish – the remains of an old Fordson tractor, some sacks of seed, a few bales of mouldy straw – the barn was empty. A ladder led up through a hatchway[5] to what I guessed was another floor. I thought about taking a look, but the ladder didn't look too sound[6], and there probably wasn't anything up there anyway, so I decided not to bother.

I went back out into the yard and headed over to the outhouses. It was hard to tell how many individual buildings there were, as they were all cobbled[7] together with corrugated plastic and scrap timber[8] and twine[9] into one big mutant shack[10]. I could only find two doors, though, so I guessed the whole thing had originally been two buildings. Both of the doors were padlocked[11] and chained, and the windows were all boarded up. The padlocks were no problem – I

1 remnants (pl): remaining parts **2** hedge: line of bushes **3** merge into sth.: gradually change into sth. else **4** timber: *Holzbalken* **5** hatchway: opening in a deck or a ceiling **6** sound: stable, strong **7** cobbled together: joined together **8** timber: *Bauholz* **9** twine: strong kind of string **10** shack: roughly-built hut **11** padlock sth.: *etw. mit einem Schloß verschließen*

could have picked them with my eyes closed. But I was in full view of the farmhouse, and it was broad daylight, and I could feel that someone was watching me.

As I moved away from the outhouses and ambled[1] across the yard towards the lane, I glanced back at the farmhouse. I couldn't see Abbie watching me – I couldn't see *anything*. The sun's reflection was blazing in the windows like a bright red ball of fire, obliterating[2] everything behind the glass. But as I shielded my eyes and looked away, and the after-image burned in my mind, I saw a velvet-framed orange disc, rimmed with electric blue, and somewhere behind it, floating in space, I saw a flickering face in the window.

The lane led upwards, away from the farmhouse, winding tightly through the moorland fields. Pale dots of sheep were grazing in the distance, and away to my right I could see the darker dots of cows or ponies scattered across the open fields. Apart from that, and the occasional black trace of passing crows in the sky, the moor was empty.

I didn't know where I was going. I was just walking – walking and thinking and drifting in silence. My eyes were open but my outside senses were closed. I was trying to get a fix on Cole – where he was, what he was doing, what he was thinking about. I didn't really expect to get anything from him, because that's not the way it works. I can't just feel something whenever I want to – it has to be there. *Trying* to feel something is a bit like trying to hear something. If it's not there, you can't hear it – no matter how hard you try. But that doesn't mean it's not worth trying, does it?

So I kept on trying as I walked up the lane, keeping my heart and my mind open – just in case – but nothing came to me. I wasn't too bothered. It didn't necessarily mean that everything was OK, but I was pretty sure that if Cole was in any kind of trouble, I'd know about it.

1 amble: walk slowly **2** obliterate sth.: (here) prevent sth. from being seen

I drifted on, lost in my mind, not really aware of where I was or what I was doing. I could feel the warmth of the air on my skin. I could sense the blue height of the sky above me, and the solidity of the earth under my feet. It made me feel small again, as small as the things underground, the virus trails and the beetles and worms ... but that was a world away, and the surface of the lane was hard and reassuring, and that, in turn, made me feel incredibly *big*. It also made me think – for a solitary moment – that I could do anything.

I *knew* it: in that tiny moment, I could do *absolutely anything.*

'Hey.'

The voice came from nowhere.

I shut myself down and refocused my mind and saw that I was approaching the top of the lane. There was a junction up ahead where the lane joined the road from the village, and across the road – on the other side – a line of granite boulders formed a low-lying wall at the edge of a pine forest. There was a gap in the wall, a gateway through to the trees, with two standing stones on either side – and that's where the gypsy girl was standing.

It was the girl we'd seen the day before with the old man and the baby. The two dogs were with her again – the lurcher and the three-legged Jack Russell – and the three of them were just standing there, watching me. They all had that same unsettling steadiness in their eyes, and as I walked towards them across the road I didn't know where to look. I didn't know how to walk, either. The process of walking had suddenly become really complicated – legs, feet, knees, arms, muscles, bones, joints, nerves ... I couldn't remember how any of it *worked.*

'Are you all right?' the girl said as I wobbled to a stop in front of her. I nodded, swaying slightly on my feet. She pulled a bottle of water from her back pocket and passed it over. 'Here,' she said, smiling. 'You look a bit hot.'

'Thanks.'

I uncapped the bottle and took a long drink. The girl watched me, still smiling. She was wearing a loose-knit black jumper and jeans and a pair of scruffy old purple DMs[1]. Up close, she was even more beautiful than before – pale and dark, clear and bright, a purity of curves and lines and contours …

'Are you going to drink *all* that?' she asked me.

I stopped drinking and started to apologise, but I'd forgotten to swallow what was in my mouth, so instead of apologising I just blurted out a mouthful of water. The girl and the dogs stepped back in surprise.

'Shit,' I said, wiping my mouth. 'Sorry …'

The girl laughed quietly. 'Are you always this cool?'

'I do my best.'

She took the bottle from me and put it back in her pocket. She gazed up at the sky for a moment, squinting into the sun, then she ran her fingers through her hair and looked back at me. 'I'm Jess Delaney,' she said.

I nodded, not sure what to say.

She looked down at her dogs and touched the lurcher's head. 'This is Finn,' she told me. 'The little one's called Tripe.'

I looked at the three-legged Jack Russell. He was old and scruffy and he couldn't care less about me. 'Tripe?' I said.

'It's short for Tripod[2]. He lost his leg when he was a puppy.'

For a moment I thought she meant lost as in *mislaid*, and I found myself wondering how a puppy could mislay one of its legs.

Jess said, 'He caught it in a rabbit trap.'

And I felt really embarrassed again. I looked around for something else to look at – anything but Jess's green eyes – and I settled on Finn the lurcher. He was tall and tan[3] and smooth and sleek[4] and his eyes were ringed with sooty[5] grey circles that made him look really sad. I carried on looking at him for a while, but then the silence got the better of me and I looked back at Jess again. She was smiling at me.

'You're Ruben Ford, aren't you?' she said.

1 DM = Doc Martens: brand name of heavy boots **2** Tripod: *Dreifuß* **3** tan: brown **4** sleek: soft and shiny **5** sooty: (here) black

'How do you know—?'

'I saw you yesterday with your brother. My uncle told me who you were.'

'Sorry?'

'My uncle – the old guy with the broken nose? He told me you were Baby-John Ford's boys.' The stunned[1] expression on my face seemed to amuse her. 'Don't look so surprised,' she grinned. 'Your dad's famous. Everyone's heard of Baby-John Ford.'

'Have they?'

'Yeah – he was one of the best bare-knuckle fighters of his time. They still tell stories about him. And then there was the trial[2], of course. And now this ...' Her face suddenly dropped. She lowered her eyes, rubbed her forehead, then looked up again. 'Sorry ... you know, about your sister ... I know it's no good saying sorry –'

'No, it's OK. It's fine.' I smiled at her. 'It makes a nice change from getting told to go home and forget all about it.'

Her face began to lighten again. 'Is that what's been happening?'

'Yeah, pretty much.'

'And is that why you're staying at the Gormans' place?'

I thought about it, then nodded. 'Yeah, I suppose it is.' I looked at her. 'Do you know Abbie and Vince?'

'Not really. I mean, I know who they are ...' She glanced down at her dogs. 'I saw your brother with Vince earlier on. They were driving towards the village.' She paused for a moment, then raised her head and looked at me, her eyes slightly hesitant. 'Your brother's not thinking of stirring things up[3] in the village, is he?'

I stared at her, wondering how much she knew and how much she was just guessing ... and for a moment I saw something of myself in her eyes. Not just my vision of her vision of me, but something beyond that – a *feeling* of me. My feeling for Cole, his feeling for me, all wrapped up in her eyes. She was something else, this Jess Delaney.

1 stunned: surprised **2** trial: legal process in a court of law **3** stir sth. up: cause trouble

'Do you know where Rachel's body was found?' I asked her.

'Yeah,' she said. 'It's not far from here.'

'Could you take me there?'

She looked at me for a moment, then without another word she turned round and headed off into the forest. I watched her dogs trailing after her – Finn loping[1] easily, Tripe scuttling[2] along beside him – and then I shrugged to myself and followed them through the gateway and into the shade of the trees.

1 lope: *locker laufen* **2** scuttle: hurry with short steps

Eight

Inside the forest it was dark and cool and eerily[1] still. Towering pine trees blanked out the sky, turning the daylight to dusk, and the thick carpet of needles under our feet soaked up the sound of everything. Nothing moved. Nothing stirred. Even the birds were quiet. It was like walking through the belly of an ancient cathedral.

We walked on in reverent[2] silence: up through the forest, across a dirt road, then over a ditch[3] and along a narrow pathway that wound its way through thick patches of gorse before finally bringing us out onto a broad track of open ground that stretched up into the hills. As we followed the track up a gentle slope, I began to feel something I didn't understand. The moor felt different – out of place and out of time – and there was something in the air that made me think of sadness and longing, of tears and sweat, of a death-white mist creeping down from the hills and shrouding the land in stillness.

I looked over at Jess, and I could see that she was feeling it too.

'It's the Lychway,' she said.

'Sorry?'

'This path we're on, it's called the Lychway. Apparently, if you lived around here before the thirteenth century and you wanted to bury your dead in a churchyard, you had to carry the body all the way across the moor to the parish church at Lydford. The funeral route became known as the Lychway.' Jess looked at me. '*Lyche* means corpse.'

I gazed into the distance, imagining medieval funeral processions toiling their way up the hill, clambering over rocks and streams, trailing this desolate path across the moor ...

'Some people call it the Road of the Dead,' Jess said.

1 eerie: scary **2** reverent: respectful **3** ditch: long and narrow space dug in the ground

I looked at her.

'The Lychway,' she explained, 'that's what it means – the Road of the Dead.'

We carried on walking in silence.

Every now and then we lost track of the path and found ourselves struggling through mossy boulders and knee-high clumps of tussock grass[1]. I kept losing all sense of direction, but Jess and the dogs just floated over the ground with the uncaring confidence of creatures who'd never been lost in their lives. While Jess forged ahead in an unerringly straight line, and I followed closely beside her, the two dogs trotted along in front of us, criss-crossing the ground, sniffing out birds and rabbits. They looked good – quiet and wild and content.

We'd left the forest behind now. It was still visible – darkening the flanks of the hill – but as we climbed higher and higher, the trees gradually thinned out and fell away until all that was left was a hilltop wilderness of dry grass and rocks and the occasional wind-withered shrub.

'I thought you said it wasn't far,' I said breathlessly to Jess.

'It's not as far as it seems,' she replied. 'We've only come about half a mile.'

I found that hard to believe – it felt like a thousand miles from anywhere. But then I wasn't really used to walking through forests and climbing up hills. I was used to roads, buses, tubes and trains.

Jess said, 'You didn't answer my question about Cole.'

'What question?'

'About him stirring things up in the village. Is that what he's doing?'

'Probably,' I said. 'Not that it needs much stirring up. You saw what happened yesterday near the petrol station?'

'Yeah,' she grinned, 'I saw it.' She looked over at me. 'Do you know what Uncle Reason said when he saw Big Davy going down?'

'Reason?'

1 tussock grass: type of long grass

'My uncle. I told you about him. He was with me when you saw us by the camp.'

'He's called Reason?'

'Yeah.'

'Right ...' I looked at her. 'Who were the others with you? The young girl and the baby.'

'The girl's my little sister – Freya.'

'What about the baby?'

'What about him?' Jess gave me a playful look. 'What's the matter? What are you looking at me like that for?'

'Like what?'

'Like this.' She pulled a face, which I guessed was supposed to be me looking shocked. Then she smiled and said, 'Did you think the baby was mine?'

'I didn't think *any*thing.'

'Liar,' she said, still smiling. 'Anyway, when my uncle saw your brother whacking Big Davy, he said to me – "That's a Ford, there. I seen that punch before. That's a Ford if ever I seen one."'

'Really?'

She nodded. 'Uncle used to fight a bit when he was younger. He saw some of your dad's fights. Bet on them, too. I think he won a lot of money on him once. He always rated[1] your dad.'

'What does he think of him now?'

'How do you mean?'

'Well, you know ...'

'What?'

'He married a non-gypsy ...' I shrugged awkwardly. 'You know what it's like. When Dad married Mum and bought a house and everything, a lot of the gypsies didn't want to know him any more. Even some of his own family still won't talk to him.'

Jess didn't say anything for a while. I don't think she was embarrassed or anything, but I knew it was a tricky thing to talk about. Some gypsies think that marrying into the non-gypsy world is a bad

1 rate sb.: (here) bet on sb.

thing. They don't like the *gadje*[1], or *gorgers*[2], as some of them call us. They think we're dirty and corrupt and impure. And I can't say I blame them really – most of us probably are. Personally, I don't care what anyone is – tinker[3], tailor, soldier, sailor, rich man, poor man, beggar-man, thief[4]. I just can't see how it makes any difference. If someone's all right, they're all right; if they're not, they're not. The trouble is, other people don't see it like that. They don't see people, they just see People. They see Gypsies, and they don't *like* Gypsies. They see Gorgers, and they don't *like* Gorgers. They see a Gypsy married to a Gorger, and they *double* don't like[5] either of them.

'Is it true what they say about your dad?' Jess asked me.

'Why – what do they say?'

'He killed a man in a bare-knuckle fight, didn't he?'

'Yeah ...'

'One of the Docherty brothers?'

I nodded. 'The youngest one – Tam Docherty. It was a fair fight. There was nothing wrong with it. Dad just threw a good punch and Tam went down and smashed his head on a rock. No one blamed Dad for it. If the cops hadn't been there, nothing would have happened.' I closed my eyes, remembering it all as if it was yesterday – the midnight phone call, the half-heard voices, then Cole coming into my room, trying to explain, while Mum was crying and shouting and cursing[6] Dad for giving in to his stupid sense of pride. He hadn't even *wanted* to fight Tam Docherty. He'd retired from fighting a long time ago. He was a family man now. A businessman. But Tam had kept on calling him out – taunting[7] him, insulting him, humiliating him – and in the end Dad couldn't take it any more.

'The police were already there,' I told Jess. 'They arrested Dad and took him in, and the next day he was charged with murder.'

'They say it was all a set-up,' Jess said quietly.

1 gadje (derog Gypsy sl): sb. who is not a Gypsy **2** gorger (derog Gypsy sl): gypsy who lives in a house **3** tinker: person who travels around like a gypsy mending pans, etc. **4** tinker ... thief: children's rhyming game **5** double don't like sb. (infml): don't like sb. twice as much **6** curse sb.: swear at sb. **7** taunt sb.: make sb. angry by saying unkind things about them

'Who's *they?*'

'Everyone – they say the Dochertys set up the fight and tipped off[1] the gavvers[2] to pay back your dad for taking out[3] Billy McGinley.'

'Who's Billy McGinley?'

She looked at me, knowing that I knew who he was, but wanting to tell me anyway. 'He's a cousin of the Dochertys.'

'Yeah? And why would my dad want to take him out?'

'Because Billy messed up[4] his best friend's daughter. And she was just a little girl. And your dad's a decent[5] man.' She reached out and touched me lightly on the arm. 'That's what my family think of him, anyway. We think he's a decent man who got an unlucky break. The other stuff, the stuff about marrying a *gadje* and buying a house ... well, I know some of the families don't like it, especially the older ones, but most of us are fine with it. There's more and more of us settling down now.' She smiled sadly at me. 'There's nowhere to go any more. People don't like us when we travel, and they don't like us when we stop. Sometimes the only way out is to disappear.'

We were walking slowly now, both of us beginning to tire. Up ahead, away in the distance, I could just make out the hazy grey peak[6] of a tor, shimmering in the sunlight. In the wavering air, it seemed to have a face – a flat head, a wide nose, the sockets[7] of amber eyes ...

'It's going to be the same for you if you stay here,' said Jess. 'They won't leave you alone.'

'Who won't?'

'Davy, Red, Bowerman ... the rest of them. They don't want you here. They won't leave you alone until you've gone. They've got too much to lose.'

'What do you mean?'

She wiped sweat from her brow. 'I don't suppose Abbie and Vince told you anything about the hotel, did they?'

1 tip off sb.: tell sb. (e.g. the police) that sth. is going to happen **2** gavver (derog Gypsy sl): policeman **3** take out sb. (sl): kill sb. **4** mess up sb. (infml): (here) abuse sb. **5** decent: good **6** peak: top **7** socket: (here) eyehole

'You mean the Bridge Hotel?'

'Not exactly –'

She stopped suddenly as a distant gunshot rang out from the other side of the hill. I stopped beside her. The dogs stopped, too – perfectly still, their ears cocked[1], their eyes alert[2]. As the sound of the gunshot echoed dully around the hills, I looked at Jess and saw her shielding her eyes and staring intently into the distance.

'What is it?' I asked her.

She didn't reply.

'Jess?' I said. 'What is it?'

This time she lowered her hand and looked over at me. Her eyes were masked with that silent steadiness again, but I knew her well enough to see through it now, and when she smiled and shook her head and told me it was probably just someone shooting rabbits, I knew she was lying. There was more to it than that.

She sat down on a lichen-covered rock and drank from the bottle of water. When she held out the bottle to me, I went over and sat down beside her. The mask had slipped from her eyes now, and I could see that she was about to tell me something. I thought – thoughtlessly – that she was going to explain why she'd just lied to me, but she didn't. Instead, as I took a long drink from the bottle, she started telling me about a big hotel and a man called Henry Quentin.

The essence of it all was that the entire village of Lychcombe was in the process of being bought up. Everything in and around it – every house, every farm, every shop, every building – was either sold already, being sold, or under offer.

'It's been going on for a couple of years now,' Jess explained. 'Most of the villagers wouldn't have anything to do with it at first. A lot of them have lived here all their lives – their families are here, their roots, their history. This is their home. They don't *want* to live anywhere else. But as the offers kept coming in, and kept getting

1 cock one's ears: *die Ohren spitzen* **2** alert: watchful

bigger and bigger, some of them started changing their minds.' She shrugged. 'You can't blame them. I mean, it was big money, silly money, much more than the properties were worth, and after a while they just couldn't resist it. After that, everything started to snowball[1]. The ones who didn't want to sell began to realise there wasn't any point in staying because there wasn't going to be anything left to stay for – no shops, no pub, no school, no work ... no Lychcombe.' She paused, looking back down the hill in the direction of the village. 'It's pretty much all gone now,' she said. 'There's still a few left who haven't given in, but they won't last long.'

'I don't get it,' I said. 'Why would anyone want to buy a whole village? Especially this one. I mean, there's nothing here, is there?'

'Not yet, but there soon will be.' She looked at me. 'Have you heard of a place called Dunstone Castle?'

'No.'

'It's a luxury hotel on the other side of the moor, about ten or twelve miles from here. It used to be a castle ... well, it still *is* a castle, I suppose. It was bought up a couple of years ago and completely rebuilt – the buildings, the land, everything. Now it's all golf courses and swimming pools and conference rooms ... there's even a private heliport. People come from all over the world to stay there.'

'Big money,' I muttered.

'Exactly – which is why they want to build another one here.'

'Here?'

She nodded. 'Apparently, this one's going to be even bigger than Dunstone. A brand-new purpose-built hotel, restaurants, golf courses, horse-riding, shooting, fishing ... no expense spared.'

'No locals to bother you, either.'

'Just the peace and tranquillity of the moor ...'

'Your own private haven[2].'

Jess smiled at me. 'It'll make a fortune.'

'Who for?'

1 snowball: (here) go quickly **2** haven: place of safety

She shook her head. 'No one knows. Whoever's behind it, they don't get involved at this level. All the property deals are done through a third party. They appoint someone to run things, and the person who runs things appoints someone else to appoint someone else local to do all the dirty work.'

'What kind of dirty work?'

'Buying people out, basically. Persuading them to sell.'

'Persuading?'

She shrugged. 'Not everyone knows what's good for them.'

I was beginning to understand things now. I was beginning to see the missing pieces – the layers, the shades ... the things that make up what's supposed to be there.

'Who's the persuader?' I said.

Jess looked at me. 'His name's Henry Quentin. You probably saw him in the Bridge the other night.'

'The man with the beard?'

'Yeah.'

'Does he live in the village?'

She nodded. 'In the big stone house at the end of the High Street. I don't know much about him, but I know he's making a lot of money out of this. He gets a fee from the hotel people, plus a commission on everything he buys, and a big bonus payment when the whole deal's done. I've heard he's got a few things going on for himself, too – things the hotel people don't know about.' She looked at me again. 'That's why no one wants you around, poking your nose in. Henry's not the only one making money out of this – he's got half the village in his pocket. And if they think you're stirring things up too much ... well, they're not going to like it.'

She uncapped the water bottle and took another drink. I watched her, wondering why she was telling me all this. Was she simply giving me a friendly warning, just letting me know how things were? Or was there something else, something she hadn't told me yet?

I guessed I'd just have to wait and see.

The sun was directly above us now, glaring down with a pale white heat that shimmered in the air like an unseen mist. In the timeless silence I could feel Rachel's breath on the wind. She wasn't far away now. I could feel her presence, her pain, her death. She was *with* me. She'd been with me all along – with me, with Jess, with the dogs – in the forest, on the hill ... she'd been with us all the way. But now she was right here, right now, in this time.

Jess stood up and put the bottle of water in her pocket. 'Ready?' she said, looking down at me.

I got to my feet and we carried on up the hill.

'She was found just there,' Jess said quietly. 'Under the thorn tree.'

We were standing beside an ancient stone circle at the end of a short grassy track near the top of the hill. The old granite stones were half-buried in the ground, spaced about a metre apart, forming a ragged ring about four metres across. Grass was growing inside the circle – lush and thick and green – but outside the ring there was nothing but dry grass and rock. I didn't understand it – the geography, the history, the shape of the land – but it didn't matter. I didn't have to understand it.

This was the place.

The ring of stones, the stunted thorn tree, the dying wind ...

This was where it had happened.

It should have looked different in the daylight. Without the storming rain, without the night, without the purple black light that rolled the sky to the ground ... it should have been harder to believe – but it wasn't. It was midnight in the middle of the day, and I could see Rachel lying there naked and dead in the dark.

I could see it all too clearly.

I could feel her death.

Jess's dogs could feel something, too. They were sitting off to one side of the circle, both of them whining quietly. Their hackles[1] were up, their ears were flattened against their heads, and their backs were arched[2] in fear. I didn't know if it was Rachel's death they could sense, or if there was something else within the stone circle that

1 hackles (pl): hair on a dog's neck **2** arch your back: *einen Buckel machen*

frightened them, something that only they could feel – an aura, a power, an unknown force. I didn't know if I believed in such things, but as I gazed around at the lichened rocks and the wind-sculpted thorn tree in front of me, I knew what I could feel: I could feel Rachel dying, the Dead Man breathing, the rain running red with blood.

And I believed in that.

I could see the Dead Man in the shadows of the thorn tree. He was dark and sharp and dirty … his face a broken black knife. His hands were scarred[1]. He was bleeding, scratched, bitten. Yellow-eyed. He had nowhere to go. Nowhere to hide.

I turned round and looked at Jess. She was standing a few paces behind me. The dogs were lying down beside her now, their heads held low to the ground.

'Who is he?' I asked her.

'Who?'

'You *know* who.'

Her eyes flickered, and for a moment I thought she was going to lie to me again, but when she spoke her voice was true. 'I'm sorry,' she said. 'I was going to tell you … I just didn't know if I ought to or not. I mean, there's no proof or anything … it's all just rumours[2], really—'

'Tell me his name,' I said quietly.

She looked at me. 'Selden. His name's John Selden.'

'Selden?'

She nodded.

I brought the Dead Man into my mind and tried putting the name to his broken face – *Selden, Selden, John Selden …?* The words fit. The name *became* him – he *was* John Selden.

'Who is he?' I asked Jess. 'What does he do?'

She shook her head. 'He's nothing … he doesn't *do* anything. He just hangs around on his own most of the time – skulking around[3]

1 scarred: full of marks that are left on the body after an injury **2** rumour: news or story passed around by people which may not be true **3** skulk around: move around secretly

in the woods, or on the moor …' A look of disgust crossed her face. 'He's a creepy little shit. I caught him watching me once. I was out walking the dogs and they started barking up a tree, and when I looked up I saw Selden sitting in the branches with a dirty little grin on his face …' She looked at me. 'He hasn't been seen since Rachel was killed. The police have been looking for him, asking questions, searching his room –'

'How would he have got here?' I asked her. 'How would he have got Rachel up here?'

'The village road's just down there,' Jess said, pointing down to the right of the hill. 'See? Behind that little copse[1].'

There was a lay-by at the side of the road, a little gateway through to the copse, a pathway up the hill … it wasn't far. Less than a hundred metres. It wasn't too far to carry a body. I gazed down the slope, imagining the Dead Man toiling his way up the hill, clambering over the rocks, carrying my sister's body through the storming rain …

Why?

Why did he do it?

Why did he kill Rachel?

Why did he bring her up here?

Why?

I could feel my head spinning with questions now. Why had no one mentioned John Selden before? Why was Jess telling me about him now? Who was he? Where did he come from? Who'd killed him? And why? And what had they done with his body …?

And then suddenly I was feeling something else – a familiar race of blood in my heart. It was the same sudden fear I'd felt on the night Rachel died, only this time it was coming from Jess. I looked over at her. She was staring up ahead, beyond the ring of stones, where three slouching[2] figures were coming down the hill towards us. They were walking side by side. The two on the outside were carrying shotguns; the one in the middle was Red.

1 copse: small group of bushes or trees **2** slouch: walk with shoulders hanging forward

Nine

I studied the three men as they approached the circle of stones. Red hadn't changed one bit – he was still wearing his grubby red suit, still smiling his sharp-toothed smile, still fixing me with his wrong-looking eyes. With his hands in his pockets and his suit collar turned up, he looked like some kind of weird rural gangster. The other two were walking vegetables. The one on Red's right was a Potato Man – fat head, seedy[1] eyes, flaky brown skin – while the one on his left looked like a bean sprout[2] on legs. Tall and skinny, with a bulbous[3] head and horseradish fingers[4] and eyes that could make an onion cry. Potato Man was wearing an army jacket and boots; the skinny one was in a sleeveless nylon jacket and a baseball cap. They both had their shotguns slung over their shoulders, and neither of them were smiling.

As they reached the edge of the stone circle, I felt Jess move up beside me. She didn't say anything, but she didn't have to – I was *with* her now, sharing her senses, seeing the three men through her eyes. She recognised Red and Potato Man, but she hadn't seen Skinny before. She knew what he was, though. She'd seen the likes of him a thousand times before – we both had. He was a fear-sucker, the same as the other two. And they were all getting ready to feed.

We could see their mouths drooling[5] at the scent[6] of our fright, and there was nothing we could do to hide it. We were *scared* – full stop. But we could still function. We could see the dull glint of their double-barrelled shotguns. We could see the dead rabbit stuffed in Potato Man's pocket. We could see the finger of rabbit's blood smeared on his face.

1 seedy: dirty and unpleasant **2** bean sprout: *Bohnensprosse* **3** bulbous: *knollig* **4** horseradish fingers: fingers that look like horseradish (= *Meerrettich*) **5** drool: get watery **6** scent: smell

We both thought they might stop at the edge of the stone circle, but they didn't. They were senseless – unaware of unseen things. They just walked straight across the circle without so much as a thought – under the thorn tree, over the ghost of Rachel's body, through the shifting shadows of the Dead Man, and right up into our faces.

'Hey,' said Red, flicking a smile at me. 'How's your luck?'

It was the kind of question that fear-suckers use to start a fight – *what are you looking at? what's your problem?* – and we both knew it was pointless trying to answer it. Red knew it, too. I could tell by his laughing eyes, by his nodding head and his twitching shoulders. I could tell by the way he grinned and wiped his nose on the sleeve of his jacket.

'All right?' he said.

My mind flashed back to the day before. *All right?* he'd said to me then, and then I'd just kept my mouth shut and waited for Cole to do his stuff. But now I was on my own. With Jess.

Red smiled at me. 'Where's Jackie Chan[1]?'

'Who?'

He punched the air, making me flinch, but when he grinned again and grabbed his throat and groaned, I realised he was reminding me of what Cole had done to Big Davy.

'Must be nice having a big brother like that,' he said, taking his hands from his throat and grinning again. 'I wish I'd had a brother to keep all the nasty big boys away.' He made a show of gazing around the stone circle, then he turned back to me. 'Looks like you're on your own today, though.'

'I wouldn't say that.'

'No?' He looked around again, staring through Jess as if she wasn't there. 'I don't see anyone else,' he said, turning to the Potato Man. 'You see anyone else, Nate?'

'I don't see shit,' Potato Man grunted.

1 Jackie Chan: Chinese actor of martial arts movies

Red turned back to me. 'You must be seeing ghosts, boy. There's plenty up here – pixies[1] and shit, ghouls[2] and ghosties …' He raised his hands, widening his eyes and moaning, like a child playing at ghosts. Then he dropped his hands and winked[3] at me. 'Oh, yeah – we *always* got plenty of dead stuff.'

I was thinking of Cole now. Wishing he was here, wishing I was him, wishing I could take this stuff without my heart jumping up and down like a frog. I wished I had some control over the things inside me – the mechanisms, the signals, the reactions – but I knew I was wasting my time.

'What you doing up here, anyway?' Red said to me. 'This is Forestry land. It's private. You're trespassing[4].'

'You're breaking the law,' added Nate, the Potato Man. His voice was so lazy and his accent so thick I could barely understand what he was saying. I looked at him. His lips were loose and his tongue was too fat for his mouth.

'What?' I said.

'Whut?' he echoed.

Jess suddenly let out a sigh – a loud and exaggerated yawn of boredom – and all at once everything switched to her. Nate and Skinny just swivelled their heads and stared at her, but Red made a big show of it – widening his eyes and stepping back in mock surprise as if Jess had suddenly appeared from nowhere.

'Shit,' he grinned, clamping his hand to his chest, 'where d'you come from? You nearly gave me a heart attack, man. How d'you *do* that?'

Jess said nothing, just stared at him with a slight shake of her head.

Red leaned forward and cupped a hand to his ear. 'Say what? Come on, speak to me. Tell me how you do it. Come *on*, don't be shy – I won't bite.' When Jess still didn't answer him, he grinned again

1 pixie: *Kobold* **2** ghoul: evil spirit that eats dead bodies **3** wink: *zwinkern*
4 trespass: enter private property illegally

and spoke to her in a stupidly simple voice. 'You ... speakee ... English? No? You ... Pikey[1] ... yes?'

Jess's eyes showed nothing.

Red leaned back and spoke to Potato Man. 'You know any Pikey words, Nate?'

'Tarmac,' he grunted, 'caravan ... not guilty ...'

'Hedgehog[2],' added Skinny.

Red laughed. 'Hedgehog?'

'They eats 'em.'

'They eats anything,' Nate said.

'You wish ...'

They all laughed again. It was the same old sound – the sound of the grown-up playground – and I could tell that Jess wasn't bothered about it. She knew as well as I did that, in itself, it was nothing. It was just a warm-up, a bit of sparring[3], a blast of hot air to get things going. When the laughing stopped – that was the time to start worrying.

I glanced at Jess and saw that she was standing with her hands held down at her sides, the palms facing backwards, keeping her two dogs behind her. They were sitting motionless, their jaws set tight and their eyes fixed on Red and his boys.

Red said to Nate, 'Give her the rabbit.'

'What?'

'The rabbit ... give her your rabbit.'

'What for?'

Red ignored him, turning to Jess. 'You want a rabbit? A nice little bunny?' He started making eating motions, smacking his lips and rubbing his belly. 'Yum yum, very nice ... you like?' He grinned his grin. 'You likee[4] fresh meat? Nice and tasty –'

'Hey, shit-head,' Jess said quietly. 'Let's just get it done, OK?'

Red leaned back, doing his mock-surprise thing again. 'I'm *sorry?* Did you *say* something?'

1 pikey (derog sl): Gypsy **2** hedgehog: *Igel* **3** sparring: exercising in order to get ready **4** likee: like (pronounced as a foreigner might say it)

'Look,' she said patiently, 'we've all got better things to do than stand around here listening to you all day, so why don't we just cut the crap[1] and get on with it. We've done the funny gypsy stuff and the dirty little jokes ... what else do you want to do? You want to scare the kid some more? Impress your friends? You want to say some naughty words?'

Nate and Skinny were smirking[2] at each other now, but Red didn't think it was funny. His smile had thinned to a white-lipped scar.

'Come on,' Jess taunted him, 'say something funny. Insult me. Let's have some more of your gypsy stuff.' She clicked her fingers. 'I know, how about the interbreeding thing? That's always a good one – incest *and* race. Two insults for the price of one.'

Red's staring face had drained to a pale white mask, the whiteness stained with angry red blotches. His skin was so tight that when he spoke, his lips barely moved. 'Race?' he hissed at Jess. '*Race?* You're not a *race*, you're just a waste of blood.'

'That's more like it,' Jess said, clapping her hands. 'That's *excellent*. What else have you got?'

I could feel the bad stuff coming now, and I guessed that was Jess's intention – get it on, get it over, get it done. Normally, I might not have minded – but this wasn't normal. This was a twitchy[3] red lunatic and two big vegetables with double-barrelled shotguns.

I looked around. Red was wired up[4] – his head nodding, his elbows twitching, his face a mess of pale-skinned tics[5] – and the other two were beginning to get the message. Their smirks had gone and they'd put their dead faces on. Their eyes were jumpy and white. Nate had taken the dead rabbit from his pocket and was holding it by its ears, swinging it gently against his leg, and Skinny was leering[6] at Jess and scratching his crotch[7].

1 cut the crap (sl): *mit dem Mist aufhören* **2** smirk: smile in a self-satisfied, mean manner **3** twitchy: nervous, irritable **4** wired up (infml): nervous, excited **5** tic: unusual repetitive movement of the body **6** leer at sb.: look at sb. in a sexually interested way **7** scratch your crotch: scratch yourself between the legs

There was absolute silence for a moment, a silence with no time and no feeling. I could hear the world ticking inside my head – tick, tick, tick ...

And then Jess said to Red, 'Is your boyfriend going to give me that rabbit or what?'

And that was it. Everything just *erupted.* It was all so cold and quick and dull, that at first I didn't know what was happening. Nate's arm came up and I saw something shoot through the air and smack into Jess's face with a muffled thump, and then she was staggering backwards with blood on her face, and the dead rabbit was lying on the ground at her feet. Before I could tell if the blood was hers or the rabbit's, Skinny had stepped over and levelled his shotgun at my head.

'On the ground, boy,' he hissed.

As I lowered myself to the ground, I looked over at Jess and saw her setting her dogs on Red and Nate. Red had turned round and was snatching the shotgun out of Nate's hands, and as the two dogs raced towards them, Red pushed Nate in front of him and shouted in his ear – 'Get the bastards!' Nate swung a booted foot at Finn, and as the lurcher yelped and jumped to one side, Tripe zipped through Nate's legs and went for Red's ankles. Red swung the shotgun and cracked the barrel[1] into Tripe's head, and the little dog went down. It whined a little and tried to get up, but Red hit it again, harder this time, and I heard something crack ... and this time it didn't get up.

Jess screamed.

It was a terrible sound, the scream of a torn heart, and it ripped the air to ice. Nate was grinning now, stomping after Finn, and Jess was screaming at him and screaming at Finn to get away and screaming at Red that she'd kill him ...

And I couldn't do anything. I was kneeling on the ground with a shotgun barrel pressed between my eyes. Skinny was shoving it into my head, trying to push me right down into the ground, trying to buckle me, trying to *bury* me ...

1 barrel: *Gewehrlauf*

But I wasn't going down there.

I strained[1] my head against the pain and kept my eyes fixed on Red as he walked up to Jess with the shotgun in his hands. He had his smile back now. It was tight and hard and flecked with spit. Jess was still screaming at him.

'You *bastard!* You shitty red *bastard!* You're gonna –'

'What?' said Red. 'I'm gonna what?'

'You're *dead*,' she spat.

'I don't think so.' He smiled. 'I think you'll find that crippled rat over there's the dead one –'

Jess lunged[2] at him, but he quickly raised the shotgun and aimed it at her head. She stopped right in front of him, staring down the barrel of the gun, and I could feel her torn between fear and anger. She wanted to rip Red to pieces, and she was almost sure he wouldn't use the gun ... but she wasn't quite sure enough.

'Go on,' he said to her, 'try me – see if I've got the guts.'

She stared at him for a long time, staring painfully into his eyes, and then finally she took half a step back. 'I'll see your guts[3] soon enough,' she said quietly. 'I'll see them ripped from your belly and thrown in the dirt.'

Red just smiled at her. 'Pick up the rabbit,' he said.

'What?'

He waved the shotgun at the dead rabbit on the ground. 'Pick it up.'

Jess looked at the rabbit. She wiped some blood from her face, then looked back at Red. 'Go to hell,' she told him.

He smiled at her again, then looked over at Nate. He was stomping around in a patch of tussock grass away to the left of the stone circle.

Red called out to him, 'You got that dog yet?'

'I think he's gone,' Nate called back, still looking around. 'I lost the bastard.'

1 strain sth.: (here) force yourself to ignore the pain in sth. **2** lunge at sb.: attack sb. **3** guts: *Eingeweide*

Red shook his head and looked over at Skinny and me. I was hurting now. The barrel of the gun had broken my skin and I could feel a trickle of blood running down my nose. My legs were numb[1] from kneeling in the dirt.

'Hey, kid,' Red said to me. 'What d'you reckon your life's worth?'

Even with a gun at my head, I thought it was a pretty strange question, and for a moment I actually found myself thinking about it – what *is* my life worth? – but the thought didn't last for long.

Red said to Jess, 'What do *you* think his life's worth?'

Jess shook her head. 'I don't even know what you're talking about. Why don't you just—'

'Shoot him,' Red said to Skinny.

Skinny looked at him. 'What?'

'Shoot the mongrel bastard[2].'

Skinny hesitated a moment, then turned back to me and slowly cocked both barrels of the shotgun – click, click. I felt the faint vibrations echoing through my skull.

'Don't be stupid –' Jess started to say.

'Pick up the rabbit,' Red told her.

'What?'

'Just *do* it. Pick up the rabbit and I'll let the kid keep his head.'

She looked over at me. We were only a few metres apart, but it seemed like a thousand miles. Our eyes met for a moment, and in that moment neither of us knew anything. Jess looked away and I saw her bend down and pick up the rabbit.

She held it out to Red. 'There – satisfied now?'

'Eat it,' he told her.

'What?'

'Eat it.'

'I'm not going to –'

'It's only raw meat,' Red smiled. 'I'm sure you've eaten worse. Come on ... it's not a lot to ask for the sake of a little kid's life, is it?'

1 numb: unable to move **2** mongrel bastard: offensive term for a person of two different races

'You're out of your *mind*.'

'I'll count to three.'

'Listen –'

'One ...'

Jess was sweating now, the moisture mingling with the blood on her face. Her eyes were sick and confused. As she looked over at me and tried to speak, I suddenly felt my brother's heart inside me. I couldn't feel *him*, but I could feel what made him, and I just didn't care any more.

'It's all right,' I said calmly to Jess. 'Just tell him to piss off. He won't do anything.'

Red smiled. 'Two ...'

I smiled back at him, then looked up at Skinny and said, 'Three.'

Skinny blinked once, then his finger tightened and he pulled the trigger and a deafening blast ripped through my head.

Ten

The blast came from Red's gun,' I told Cole later that night. 'Skinny's wasn't loaded. Red fired his shotgun into the air just as Skinny pulled the trigger.' I paused then, reliving the memory of the moment – the dull metallic click, the simultaneous crack of Red's shotgun, the nothingness ... and then the trickle of warm liquid running down my leg ...

'Christ, Rube,' breathed Cole, 'what were you *thinking?* You could have been *killed*.'

'I knew Skinny's gun wasn't loaded.'

'*How* did you know?'

'Come on, Cole – they weren't going to shoot me, were they? They might be dumb, but they're not stupid. Skinny didn't have the guts for it, anyway. He couldn't have killed me to save his life. I could see it in his eyes.'

'That's *it?*' Cole said incredulously[1]. 'You could see it in his *eyes?*'

'Yeah.'

'Shit, Ruben ...'

'What?'

He looked at me, shaking his head. I tried to smile at him, but the look in his eyes was too much for a smile, and I felt instead the moist tingle of tears welling up in my eyes.

I hadn't felt anything at the time – not consciously, anyway. I suppose my body must have been shocked at the sudden blast of Red's gun – otherwise I wouldn't have wet myself – but there was nothing going on in my mind. Nothing at all. I didn't have time to think or feel anything. There *was* no time. No time for flashing lives or final regrets, no time for fears or prayers ...

No time at all.

1 incredulous: unwilling to believe

Just – *BAM!* – and everything stopped – the air, the world, the hour, the day – and then moments later everything suddenly started again. I was Ruben Ford. I was kneeling on the ground. My mouth was dry and my trousers were wet and my head was bloody and I wasn't dead. I could see the blue sky, the white grass, the granite-grey tor in the distance. I could see the red maniac. I could hear his gunshot echoing around the moor and the sound of his laughter staining the air as he walked away up the hill without even bothering to look back.

And then Jess was there, kneeling down beside me, tearfully asking me if I was all right, and I was telling her not to worry about me, that I was fine, that she ought to go and see to her dog. And then she was running over to Tripe's lifeless body and picking it up and crying herself to death.

We'd walked back in silence. Down the hill, down the Lychway, down the Road of the Dead – adding to its sadness and longing – then through the forest's cathedral light and out through the stone gateway at the side of the road where our journey had first begun. Here, Jess had gently laid her dog on a sunlit boulder and we'd embraced each other in the dying shadows of the afternoon.

'I'm so sorry,' she whispered into my ear. 'I should have kept my big mouth shut. I just didn't –'

'You don't have to say anything,' I told her. 'There's nothing to say.'

She'd kissed me then, touching her lips to the shotgun-graze on my forehead, and then she'd turned round and picked up Tripe and walked away down the road with Finn trailing sadly behind her. I'd watched her until she'd disappeared around a corner, then I'd turned round and started walking back to the farmhouse.

As I headed down the lane, the image of the dead dog began haunting[1] my mind – his sad little body splayed out on the moor, his three legs limp, his mouth hanging open, his dog-brown eyes staring at nothing. The picture was clearer to me then than it had been at the time. In my mind I could see one of his ears moving, and for a

1 haunt sb.: keep coming back to sb.'s mind

witless moment I'd thought of miracles – *he isn't really dead, he's only stunned, knocked out, in a coma* – but of course it was only the wind, breezing over the hill, ruffling his fur.

I wished I'd done something.

All I could imagine was putting my hand on his body and feeling the cold stillness of death, and that made me shiver and cry.

By the time I'd got back to the farmhouse, the sun was starting to cloud over and there was a faint scent of rain in the air. The house and the yard looked quiet. There were fresh tyre tracks in the yard, but no sign of the Land Rover, so I guessed Vince had come back and gone out again. The front door of the farmhouse was unlocked. I let myself in and went quietly upstairs, not wanting to bump into Abbie, and I'd found Cole waiting for me in the bedroom.

'Where've you been?' he said impatiently as soon as I opened the door. Then almost immediately he saw the cut on my head, and suddenly his voice went cold. 'Who did that?'

I'd told him everything then – what happened with Abbie, how I'd met Jess, what she'd told me about the village and the hotel and John Selden, and then all the stuff about Red and Nate and Skinny – and now here we were, sitting together on the bed, my eyes filling up with tears and Cole's filling up with a cold calm rage.

'Did they do anything else?' he asked me. 'Did they hurt you or anything?'

I shook my head. 'They were just trying to scare us. I don't think anything much would have happened if Jess hadn't started making Red look stupid. He's a psycho, Cole. He killed her dog without even thinking about it.'

Cole nodded. 'But he didn't hurt you?'

'No.'

'Did they say anything about Rachel?'

'Not really. Red made a crack about ghosts or something, but that was about it. They were just doing the usual stuff, you know –

dumb threats, scary looks, taking the piss. Jess got the worst of it. I mean, they really laid into her[1].'

'Yeah, well,' Cole shrugged, 'she's a gypsy. She'll have been through it all before.' He looked at me. 'If she's anything like the rest of the Delaneys, she's tough enough to deal with it.'

'Do you know them?'

'The Delaneys? Only by name. Dad knew some of the Essex Delaneys a few years back – I think they lived on the same site for a while. They're a big clan, though, so I'm not sure how close they are to Jess's family.'

He got up and went over to the window and lit a cigarette. I watched him for a while, wondering if I ought to tell him what Jess had said about Dad and the Dochertys and Billy McGinley, but I decided that we both had enough to think about just now without delving back into the past and stirring up all the bad stuff again. It wasn't all history, though – and I knew we'd have to talk about it some time soon. But not right now.

'How did it go in the village?' I asked Cole.

'It didn't,' he said, puffing moodily on his cigarette. 'No one's talking. No one would even come near me, let alone talk to me. It was like I was a leper[2] or something. I managed to ask a few questions in the post office, but it didn't do me any good.' He stubbed out his cigarette. 'It was like talking to a bunch of bloody zombies.'

'Did you go up to the gypsy camp?'

'Yeah.'

'And?'

He nodded. 'Yeah, it was OK. They didn't talk much, but I didn't really expect them to. They knew all about us, though – me, you, Rachel, Dad. They know who we are.'

'Jess told me that her uncle used to watch Dad fight,' I said. 'He told her you punched like a Ford.'

'Yeah, I know – I talked to him.' Cole frowned. 'Well, actually, he did most of the talking. I just listened.'

1 lay into sb. (infml): attack sb. **2** leper: *Leprakranke/r*

'What did he talk about?'

'Fighting, mostly. I kept trying to ask him stuff about Rachel, but all he wanted to talk about was bare-knuckle fighting – the good old days, the big fights, the famous names ... all that kind of stuff.' Cole shook his head. 'There's something a bit weird about him.'

'What do you mean?'

'I don't know – I couldn't work it out. I mean, he's all *right* ... I'm not saying he's whacko[1] or anything. There's just something a bit strange about him. It's like he hasn't got any grip on reality.'

'Jess said he used to fight.'

'Yeah, I know. He told me all about it.'

'Maybe he took too many punches.'

'Maybe ...'

'So what's so strange about that? He's just a punchy old guy with a few screws loose[2] – there's plenty of them around.'

'Yeah, I know – but he's the *guvnor*, Rube. He's the one they all look up to. When I first got to the camp and started asking around, all I kept getting was – "Best see the guvnor, mate ... best ask Reason about that ..." – and they all kept looking over at the old man's trailer. Then, when he finally came out and invited me in, they all backed off and left us alone.' Cole looked at me. 'He's not quite right in the head, Rube. Don't you think that's a bit odd for a guvnor?'

'Maybe that's why they're here,' I suggested.

'What do you mean?'

'You said it yourself – there's nothing here for them, is there? No work, nowhere to sell anything, no fairs. Maybe that's what happens when you listen to a whacked-out old fighter like Reason – you end up in the middle of nowhere.'

'No,' said Cole, 'there's more to it than that.'

'Like what?'

He shook his head. 'I don't know. I'm pretty sure there was something he wasn't telling me.'

1 whacko (infml): weird, crazy **2** have a screw loose (infml): *eine Schraube locker haben*

'About Rachel?'

He shrugged. 'I'm not sure ...'

'Do you think the rest of them know anything?'

'I'd be surprised if they didn't, but I don't think they're going to tell us. They don't want to get involved. I don't blame them. They've got enough crap of their own to deal with, without getting dragged into ours.'

We were silent for a while then, both of us just thinking things over, weighing things up, trying to work out if anything meant anything.

After a couple of minutes, Cole lit another cigarette and started gazing out of the window again. I went over and stood beside him. The afternoon light was beginning to pale now, the lowering sun casting faded shadows across the distant hills. The yard below was empty and quiet.

'So,' I said to Cole, 'you didn't find out anything in the village, then?'

'Only that it stinks.'

'No one said anything about this hotel complex?'

'No.'

'Or Henry Quentin?'

'No ...'

'And no one mentioned John Selden?'

Cole looked at me. 'Yeah, all right, Rube – I get the point. You found out everything and I found out nothing.'

I smiled at him. 'Don't feel bad about it.'

His face remained blank, but I could see a half-smile in his eyes. 'How's your head?' he asked me.

'It's all right ...' I started to say, brushing the graze[1] on my forehead, but then I realised what he meant. And I guessed he was right: I might have found out a lot more than he had, but it'd cost me a lot to find it. 'Yeah, well,' I told him, 'at least I didn't come back empty-handed.'

1 graze: (here) small injury

'You nearly didn't come back at all.'

I lowered my eyes as the sudden realisation hit me again – that I might *not* have come back, that I could have ended up as another cold body on the moor, another Tripe ... another Rachel. The thought was so frightening it made me feel sick. But that wasn't the worst of it. The worst of it was knowing how close I'd come to putting my family through hell again. I knew what that hell was like, and I couldn't bear thinking of anyone going through it for me – *because* of me.

'Hey,' said Cole, resting his hand on my shoulder, 'don't worry about it. You did all right.'

I looked at him.

He smiled at me. 'If I wasn't such a heartless bastard, I'd be proud of you.'

'Thanks.'

We looked at each other then, and something passed between us – something that hadn't been there for a long time. It was an intimacy, a closeness beyond our everyday closeness, and it reminded me of when we were kids. It was a good feeling.

Just as I was beginning to enjoy it, though, Cole's smile faded and he drew himself back into his shell again.

'All right,' he said, putting out his cigarette, 'I want you to tell me everything again – and this time I mean *everything*. Rewind that camcorder you keep inside your head and play it all back to me – word by word, scene by scene – from the moment I left this morning until the moment you came back.'

A couple of hours later we left the farmhouse and headed up the lane towards the village road. The moorland light was dimming under a cover of darkening clouds, and the murky[1] air felt heavy and damp. Everything seemed blurred and muffled – sounds, colours, surfaces, shapes – and I wished there were some lights around. I

1 murky: (here) unclear, difficult to see through

missed having lights. I missed their sharpness, their brightness, the way they define things ... the way they show you where you are.

I was tired and hungry.

Vince had come back while we were talking in the bedroom. We'd heard him arguing with Abbie about something, then a short time later Abbie had come upstairs and asked us if we wanted anything to eat. It was the first time I'd seen her since she'd stormed out on me that morning, and I could tell by the way she looked at me that she hadn't forgotten about it. She wasn't exactly *un*friendly towards me ... but she wasn't particularly friendly, either. Cole had given her his nice-guy smile and told her that we were going out, but thanks for the offer anyway ...

So we hadn't eaten.

And it was getting cold.

And my head was throbbing and my legs were aching from all the walking I'd done earlier, and now I was trying to keep up with Cole as he marched on ahead of me up the lane ... and I wasn't looking forward to the next few hours.

'What did Abbie say about not leaving the farmhouse?' Cole said to me over his shoulder.

'What?'

'Abbie – she told you she didn't want to move out.'

'Hold on,' I said, scuttling up behind him.

He stopped and waited for me to catch up, then we carried on walking side by side.

'It was her mum's house,' I told him, remembering what Abbie had said. 'That's why she could never leave it. It means too much to her. Her mum was born there, she died there.'

Cole nodded thoughtfully. 'If what Jess told you is true, she must be one of the last ones left who haven't sold.'

'Yeah, I suppose ... unless the hotel people don't want her place.'

'Why shouldn't they want it? This Quentin guy has bought up everywhere else, hasn't he? And he doesn't sound like the kind of man who'd take no for an answer. I bet he's offered them a pretty good deal. And it's not as if they don't need the money. The farm's not theirs any more, and neither of them's got a steady job.'

'What about Vince?'

Cole shook his head. 'All he knows is farming. I asked him about it when he gave me a lift to the village. He picks up a bit of farm work now and then, but he spends most of his time just buying and selling stuff.'

'What kind of stuff?'

'Anything – motorbikes, cars, horses, all sorts of crap. I don't think he makes much money, though ...'

Cole was quiet for a while after that, and as we carried on walking through the moorland dusk I could feel him thinking slowly and carefully about all the things I'd told him – and more. I couldn't tell *what* he was thinking about them, but I knew he was putting things together in his own deliberate way.

He's always been a cautious thinker, never quite trusting his mind in the same way that he trusts his fists, and I've always kind of envied him for that. In some ways we're very much alike, but when it comes to cautiousness we're polar opposites: my mind works as furiously as his fists, and my fists work as slowly as his mind. Not that there's anything wrong with having a furious mind, I just sometimes wish that mine would slow down a bit and let me see what it's doing.

We'd reached the end of the lane now, and as we turned right onto the village road and passed alongside the forest gateway, I glanced across at the black mass of pine trees and hillside beyond, searching for the Road of the Dead. But I couldn't see it. The hills were slumbering under a blanket of cloud, and all I could see was a spectral grey mist creeping down from the heights, smothering the moor in stillness.

I looked away and followed Cole along the darkening road.

He had his rucksack slung over his shoulder. As he walked, it was jogging up and down, bouncing lightly against his back. I watched it for a while, focusing on the rhythm, the constant *thunk-thunk-thunk*, and I let the sound burrow into my mind and hypnotise the part of me that wanted to forget the things I had to talk to him about.

I don't know how long it took – maybe five minutes or so – but eventually I found myself catching up with Cole again and walking alongside him without the fear that had been niggling at me for days.

He turned his head and saw me staring at him. 'What?' he said. 'What's the matter with you?'

'Nothing – I need to talk to you about something.'

'What?'

'When I was with Jess today, she mentioned Billy McGinley.'

'Who?'

I smiled. 'Yeah, that's what I said. It didn't fool her, either. We both know what happened.'

'Yeah? And what was that?'

'I'm not stupid, Cole.'

'I never said you were.'

'Just because I don't talk about it, that doesn't mean I don't know about it.'

'Know about *what?*' he said irritably. 'How am I supposed to know what you're talking about if you don't tell me?'

'All right,' I sighed, 'if that's how you want to play it.' I looked at him. 'I'm talking about Dad's fight with Tam Docherty – OK?'

'What about it?'

'It was a set-up[1], wasn't it?'

He hesitated briefly, then nodded. 'Yeah, the gavvers were after Dad for a bunch of stuff he'd done years ago – blank MOTs, ripped-off[2] cars, that dodgy[3] Range Rover deal he had going ...' He shook his head. 'It was all nothing stuff, but he'd got away with it for so long the gavvers were desperate to nail him for anything. So when they heard about the fight '

1 set-up: *Falle* **2** ripped-off (sl): stolen **3** dodgy (infml): suspicious, not trustworthy

'Who tipped them off? The Dochertys?'

'Probably.' He looked at me. 'They never liked Dad.'

'Why not?'

'I don't know ... it's just one of those family feud[1] things, I suppose. The Dochertys and the Fords have hated each other for years. It's been going on for so long now that no one can remember what started it.'

I looked into his eyes. 'That's bollocks[2], Cole – and you know it.'

He stopped walking and stared back at me. 'What?'

'There's no family feud,' I told him. 'There never was. The reason the Dochertys tipped off the cops was to pay back Dad for taking out Billy McGinley.'

Cole shook his head. 'I don't know what you're talking about.'

'Yeah, you do,' I told him. 'Billy took a little girl from a site in Norfolk and kept her locked up in his trailer for two days. The girl was Jem Rooney's daughter – Jem was Dad's best friend.' I looked at Cole. 'You used to call him Uncle Jem – remember?'

Cole didn't say anything.

'I don't know exactly what happened,' I went on, 'but a couple of days later Billy McGinley was found dead in a field near Cambridge. He'd been shot in the back of the head.'

'So?' Cole shrugged.

'So the night Billy was killed, you and Dad went out and didn't come back till late. And when you got back to the yard, you stashed something in the boot of that Volvo where Dad keeps all his dodgy money and stuff.'

'You *know* about that?'

'I've known about it for years. I used to break into the boot when I was a kid and help myself to a few fivers.' I looked at him. 'That's how I know you put the pistol in there that night. I saw it the next day.'

Cole went to say something, then changed his mind and closed his mouth.

1 feud: long-lasting quarrel **2** that's bollocks (sl): *das ist Schwachsinn*

'I know you've got the pistol in your bag,' I told him. 'I saw you take it out before you left the yard.'

He shrugged again and started walking, his eyes fixed intently on the village up ahead. We were nearly there now, just passing the old stone house at the end of the street. The streetlights were on, but it hardly seemed worth it. The grey of the village just soaked up the dim orange light like it soaked up everything else – sound, colour, life, death. Everything just faded to grey.

'You're not denying[1] it, then?' I said to Cole.

'Denying what?'

'The pistol ...'

'No,' he said blankly, 'I'm not denying it. Why should I? It's only a gun. It's no big deal. I just thought we might need it, that's all.'

'Like you needed it before?'

'When?'

'When Billy McGinley was killed.'

He stopped again – stopped, turned round, and looked me in the eye. 'Billy was sick,' he said quietly. 'Whatever he did, it wasn't his fault. He just got sick, like a mad dog gets sick. Locking him up wouldn't have done any good. He'd have got out eventually and done it again. Some other little kid would have suffered.'

'So you killed him.'

Cole shook his head. 'I've never killed anyone. I'm not saying I don't know what happened to Billy, but I can promise you that I've never killed *any*one.'

'What about Dad?'

Cole blinked once. 'He killed Tam Docherty, but that was an accident –'

'I'm not talking about Docherty, I'm talking about Billy McGinley. Did Dad shoot him? Is that why the police were *really* after him, because they knew he'd killed Billy but they just couldn't prove it?'

Cole touched my arm. 'I'm sorry, Rube,' he said softly. 'I can't tell you anything else.'

1 deny sth.: say that sth. is not true

'Why not?'

'I just can't.'

We stared at each other for a long time then, both of us greying in the village light, and I didn't know what to think. I couldn't feel anything – there was nothing from Cole, nothing from me – but somehow it felt OK. I didn't understand it, and I wasn't sure if it was right, but it was what I felt – and that's all I had.

'All right,' I said eventually, 'but whatever happened with Billy McGinley, this had better not be the same.'

'What do you mean?'

'We're just here to do what we can to get Rachel's body back – right?'

'Right.'

'And that's all?'

'That's all.'

'You're not after anything else?'

'Like what?'

'Vengeance, justice, reckoning, revenge ... all that Hollywood shit. Tell me the truth, Cole – is that what you want?'

'No,' he said simply. 'That's not what I want. *I* don't want anything. I'm not doing this for myself, or for you, or even for Rachel – I'm doing this for Mum. It's all I *can* do. Look, I'm not saying that no one's going to get hurt, because I think they probably will, but it won't have anything to do with revenge or punishment or justice, it'll just be because that's how it has to be – OK?'

I looked at him, seeing the truth in his eyes, and I nodded.

He gave my arm a gentle squeeze, then he looked away and gazed down the street.

'Are you ready?' he asked me.

'I suppose ... what do you think's going to happen?'

'I don't know,' he said, moving off down the street. 'Let's go and find out.'

When we entered the bar at the Bridge Hotel, it was like walking into a time warp[1]. Nothing had changed from the night before – it felt the same, looked the same, sounded the same. Loud voices, glasses chinking, drunken laughter ... there was even the same sudden silence as we walked through the door. Sky Sports was still flickering on the TV, and the bar was packed with the same sour faces that had welcomed us before. They were all there: Nate and Big Davy, his neck in a brace[2]; Red and Henry Quentin; Skinny and the metal-heads; the hoods in tight T-shirts; Ron Bowerman; Will the barman. A bunch of boys I hadn't seen before were hanging around by the window, and from the way they kept glancing outside at the street, I guessed they were keeping an eye out in case any of the Delaneys came looking for Red to pay him back for killing Jess's dog.

Red himself was sitting at an alcove[3] table with his back to the wall, raising his glass and smiling across the room at us. Henry Quentin was sitting beside him, with Big Davy and Nate standing guard behind them.

My belly felt sick and my legs were shaking. I wanted to *do* something – move, talk, turn round and leave ... *any*thing to take my mind off those staring faces – but Cole just stood there, gazing quietly around, soaking it all up. The looks, the smiles, the whispers – they didn't exist for him. They were nothing.

I saw his eyes settle on someone at the back of the room, and when I looked over I caught sight of Vince trying not to be seen. He was with a plump-faced blonde girl in a very short dress. They were sitting close together in a cosy little nook[4] in the corner, all lovey-dovey[5] and holding hands. The girl couldn't have been much more than seventeen. When Vince saw us watching him, he dropped the girl's hand and quickly moved away from her, but he knew he wasn't fooling anyone. I could see the realisation dawning in his face. In less than a second his eyes went from troubled to angry, from angry

1 time warp: *Zeitschleife* **2** brace: *Halskrause* **3** alcove: *Nische* **4** nook: *Nische* **5** lovey-dovey (infml): *Turteltäubchen*

to scheming, before finally settling on casual defiance – *yeah, all right, so you've seen me – so what? What are you going to do about it?*

Cole didn't care – it was nothing more than information to him.

'Come on,' he said to me, putting his hand on my shoulder and guiding me towards the bar, 'let's get a drink.'

We squeezed into a space at the bar between a couple of gnarly[1] old farmers and a tough-looking lunk[2] with a teardrop tattooed under his eye.

'What do you want?' Cole asked me.

'I don't know,' I mumbled. 'A Coke, I suppose.'

'Any crisps?'

'Yeah, cheese and onion.'

Cole took a £20 note from his pocket and waved it at Will the barman. After pretending not to see us for five minutes or so, he eventually made his way over.

'Yeah?' he said to Cole.

'Two Cokes and a packet of cheese and onion crisps,' Cole told him.

The Teardrop Man snorted into his drink, and at the end of the bar I saw Ron Bowerman smirking drunkenly to himself.

'Two *Cokes?*' the barman grinned.

'Yeah,' Cole told him, 'and a packet of cheese and onion crisps. Do you want me to write it down for you?'

The barman stopped grinning and glared at Cole for a moment, then he shook his head and started fetching the drinks.

There was a mirror at the back of the bar. I could see the rest of the pub behind us, and I could see that everyone had started talking and drinking again. Just like before, the bar was gradually returning to normal. We were still being watched, though, and watched very closely – particularly by Ron Bowerman and the Teardrop Man. In the mirror I could see Teardrop staring at Cole. Cole was just ignoring him. Teardrop kept staring at him for a while, sucking dumbly

1 gnarly (infml): (here) wrinkled **2** lunk (infml): person with a lot of muscles but not very clever

on his lower lip, then suddenly he snapped his mouth and started looking around the room, sniffing loudly.

'Hey, Will,' he said, turning to the barman. 'You got rats in here or something? This place is really starting to stink.' He stared openly at Cole again. 'What do you think, mate? D'you smell anything bad?'

'Only you,' Cole said calmly, without looking at him.

Teardrop slammed his beer glass on the counter and leaned into Cole, but before he could do anything the barman reached over and shoved him away.

'Not in here,' he said, glaring into his eyes. 'I don't want any trouble in here – OK?'

Teardrop gave him a look, glanced at Cole again, then swore under his breath and went back to his beer.

The barman turned his glare on Cole. 'Here,' he said, passing him the drinks, 'but when you've finished those, I want you out.'

Cole slid the £20 note across the counter and picked up the Cokes. As he passed one to me and took a sip from the other, Teardrop pushed past us, heading for a door marked *Gents,* giving Cole a sly shove[1] in the back as he went. When Cole jerked forward and spilled his drink, I fully expected him to turn round and smash the glass into Teardrop's face – but he didn't. Incredibly, he didn't do anything. Didn't even look at him. Just wiped the spilled Coke from his sleeve, wiped his mouth, and lit a cigarette.

'You all right?' I asked him quietly.

He nodded, blowing out a stream of smoke. 'Was that one of them?'

'Who?'

'The tattooed guy – was he one of the ones you met on the moor?'

I shook my head.

'Are they in here?' he said.

I nodded.

'Don't look at them,' he told me, 'just tell me who they are.'

1 shove: push

I looked in the mirror. 'Nate's the fat one in the army jacket standing behind Red. Skinny's at the table with the metal-heads – he's the one in the hat.'

Cole glanced casually in the mirror. 'The baseball cap?'

'Yeah.'

Cole nodded.

The barman had crossed over to the other side of the bar now. He was talking to Ron Bowerman and gesturing in our direction. He didn't look very happy.

'What are we going to do?' I said to Cole.

'Nothing.'

I looked at him. 'We can't just stay here –'

'It's all right,' he said calmly. 'We're going in a minute. I just want to see what this piece of shit has to say.'

I followed his eyes and saw Ron Bowerman heading towards us with a pint of beer in his hand. His eyes were glazed and his bald head was sweating under the gleam of the bright pub lights.

'Mr Ford,' he slurred at Cole, leaning on the bar beside him, 'nice to see you again. I see you decided not to go home, then?'

'We'll be gone soon,' Cole told him.

'Glad to hear it. Now then ...' Bowerman paused and drank deeply from his glass. Wiping the froth from his lips, he tried to focus on Cole. 'Sorry – what was I saying?'

'Do you always do what the barman tells you?' Cole said to him.

'What?'

'He doesn't want us in here, doesn't want any trouble, so he gets you to tell us to leave and you get your slate wiped clean[1]. Is that it? Or maybe you're just following Henry Quentin's orders like everyone else around here. What's he like to work for, anyway? Good man, is he? Good money?'

The bar had gone quiet again. Everyone was listening and staring as Bowerman leaned his reddened face into Cole's. 'Listen, sonny,' he hissed, 'I don't know what you think –'

1 wipe the slate clean: *reinen Tisch machen*

'How did you feel?' Cole interrupted him.

'What? How did I feel about *what?*'

'When you were waiting on the hill with my sister's body. How did you feel? I mean, she must have been a hell of a sight – all ripped up and naked and dead. How did that make you feel?'

'Christ, you're *sick*.'

'You think so?'

'I've never heard anything so dis*gus*ting –'

'Have you found John Selden yet?'

Bowerman froze. 'What?'

'John Selden – have you found him?'

Bowerman's eyes darted briefly across the room, and in the mirror I saw Henry Quentin watching him. It was a look of pure domination. When Bowerman turned back to Cole, his face was marked with fear.

'Who told you about Selden?' he said under his breath.

But Cole wasn't listening any more – he was staring intently at Henry Quentin. Quentin stared back at him, and their eyes split the silence like a white-hot poker[1] cutting through ice. As Quentin studied Cole, I studied Quentin in the mirror. He was an ageless man, stern and dark and motionless. He had amber eyes and greased black hair and a face that belonged to another century. He was wearing heavy black trousers and dull black boots and a brass-buttoned soldier's coat with the sleeves rolled up to his elbows. His eyes were the eyes of a travelling preacher man.

'I asked you a question,' Bowerman said to Cole.

Cole said nothing. Keeping his eyes fixed on Quentin, he stubbed out his cigarette and started walking across the room towards him. He moved steadily, drifting like a ghost through the clouds of cigarette smoke hanging in the air, his footsteps soundless in the silence. As he passed the table where Skinny was sitting, he briefly glanced down at him.

'All right?' he said.

1 white-hot poker: *glühender Schürhaken*

Skinny grinned nervously and looked away, and Cole carried on across the room. He stopped at Quentin's table. No one moved for a moment. Red and Quentin just sat there, looking up at Cole, and Nate and Big Davy remained motionless behind them. Then Red raised his glass and winked at Cole, and Nate and Davy started lumbering out from behind the table. Cole didn't move, just carried on staring at Quentin, and after a moment the bearded man held up his hand and waved Nate and Davy back. Cole stared briefly at Nate, then turned his eyes back to Quentin.

'Henry Quentin?' he said.

Quentin didn't reply.

Cole said, 'Are you Henry Quentin?'

'What can I do for you, Mr Ford?'

His voice was hollow[1] and heartless.

'Where's John Selden?' Cole said.

'Who?'

'John Selden – the man who murdered my sister. Where is he?'

'I'm afraid I don't know what you're talking about,' Quentin said.

'Yeah, you do.'

'I'm sorry? Are you calling me a *liar?*'

'Listen, mister,' Cole said calmly, 'I just want to know where Selden is. You can either tell me now or you can tell me later. It's your choice. But if I were you, I'd do it now.'

Quentin smiled, showing cracked grey teeth. 'Is that a threat, Mr Ford?'

'Absolutely.'

1 hollow: (here) *dumpf*

Eleven

It was raining when we left the Bridge, a warm summery rain that fell to the ground with barely a sound, deadening the night to a moist black silence. Cole was quiet, too. He lit a cigarette and gazed up and down the High Street.

'Are you OK?' I asked him.

He nodded.

'I ought to ring Mum,' I said. 'Let her know we're all right.'

Cole just nodded again, then turned round and started walking up the street towards the telephone box. I followed him. When we got there, he pulled some coins from his pocket and handed them over.

'Don't be long,' he told me.

I wasn't long.

Mum sounded really low on the phone. She tried to hide it from me by asking all the usual questions – *are you OK? have you got enough money? are you eating properly?* – but I could tell she was in a bad way. I wanted to talk to her – not necessarily about Rachel … I just wanted to talk – but Cole was waiting impatiently outside, and Mum was waiting for Dad to call, and I guessed there wasn't much to talk about anyway. So we kept it short and said our goodbyes and I went back out to Cole.

'How's she doing?' he asked me as we headed back down the street.

'You could try asking her yourself.'

I felt his reaction as soon as the words left my mouth, and when I looked at him he suddenly seemed small – small and young and vulnerable. And I wished I hadn't said anything.

'It's different,' he said quietly.

'What is?'

'You know … the way it works. I talk to Dad, you talk to Mum …' He looked at me. 'I mean, why didn't *you* talk to Dad when he rang the other day? It doesn't mean anything, does it? It's just the way it works.'

'Yeah, you're right – I'm sorry.'

He nodded his head and shrugged his shoulders – getting himself back to his normal size – then he looked at me again. 'So – is she doing all right?'

'Yeah, just a bit down, I think.'

'She misses you.'

'She misses Rachel.'

Five minutes later we were sheltering in an alleyway[1] across the street from the Bridge – sheltering, waiting, watching the hotel door. Cole hadn't told me what we were waiting for, but I had a pretty good idea.

'Can I ask you something?' I said to him.

'What?'

'All that stuff in the bar just now ... you know, when you were asking Quentin about Selden?'

'Yeah?'

'You know he's dead, don't you?'

'Who – Selden?'

'Yeah.'

'Yeah, I know he's dead. You told me – remember?'

I looked at him. 'So when you were asking where he is ... you meant his body – right?'

'Right.'

'You realise it's probably buried somewhere on the moor?'

'So?'

'The moor's a big place.'

'Everywhere's a big place.' He looked at me. 'Look, it's simple, Rube. We find out where Selden's buried, we tell the cops, they dig him up. Once they've done their forensic stuff and proved he's the killer, they can release Rachel's body back to us.'

1 alleyway: narrow path

'That simple, eh?'

'Yeah.'

'Do you really think Quentin knows where the body is?'

'I don't know,' he shrugged. 'I was just stirring the barrel[1].'

'What barrel?'

'The barrel of bees.'

'Bees?'

He shook his head, suddenly embarrassed. 'It's nothing ...'

'What do you mean – *it's nothing?* You can't just start talking about a barrel of bees and then suddenly tell me it's *nothing*.'

'Just forget it, OK?' he said, lighting a cigarette. 'I don't want to talk about it.'

'Talk about what?'

He sighed, realising that I wasn't going to give up. 'It was just a stupid dream,' he said awkwardly. 'It doesn't *mean* anything. I just saw this picture ... last night ... you know, like an image in my head.' He paused for a moment, staring into the darkness, then he closed his eyes and began telling me what he'd seen. 'It was really weird ... I can still see it now. There's this boy, he's about my age, and he's standing beside a tar-stained[2] barrel. He's dressed in a black suit and he's got a stick in his hand, some kind of cane. There's a sound coming from inside the barrel – a buzzing sound.' Cole opened his eyes and looked at me. 'The barrel was full of bees – black bees. There were thousands of them, millions, all swirling around inside this barrel, and they couldn't get out. They couldn't get out because there was a lid on the barrel. And the boy, this boy in the black suit ... I don't know ... I didn't actually *see* him doing anything, but somehow I knew what he had to do. All he had to do was lift the lid off the barrel and poke his stick into the mess of bees and stir it all around, then step back and see what happened. That was it. He just had to see what came out.'

'Why?' I said.

Cole looked at me. 'What?'

1 barrel: container made of wood **2** tar-stained: *mit Teer befleckt*

'Why did he have to step back and see what came out? He must have known what was going to come out. I mean, it was a barrel full of bees. The only thing coming out of a barrel of bees is bees.'

Cole sighed and shook his head. 'See? That's exactly why I didn't want to tell you. Why do you always have to *analyse* everything, Rube? It was just a dream—'

'Yeah, I know.'

'It doesn't mean anything.'

'I *know*. I just thought it'd be better if there was something else inside the barrel, that's all.'

'Better?'

'Yeah. I mean, the rest of it makes sense. The barrel is obviously the village, the boy in the black suit is either you or me or both of us –'

'Christ, Ruben – it was a *dream*. Dreams aren't *supposed* to make sense. If they made sense they wouldn't ...'

His voice trailed off and he stared across the street. The two metal-heads and some leather-clad bikers were coming out of the hotel – talking, smoking, laughing, grunting ... their muffled voices cheapening the night. They slouched their way over to a line of parked motorbikes, mounted up, started the bikes, then rode off into the rain. The roar of the engines took a long time to fade.

'Bees?' I said, turning to Cole.

'Bees,' he agreed.

'Not the ones we're after, though.'

'No.'

We had to wait another half-hour before the ones we were after finally came out. While we were waiting, a steady stream of now-familiar faces rolled out of the bar. It felt good to be watching them for a change, instead of them watching us. We watched them all in silence: Ron Bowerman staggering through the door, trying to light a cigarette, his face a beacon of beer-sweat; the hoods in tight T-shirts, their drunken voices cracking the night; Big Davy, jawing his mouth and rubbing his neck; Vince and the plump girl, their arms around each other's waists; Teardrop; the look-out boys ...

As we stood together in the alleyway, watching and waiting in the darkness, I could feel Cole's stillness beside me. There were no thoughts coming from him, no feelings, no nothing – he was just there. Watching. Waiting. Breathing. Being.

'There,' he said under his breath.

I looked across and saw Nate and Skinny coming out of the hotel. They stopped in the doorway and looked up and down the street, then, satisfied that everything was OK, they stepped out onto the pavement and stood aside as Red and Quentin came out after them. Quentin was explaining something to Red. Red was nodding his head up and down like an idiot. They stopped on the pavement and carried on talking for a while, with Nate and Skinny standing guard on either side of them, then Quentin slapped Red on the shoulder and walked away up the street. Nate and Skinny started after him, but Quentin turned them away with a dismissive[1] wave of his hand.

I felt Cole tense beside me.

I thought we were going to get moving then. I thought we were going to follow Henry Quentin up the street. But Cole didn't move. He just stayed where he was, his eyes fixed on the others. They were just hanging around now – lighting cigarettes, joking, jostling[2] each other. They seemed a lot more relaxed now that Quentin had gone.

'Cole?' I whispered. 'What are we –?'

He held up his hand – *shut up.*

I shut up.

I heard someone making a barking sound, then whining, then laughing – and when I looked across the street again I saw Red and Skinny and Nate re-enacting the death of Jess's dog. I saw lifeless paws[3], rolling eyes, lolling tongues ... stupid grinning faces. I saw redness and blackness and bone-white fury ... I saw violence ... pain ... I saw myself doing things I'd never thought possible.

'You ready?' Cole whispered.

'What?'

1 dismissive: showing he does not need and want them **2** jostle sb.: push sb. roughly **3** paw: foot of an animal

'Come on, before we lose them.'

The three men had split up now. Red was driving off in his Toyota pick-up; Nate and Skinny were crossing the street towards a dark-blue Astra estate. Cole had taken the rucksack off his back and was holding it in front of him, his right hand inside the bag.

'Come *on*,' he hissed at me, tugging my arm.

The Astra was parked on our side of the street, about ten metres away. As Nate and Skinny opened the doors and got in, I followed Cole in a crouching[1] run up to the back of the car. I saw him glance through the rear windscreen, then he signalled me to take the left-hand side, and as the engine started, coughing exhaust fumes into our faces, he darted around to the right and yanked open the rear door and jumped in. By the time I'd done the same, getting in the other side, Cole had already pulled the pistol from his bag and was jamming it into the back of Nate's head.

'Drive,' he told him.

Skinny's head snapped around in the passenger seat, but before he could say anything Cole had cracked the gun barrel into his face, then quickly shoved it back into Nate's head. As Skinny slumped forward in his seat, holding his head in his hands, Cole leaned in close to Nate's ear.

'Drive,' he told him again.

And this time the car got moving.

Nate's hands were shaking on the steering wheel as we headed slowly up the street. Sweat was gleaming on the back of his neck, and in the rear-view mirror I could see the fear showing white in his eyes. It was an animal fear – thoughtless and dumb – and a part of me felt sorry for him. It was only a tiny part of me, though, and it wasn't hard to ignore. In the passenger seat next to him, Skinny was groaning and cursing, his face and hands streaming with blood.

'Christ,' he spat, 'shit ... my nose is broke—'

'Shut up,' Cole told him.

1 crouch: be close to the ground

Skinny started to turn round again, but then quickly jerked back with a stifled[1] scream as Cole gave him another sharp crack with the pistol, this time whacking him hard across the mouth. Skinny doubled over in the seat, his eyes screwed shut in pain, and I guessed he had a couple of broken teeth to go with his broken nose.

'Turn round at the end of the street,' Cole told Nate.

Nate's eyes darted nervously in the mirror. 'What?'

'Are you deaf as well as stupid?'

Nate frowned. 'I don't –'

'Just turn the car round.'

We were at the end of the village now. As Nate slowed the car and started turning it round, I could see Henry Quentin's big stone house glaring down at us through the darkness. A solitary light glowed brightly in an upstairs window, but the rest of the house was dark. In the light of the window I could just make out the shadow-shapes of tangled[2] trees in a vast rambling garden at the back of the house. Half a dozen vehicles were parked in a ramshackle driveway out the front. Among them were a couple of Land Rovers – one of which could have been Vince's – and the petrol tanker we'd seen at the filling station.

'Where to?' Nate asked Cole as he got the car straightened up.

'There's only one road.'

Nate flicked a look at him again.

Cole sighed. 'Just drive.'

We headed back down through the village, over the stone bridge, then up the hill towards the junction with the main moorland road. The darkness was thick and silent, the rain a mist of blackness. As we passed the gypsy camp, the pale lights of the trailers glimmered faintly behind a line of spindly trees. I wondered what Jess was doing right now. Crying? Sleeping? Thinking? Forgetting? I remembered her torn-heart screaming, and her silence in the forest, and her sad-

1 stifle sth.: suppress sth. **2** tangled: (here) standing very close together and touching each other

dened kiss in the dying shadows ... and then I closed my eyes and saw her face in the light of another time.

It's early morning, cold and bright ... some time soon. Maybe tomorrow. Jess is kneeling down, talking to someone. I can't see who it is. I'm not there. I don't know where I am. Jess looks sad, but not as sad as she's been. It's the sadness of someone who's doing what they always wanted to do, but in the wrong place and at the wrong time and under the wrong circumstances.

I can hear a gas fire hissing, and I can smell cigar smoke and coffee, and I can see Jess lowering her eyes and smiling in the light of the sleepy blue flames ...

And then I lost it.

When I opened my eyes again we'd reached the junction at the top of the hill and Cole was telling Nate to turn left. Nate did as he was told, and we drove on in silence along the empty moorland road. The night sky was huge now, like a vast black curtain of starless velvet. There was nothing to see and everything to imagine.

I looked at Cole. His eyes were dead. The gun in his hand was a silver-and-black 9 mm automatic pistol. I could tell that he'd held it before – I could feel the remembered weight in his hand – and I was pretty sure that he'd fired it, too. I could feel the muscle-memory in his arm – the sudden jerk of the gun and the whip of the recoil[1] as he flexed his finger and pulled the trigger ...

Did he kill Billy McGinley?

Did I want to know?

I looked at him again. His eyes were scanning the darkness up ahead, and I was suddenly afraid of what he was going to do.

'Stop here,' he told Nate.

'Where?'

1 recoil: *Rückstoß*

Cole said nothing, just jabbed the gun into the back of Nate's neck. Nate slowed the car and pulled up at the side of the road. The engine rattled and sighed, then settled to a low juddering rumble. No one spoke for a while. I saw Nate glance briefly at Skinny, and I guessed he was looking for some kind of support, but Skinny was out of it – slumped against the passenger door, holding his head in his hands, groaning quietly.

'You all right, Rube?' Cole asked me.

'Yeah.'

'Here,' he said, passing me the pistol, 'watch them for a second – OK?'

As I took the pistol from his hand and aimed it unsteadily at the back of Nate's head, Cole turned round and reached over the back seat. I heard him fumbling about in the dark, and then a moment later he turned round again with a shotgun gripped in his hands. I'd spent enough time staring into its barrel to recognise it as Skinny's. Cole broke it open, checked it was loaded, then snapped it shut again. Skinny flinched at the sound.

Cole looked at me, nodding his head at the pistol in my hand. 'You all right with that for a bit longer?'

'Why?' I said. 'Where are you going?'

He glanced at Nate, then back at me. 'Keep the gun at his head. If he moves or makes a sound, shoot him – all right?'

Before I could answer, Cole had opened the door and got out of the car. He walked round to the front, opened the passenger door, and levelled the shotgun at Skinny.

'Get out,' he told him.

Skinny didn't move, he just cowered in his seat and looked up at Cole with a desperate whiteness in his eyes.

Cole nudged the shotgun closer to his face. 'You want me to break the rest of your teeth?'

Skinny shook his head.

'Get out,' Cole repeated.

Skinny hesitated for a moment, then started climbing painfully from the car. Cole stepped back, keeping him covered with the shotgun, then directed him round to the front of the car. The rain had stopped now, and as Skinny moved awkwardly into the beam of the headlights, his bloodstained face appeared stark[1] and pale against the backdrop of the thick black sky. When Cole told him to stop, he seemed to just hang there in the middle of the road, floating like a wounded ghost – blood-streaked, shivering, his body angled with fear.

Cole broke open the shotgun and held it out to him, letting him see the chambers[2]. Skinny didn't have to look to know that the gun was loaded, but he couldn't help himself – his eyes darted down and he saw the truth of the two brass cartridges[3] glinting dully in the beam of the headlights. When Cole snapped the shotgun shut and took a step forward, Skinny's eyes flashed up at him, frozen in absolute fear. He could see Cole's empty heart in his eyes, and he knew what it meant. He knew without doubt what was coming. We all did.

But we were all wrong.

I watched in disbelief as Cole lowered the shotgun, turned it round in his hands, then offered it, stock first, to Skinny.

'Take it,' he told him.

All Skinny could do was stare wide-eyed at the shotgun.

'Take it,' Cole repeated.

Skinny looked at him, his fear clouded with confusion. Was it a trick? A joke? Some kind of game? Skinny glanced at the gun again, then back at Cole, then his hands started reaching out cautiously for the gun. He didn't want to take it, but he was too scared of Cole to do anything else. His hands were shaking as they slowly reached out, and his eyes kept darting from the gun to Cole, expecting him to snatch it away any second. But he didn't. He didn't do anything. He just stood there, perfectly still, watching and waiting. Skinny got one hand on the gun, then the other, and then Cole let it go.

Skinny had the shotgun.

1 stark: (here) harsh and strongly lit **2** chamber: space inside a gun where the ammunition is **3** cartridge: bullet

Still staring at Skinny, Cole took half a step back. 'All right,' he said quietly, 'let's see you do it.'

Skinny frowned, half-smiled, then shook his head in confusion. The shotgun hung loosely in his hands.

'Start counting,' Cole told him.

'Whuh ...?' said Skinny.

'Raise your gun and start counting. You can count, can't you? Just count to three and pull the trigger.'

'Yeah, but ... look ...' Skinny tried smiling again. 'Look ... I didn't mean nothing with your brother ... we was just –'

'I'm not going to stand here for ever,' Cole told him. 'Either you start counting or I will. Three seconds – you or me?'

Skinny shook his head. 'I don't wanna –'

'One ...' said Cole.

Skinny looked down at the gun in his hands, his eyes lost in fear.

'Two ...'

'No, look ... please ... I'm sorry –'

'Three.'

Skinny dropped the gun and stepped back in almost hysterical surrender[1] – bowing his body, raising his hands, shaking his head from side to side and mouthing silent nothings. Cole just stood there, watching him. I felt for Skinny for a moment – feeling his weakness, his shame, his loneliness – but I was also remembering how I'd felt when he'd had me on the ground with the shotgun pressed to my head, and although I didn't really blame him for that, there was no getting away from the fact that he'd done it. He'd made his choice. He'd sided with Red. And now he was paying the price for it.

He'd fallen to his knees now, and as Cole picked up the shotgun and turned his back on him, he buried his head in his hands and started crying. I guessed he knew that nothing would ever be the same for him again. He'd been humiliated, shamed, his mask stripped bare, and – worst of all – Nate had witnessed everything. And Nate and Skinny weren't friends. They had no loyalties. They just

1 surrender: state of giving up

did things together, like animals in a pack. And if Nate could make himself look better by telling everyone else what had happened – and I was pretty sure that he thought he could – he wouldn't think twice about doing it. The story would soon spread, getting worse with every telling, and that'd be it for Skinny – he wouldn't be worth shit to anyone.

As Cole opened the passenger door and got back in the car, I looked over at Skinny again. He was still kneeling at the side of the road, still shaking and quivering in the dark …

He was as dead as if Cole had just shot him.

'Take us to the Gormans' place,' Cole told Nate.

Without so much as a glance at Skinny, Nate turned the car around and headed back the way we'd come. I was tempted to look back at Skinny again, but I was afraid of what I might see, so I just closed my eyes and hoped that Cole had finished for the night.

I should have known better.

Twelve

As we left the moor behind and headed back to the village, the worst of Nate's fear gradually left him. He was still nervous and edgy, but his hands had stopped shaking and he was driving with a lot more confidence than before. I suppose he was thinking the same as me – that Cole had spent all his anger on Skinny. From Nate's point of view, it wasn't a bad assumption to make. He hadn't been hurt, he hadn't been shamed, and he was on his way to the relative safety of the Gormans' farmhouse. Cole wasn't going to do anything there, was he?

If I'd been in Nate's shoes, I'd probably have felt the same. But I wasn't. And – like I said – I should have known better.

'Vince's place, yeah?' Nate said to Cole as we drove up through the village.

Cole nodded, his eyes staring blankly through the windscreen. Nate gunned[1] the car and swung it past Quentin's house, and then we were speeding along the winding lane through the dead-dark shadows of the pine forest.

I realised I still had the pistol in my hand. It was heavy, and my fingers ached, so I placed it carefully on the seat beside me. When I looked up again, Cole had turned round in the passenger seat to face me.

'Everything all right?' he said.

I nodded.

'Any trouble?'

'No,' I said. 'No trouble.'

He kept his eyes on me for a little while longer, then he turned back and stared through the windscreen again. He looked tired. I saw Nate flick a glance at the shotgun resting in his lap.

'Watch the road,' Cole told him.

1 gun sth. (infml): drive at a high speed

Nate turned back and we drove on in silence, slicing through the moorland darkness like a silent beam of cold white light. I gazed through the window, imagining things I couldn't see – the night-world of the forest, the ring of stones, the thorn tree, the Road of the Dead. I imagined the ancient mourners[1] carrying their coffins[2] across the moor – trudging wearily[3] through the desolate night, cold and tired and shrouded in silence – and I realised that they were all dead now ... every single one of them. They'd been dead for centuries. All that was left of them now was bones and dust and bits of nothing. They'd lived and struggled and fought and prayed ...

And all for what?

For hope? For God? For nothing?

Go home, Ruben, Rachel had said. Let the dead bury the dead.

I still didn't know what she meant.

When I opened my eyes again, the car was slowing down and we were approaching the turn-off[4] to the farmhouse. In the beam of the headlights I could see the gateway to the forest and the boulder where Jess had laid her dead dog in the sun.

'Pull up over there,' Cole told Nate.

Nate stopped the car, and Cole turned round to face me.

'Can you make your own way back to the house from here?' he said. 'I don't want Abbie and Vince to see the car.'

'What about you?' I said. 'Aren't you coming?'

'Not yet.' He glanced at Nate. 'I want a quiet word with him. We're going for a little drive. It won't take long.'

'No,' I said, shaking my head. 'No way –'

'I'm not going to *do* anything, Rube. I'm just going to talk to him.'

'I don't care what you do – you're not doing it without me.'

As Cole looked at me, blinking slowly in thought, I could see that Nate was starting to look nervous again. I didn't blame him. The

1 mourner: person showing great sorrow for sb. who has died **2** coffin: *Sarg*
3 trudge wearily: walk with tired steps **4** turn-off: junction

idea of having a quiet word with Cole in the middle of the night was enough to make anyone feel nervous – even me.

'All right,' Cole said to me.

'All right *what?*'

'You can come with us. But you have to let me do things my way.' He glanced at Nate again, then back at me. 'Whether you like it or not – OK?'

I nodded ... but something didn't feel right. I could feel something false, and I wondered if Cole was just putting on an act to scare Nate – get him scared, get him talking. Maybe the show with Skinny had all been part of it, too.

Was Cole that smart?

I wouldn't be surprised.

'We need to swap places, Rube,' he said, struggling to adjust the shotgun in his hands. 'I can hardly move in this seat.' He opened his door, then turned round and looked at me. 'You get in the front and I'll get in the back.'

'OK,' I said, opening the door.

'Give me the pistol first.'

I passed him the pistol and got out of the car and started moving around to the front, but before I got there the passenger door suddenly slammed shut, followed almost immediately by the rear door, and I heard them both being locked.

'Hey!' I shouted, bending down to look through the windows. Cole had the pistol rammed into Nate's throat and was yelling at him to drive. 'Hey, Cole!' I cried out, rapping on the window with the flat of my hand – *bam, bam, bam.* 'Hey! HEY! What are you *doing?'*

The engine roared and the car sped off in a shower of dirt and gravel, leaving me stumbling around at the side of the road, staring after it like an idiot.

'Shit,' I muttered, angrily brushing the dirt from my clothes. 'Shit.'

The farmhouse was quiet when I got back. A light was on in the front room, and as I let myself in and crept upstairs I could hear the sound of a TV turned down low. I could sense the wary presence of Abbie and Vince behind the closed door – waiting, listening, wondering – and I wondered what they were wondering about. The same things, different things … the same things, but in different ways?

I went to the bathroom, then I went into the bedroom and shut the door and lay down on the bed and thought about Cole.

I knew what he'd done to me, and why he'd had to do it, and I was pretty sure I knew what he was going to do with Nate. It was all the same thing, really. He needed information, and he knew how to get it, and he knew he needed to be on his own to do what he had to do. I knew it, too. If I'd gone with him, I would have brought some sense of righteousness[1] with me. I might not have *wanted* to, but I would. And then Cole wouldn't have been able to do anything. Whatever it was he intended to do – and I knew he'd do whatever it took – he could only do it in an emotional void[2]: no right, no wrong, no good, no bad, no feelings at all – just do it.

My brother knew how to turn off his heart.

I wanted to turn everything off, too. Just press a button – *click* – and shut myself down. Turn off my heart, turn off my mind, turn off my body – just lie there, senseless, like a dormant tree in winter, waiting for the spring to return. Or maybe I could wait even longer …

I don't believe in life after death, but I know for a fact that matter doesn't cease to exist: it just changes. Everything that gives us life just goes somewhere else when we die. Our atoms, our molecules, our particles – they all just drift away into something and somewhere else. Into the ground, into the air, into the rest of the universe. Rachel is dead, and she's never coming back, but in a thousand years' time her atoms will be everywhere – in other people, in animals, in plants … in dormant trees waiting for the spring to return.

If only I could wait for a thousand years …

1 righteousness: behaviour that is morally right or good **2** void: emptiness

It was a nice thought, but that's all it was – just another useless thought. I had a lot more of them over the next hour or so, but none of them changed anything. I was still there, still waiting, still lying on the bed. Abbie and Vince were still downstairs, still watching TV. Rachel was still dead. And Cole was still somewhere else, still doing what he did.

My stupid head couldn't change anything.

It must have been around midnight when Cole came back. I heard a car coming down the lane, and when I looked out of the window I saw the Astra rolling into the yard, its headlights lighting up the barn and the outhouses. It pulled up in front of Vince's Land Rover and Cole got out, leaving the headlights on. In the beam of the lights I could see the shotgun in his hand and the pistol in his belt and the heartlessness in his face, and I knew that he was still in the void. It was frightening. Even the night seemed afraid of him. As he crossed over to the Land Rover and wrenched[1] open the bonnet[2] and peered inside, the darkness shivered all around him.

I couldn't see what he was doing under the Land Rover's bonnet. He was bent over the engine, reaching out for something, studying something, getting hold of something ...

'Hey!'

The voice came from the front door.

'What the hell are you *doing?*'

It was Vince. I looked down and saw him coming out of the house and marching across the yard towards Cole. I couldn't see his face, but his walk looked furious, and his voice was getting louder by the second.

'Hey, Ford! FORD! I'm *talking* to you ... Hey! *Hey! HEY!*'

Cole didn't react. He just carried on doing what he was doing – straightening up, calmly examining the tips of his fingers, angling his hand in the Astra's headlights to get a better look. It wasn't until Vince had stomped up to within half a metre of him, and was yell-

1 wrench sth.: pull sth. violently **2** bonnet: *Motorhaube*

ing right into his face, that Cole finally acknowledged his presence. Even then he barely looked at him. He just rolled his shoulder and whipped up the shotgun and hammered the barrel into Vince's head.

I ran downstairs and got to the hallway just as Cole was dragging Vince's body through the front door. I stopped and stared. Vince wasn't moving. He'd gone down hard when Cole had hit him, and now his eyes were still closed and his head hung lifelessly to one side, and I was beginning to fear the worst. He was dead ... Cole had killed him ...

But Cole didn't seem to care. As Abbie came running downstairs, screaming and crying and throwing herself at her husband, Cole just lugged[1] Vince's body into the front room, dropped it onto the settee[2], and calmly left her to it.

She was hysterical – sobbing, crazy, out of control – and I was starting to lose it, too. If Vince was dead ... that was it. That was the end. If Vince was dead, Cole was as good as dead, too. He'd be locked up for ever. Lost. Gone. Dead.

Just like everyone else.

Lost.

Gone.

Dead.

But I guess that Cole had a lot more faith than me – faith in himself, faith in his strength, faith in the thickness of Vince's skull – because ten minutes later Vince was sitting up on the settee, grunting and groaning and holding a packet of frozen peas to his head.

And no one was lost.

And no one was gone.

And no one was dead.

Abbie was still hysterical, though, pacing around the room like a crazy woman, spitting and cursing at Cole. 'Christ, what's the *matter* with you? You could have *killed* him, you stupid bastard. You're worse than a bloody *animal* ...'

1 lug sb./sth.: drag or pull sb./sth. violently **2** settee: sofa

Cole's face showed nothing. He was standing at the window, the shotgun still in his hand, and he was keeping a close eye on Vince. He didn't think Vince would do anything, but he wasn't going to take any chances.

'I want you out of here tonight,' Abbie hissed at Cole. 'Right *now*. Just get your stuff and piss off back to where you belong.' She stared at him with bulging eyes. He ignored her. She shook her head and turned her back on him. 'I've a good mind to call the police –'

'Call them,' Cole said.

She stopped and turned round. 'What?'

'Call the police. It's about time you told them the truth.'

Abbie froze, her eyes suddenly cold with fear. She tried to blink it away, but the damage was already done.

'I don't know what you're talking about,' she said, trying to sound angry again.

'OK,' Cole shrugged, 'let's call the police then.' He began moving across the room towards a telephone on the wall. 'Do you want me to call an ambulance while I'm at it?'

Abbie hesitated, darting a glance at Vince, but he was still too groggy to know what was happening. Cole picked up the phone and started dialling.

'Wait,' Abbie told him.

Cole stopped dialling, but he kept the phone in his hand.

'Are you ready to start talking?' he said to Abbie.

She looked at Vince again, then nodded. Cole put the phone down and crossed back over to the window.

'Sit down,' he told Abbie.

She sat down next to Vince and gently wiped some blood from his face. He closed his eyes and groaned. Abbie put her hand on his knee and turned to Cole.

'You didn't have to hit him so hard,' she said quietly.

'He's lucky I only hit him.'

'It wasn't his fault ...'

'What wasn't?'

'Anything … everything …' She blinked slowly, then lowered her eyes. 'Rachel … it wasn't Vince's fault. He didn't know what they were going to do. He was just—'

'Shut up,' Vince muttered, trying to sit up. 'Don't say nothing –'

'He *knows*,' Abbie told him. 'He already knows –'

'Gypsy shit … dunno shit …'

'Don't, Vince … *please* … you'll only make it worse.'

'She's right,' said Cole, stepping forward with the pistol in his hand.

Vince looked up at him, smiling crookedly[1]. 'What you gonna do – shoot me?'

Cole nodded. 'In the knees, first. Then the elbows. Then I'll string some rope round your neck and tie it to the back of your car and drag you all over the moor.' He stopped in front of Vince and pressed the pistol into his knee, then slowly leaned forward and looked him in the eye. 'What do you think? You think I'm joking?'

Vince said nothing, but he wasn't laughing.

Cole stared at him for a long time. Eventually, he said, 'I'm not sure how much longer I can put up with you, so let's just get this done – all right? No more shit. You sit there, you don't move, you don't say anything. If I ask you a question, you either nod or shake your head. Anything else and you'll never walk again. Got it?'

Vince nodded.

'Good.' Cole turned to Abbie. 'Now, I'm going to tell you what I think happened, and you're going to listen. When I've finished I'm going to ask you some questions and you're going to answer them. If I'm satisfied with your answers, you'll never see me again. If I'm not satisfied, you'll be seeing me in your nightmares for the rest of your life. Do you understand?'

Abbie nodded.

Cole went back over to the window, lit a cigarette, and started talking. 'Henry Quentin has been trying to buy up this place for a long time,' he said. 'He needs it for the hotel people, whoever they

1 crooked: dishonest

are, and he's been getting impatient because you won't sell.' He looked at Abbie. 'Am I right?'

She nodded.

He said, 'But you need the money.'

'We can manage.'

'That's not what Vince thinks, though, is it?'

Abbie said nothing. Vince just stared at the floor.

'Vince hasn't worked for a long time,' Cole went on, 'and you both know that the money you got from selling your land won't last for ever, so when Henry comes along and offers you a good deal – probably more than a good deal – Vince can't understand why you won't take it. It's good money, you can buy another house, a nice new house. Maybe a new car, too. Why *not* take the offer?'

'It's my house,' Abbie mumbled. 'It's my mother's house.'

'Right,' said Cole. 'But Vince is getting all kinds of shit from Quentin. He's putting the pressure on – offering more money, getting more impatient, starting to get nasty. And that starts getting to Vince, and *he* starts getting nasty with *you*. But whatever he says, and whatever he does, you still won't change your mind. So when Quentin suggests trying something else, like maybe giving you a bit of a fright, Vince can't see what else he can do but agree.'

'They would have done it anyway,' Abbie muttered softly. 'With or without Vince, they still would have done it.'

'Yeah, but they *didn't* do it without him, did they? Vince told them when would be the best time to do it. He told them you were going to visit his mother after Rachel had left, and he told them you'd be expecting a lift home from him, and he told them he'd pretend the car wasn't working so you'd have to walk home on your own.' Cole held his hand up to Vince, showing him the oil on his fingertips. 'I checked your carburettor – it hasn't been changed in years. You lied, didn't you?'

Vince started to open his mouth, then changed his mind and just lowered his head.

'You piece of shit,' Cole said to him. 'You set up[1] your own wife, for Christ's sake. You let her walk home in the middle of the night, knowing full well that Quentin was going to set one of his freaks on her—'

'Nothing was supposed to happen,' Abbie said. 'No one was *meant* to get hurt. I was just supposed to get frightened ...'

'And that makes it OK, does it?' Cole shook his head. 'Shit ... he's your *husband*. He's supposed to look after you.'

She shook her head. 'Vince didn't know they'd get Selden to do it. He wouldn't have gone along with that. Selden's a headcase[2].'

'You lent Rachel your raincoat, didn't you?'

Abbie nodded, starting to cry.

Cole just stared at her. 'Selden thought Rachel was you. Vince told Quentin what you were wearing and what time you'd be walking back. Quentin told Selden, and when Selden saw Rachel wearing your raincoat and walking the road back to your house, he thought she was you. But instead of just frightening her, he raped her and killed her and left her on the moor.' Cole paused, staring the truth into Abbie's lost eyes, and in that moment I could feel the pain of Rachel's death sucking the air from the room.

I couldn't breathe. I'd never felt so cold and numb in all my life. It was as if I'd only just realised that Rachel was dead.

She was *dead*.

My sister was dead.

Never coming back.

She was dead for ever, for ever pained and cold and wronged and dead dead dead dead dead dead dead ...

I was crying silently now.

Cole was with me, crying deep down inside himself, but no one else knew it – not even him. He was still staring at Abbie and Vince, speaking softly in the silence of the night.

1 set sb. up: make a trap *(= Falle)* for sb. **2** headcase (infml): person who is crazy

'What happened, Abbie? How did Quentin find out what Selden had done? Did Vince tell him? He must have been surprised when you came back that night and nothing was wrong.'

'He was drunk,' Abbie said emptily. 'I don't know what happened. I just left him on the settee and went to bed.'

Cole looked at Vince. 'Did you call Quentin?'

Vince shook his head – *no.*

'So how did he find out?'

Vince shrugged – *don't know.*

Cole looked at him for a while, then said, 'Do you know where Selden's body is?'

No.

'Do you know who killed him?'

No.

'Was it Red?'

Don't know.

'Quentin?'

Don't know.

'But Quentin ordered it?'

Maybe ...

'Yes or no?'

Yes.

'When – that night?'

Don't know.

'Is Bowerman involved? Does he know where Selden's body is?'

Don't know.

'Yes or no?'

Don't know.

The room was full of nothing now – no sound, no air, no light, no dark. No feelings. There was too much of a void to feel anything. Cole was nowhere; his black eyes soulless, his dead heart still. Vince and Abbie were just lumps of meat. And I was Ruben Ford. I was sitting in the back of a wrecked Mercedes in a breaker's yard in east London. I was watching the rain in the crystal-white lights over the gates, watching my jewels in the darkness. My mountains. My watchtowers. I was alone with Rachel, walking a storm-ravaged lane in the middle of the night, and we were cold and wet and tired and scared and we didn't know why ...

What are you doing here, Rach? I thought you were coming home tonight?

I was Ruben Ford. I wasn't dead. I could see things: a burning sky, a field of bones, a nightmare face carved out of rock. I could see a red maniac with a vision of me in his eyes ...

'What are you going to do now?' a distant voice said.

I opened my eyes to the echoed silence. Abbie was looking at Cole, her unanswered words still trembling on her lips. Cole was staring at me. I could see the flicker of my unknown thoughts in his eyes – the lights, the jewels, the skies, the faces – and I knew he could see them too. He could feel them in me. He was *with* me. For the very first time in his life, he'd sensed something from me in the same way that I'd always sensed feelings from him. And it scared the hell out of him.

'It's all right,' I told him. 'It's just you and me.'

He stared at me for a little while longer, his feelings still burdened with mine, and then he simply blinked his eyes and it was gone – all of it. The images, the feelings, the thoughts, the fears ... he just made them all disappear, and the only thing left was now.

'Get your stuff, Rube,' he said, pocketing the pistol. 'We're going.'

On the way out of the house, Abbie stopped Cole in the doorway and asked him where he was going. Her face was streaked with tears, and her eyes were haunted. But not by Rachel's ghost. The only spectres[1] plaguing Abbie were her own.

Cole didn't even look at her.

'Where are you going?' she asked him again, pleading with him, putting her hand on his arm. 'What are you going to do? About us, I mean. It wasn't Vince's fault, and I didn't know ...' She stopped, real-

1 spectre: ghost

ising that Cole wasn't listening, he was just staring at her hand on his arm. 'Sorry,' she said, letting go. 'I didn't mean –'

'You don't mean anything,' Cole told her, pushing his way past to the door. 'You never did and you never will.'

Thirteen

The air was crisp[1] and crystal-black as we drove up the lane away from the farmhouse. White moths fluttered in the beam of the headlights, dancing in the air like ghosted snowflakes in the night, and away in the distance I could see faint threads of crimson[2] colouring the raven sky. The inside of the Astra was sour with the stale scent of fear. There was a bloodstain on the passenger seat and a fresh smear of pink on a starburst crack[3] in the driver's window. Cole was as dark and silent as the surrounding moor.

'Stop the car,' I said to him.

'What?'

'Just stop a minute ... please.'

We'd just pulled out onto the village road, and when Cole slowed the car and we rolled to a halt I realised we were back at the forest again. Not that I could see it. I couldn't see anything. But I knew it was all there – the gateway, the forest, the Road of the Dead. I could feel it watching us.

Cole cut the engine and lit a cigarette. He wound down the window to let the smoke out.

'Are you OK?' he asked me.

'Not really. How about you?'

He shrugged. 'I'm all right.' He breathed out smoke and turned to look at me. 'It's nearly over now. We'll be home soon.'

We both knew it was a lie, but neither of us cared.

'Did you get all that stuff about Rachel from Nate?' I asked him.

'Not all of it. He told me as much as he knew, but he didn't know everything. I had to guess the rest. I wasn't sure I was right until I'd checked Vince's car.'

'Is that why you hit him?'

1 crisp: fresh and cool **2** crimson: deep red **3** starburst crack: crack looking like a star

'Who?'

'Vince.'

Cole shrugged. 'I needed him out of the way, that's all. If I hadn't whacked him they never would have told us anything.'

I glanced idly at the bloodstained crack in the window. 'Where's Nate?'

'I don't know,' he muttered, 'wherever I left him, probably.'

'And where's that?'

'Where he belongs – crawling around in the shit.'

'He's still alive, then?'

Cole looked at me. 'Don't start judging me, Ruben.'

'I'm not – I'm just asking if he's still alive.'

'I already told you. He's crawling around in the dark somewhere, alive as he ever was – OK?'

I nodded, satisfied that Cole was telling the truth. 'What about Skinny?' I asked him. 'What was that all about?'

'What do you mean?'

'You know what I *mean*,' I said. 'Christ, Cole – what the hell were you doing? Giving him the shotgun … shit, he could have *killed* you.'

'Yeah?' Cole smiled. 'I thought you said he didn't have the guts for it? You could see it in his eyes, you told me. Remember? According to you, he couldn't kill anyone to save his own life.'

'His gun wasn't loaded then.'

Cole reached into his pocket and pulled something out. When he held out his hand to me and opened his fingers, I saw the two shotgun cartridges nestling in his palm.

'You think I'm stupid?' he said.

I looked at him, shaking my head, not knowing what to think. I'd seen him showing Skinny the loaded shotgun … I'd seen the cartridges glinting in the chambers. He couldn't have taken them out then. He could have taken them out some time later, when I wasn't with him, but I knew he wasn't lying. He *wasn't* stupid – he *hadn't* given Skinny a loaded gun.

'Do you know what magic really is?' he said to me.

'Magic?'

'Yeah, magic – illusions, conjuring tricks[1], pulling rabbits out of hats ... all that kind of stuff. Look.'

He closed his fingers on the shotgun cartridges, held them tight, then opened his hand again. The cartridges were gone. I stared at the empty space for a moment, not quite believing my eyes, then I looked up at Cole.

'It's not magic,' he said. 'It's just fast hands.'

I didn't know what to say. I was stunned. The trick in itself was amazing enough, but what really astonished me was simply the fact that Cole could do it. That's what I couldn't believe. He was my *brother*. I knew him inside and out. I knew him as well as I knew myself. And I knew – without any doubt – that he didn't *do* magic tricks. Not in a thousand years. Magic tricks were the last thing in the world he'd do. They were frivolous, pointless, boastful, vain ... they were childish, for God's sake. My brother didn't *do* childish. He hadn't even done childish when he was a child.

'It's only a trick,' he said to me.

'What?'

'It's just a trick. You don't have to *think* about it.'

I looked at him. It was strange, suddenly realising there was a side to him I'd never known anything about. I don't think it changed anything between us, but it shifted things ever so slightly. Whatever it was that made us *us* – the bond, the dynamics, the history – whatever it was, it was now fractionally out of sync[2]. Out of tune. Our purity had been compromised by a barely audible hiss of white noise.

It didn't mean anything.

I didn't *like* it, but it still didn't mean anything. All we needed was a bit of fine-tuning.

'Are you ready?' Cole said to me, starting the engine.

'Why did you pick Skinny and Nate?' I asked him.

'What?'

1 conjuring tricks: magic tricks **2** be out of sync (infml): be not working at the same time or speed

'When we were waiting outside the hotel – what made you go after Skinny and Nate? Why not one of the others? Why not Red? I mean, he probably knows more than Skinny and Nate put together.'

'He's smarter than them, too,' Cole explained. 'That's why he didn't hang around when they split up. He was into his car and away before I had a chance to move.'

'All right,' I said, 'but what about Quentin? He was on foot, on his own ... we even knew where he was going. We could have picked him off easy.'

Cole dropped his cigarette out of the window. 'Skinny and Nate are weak,' he told me. 'That's why they do what they're told.' He wound up the window. 'There's no point trying to crack coconuts when you can get what you want by cracking eggs.'

I smiled at him. 'You're full of surprises tonight, aren't you? Magic tricks, self-styled proverbs[1] ... what else have you got up your sleeve[2]?'

He held out his hand and gave it a flick[3] – and the two shotgun cartridges dropped into my lap. I looked down at them, then lifted my eyes back to Cole. The half-smile on his face only lasted a moment, but it was more than enough for me. The white noise had gone from my head.

'OK?' he said.

I smiled and nodded. 'Let's go.'

It wasn't far to Henry Quentin's house – along the moorland road, down the winding lane, and then we were heading into the village and the big stone house was looming up on our left. As Cole slowed the car and turned off the headlights, I wound down the window and peered through the darkness at the rear of the house. The vast garden that I'd glimpsed before was completely closed off behind a high brick wall topped with razor wire[4] and broken glass.

'Any cameras?' Cole asked me.

1 proverb: saying that gives good advice **2** have sth. up your sleeve: *ein Ass im Ärmel haben* **3** flick: quick movement **4** razor wire: *Stacheldraht*

'Not that I can see.'

We kept going, rolling slowly alongside the wall, both of us looking up at the ancient stone house. It was dark, the windows unlit. Weirdly shaped chimney stacks jutted from the roof like an army of soot-black sentries[1].

'What do you think?' Cole asked me.

I shook my head. 'We'd have to go over the wall. They're bound to be watching it. And we don't know what's on the other side, anyway. There could be dogs, cameras ... anything.'

Cole thought about it for a moment, then nodded. He turned the headlights back on and accelerated[2] away down the road.

We drove into the village, turned round and parked by the telephone box, facing Quentin's house. Cole turned off the engine and we sat there in the still of the night, quietly watching the house. The driveway was still cluttered with vehicles, including the petrol tanker, and there were more cars and motorbikes parked on the road outside.

'Looks like he's got a few visitors,' I said.

Cole nodded.

I looked over my shoulder and gazed down the High Street. There was no one around. The street was dead – the hotel closed, the houses sleeping. Beyond the village, the distant moorland blurred like a dream into the grey-black horizon of the night.

'Do you think Quentin knows we're coming?' I asked Cole.

He nodded again. 'Vince probably rang him as soon as we left. He'll be waiting for us.' He looked at me. 'You don't have to come in with me, you know.'

'Yeah, I do.'

'You could wait in the car –'

'Don't be stupid. They're probably watching us right now. If you leave me here, they'll just come out and grab me as soon as you've gone. I won't stand a chance without you. And, anyway, what if you

1 sentry: soldier on guard **2** accelerate: increase speed go in on your own and then you don't come out? What am I supposed to do then?'

Cole didn't answer me. He didn't have to. I was only telling him what he already knew.

'OK,' he said after a while, 'but just stick close to me – all right?'

'I'll be in your shoes.'

'Here,' he said, pulling the pistol from his belt and passing it to me. 'It reloads automatically. The safety catch is off. All you have to do is point it and pull the trigger. If you have to shoot someone, aim for their chest. And don't hesitate. Don't warn them, don't give them a second chance, don't say anything – just shoot them. OK?'

'Yeah ...'

He reached over the back seat and picked up the shotgun. I passed him the two cartridges.

'Is that all there is?' I asked him as he loaded the gun.

He nodded, snapping the shotgun shut.

'Are you sure? Maybe there's more cartridges in the back –'

'I've already looked.'

'Do you think two's enough?'

'It's all there is.' He looked at me. 'Are you ready?'

'I suppose ...'

'OK – let's go and crack some coconuts.'

I felt faintly ridiculous – walking up a village high street in the middle of the night with an automatic pistol weighing heavily in my pocket. It just didn't *fit*. It was all out of place and out of time and out of my control. It didn't feel right. Not to me, anyway. To Cole, though, it felt perfect. The shotgun in his hand, the cool air on his skin, the rock-steady ground beneath his feet ... everything to him was just how it was. All he could feel was a straight-line emptiness in his head, and that was all he wanted.

'Trees on the left,' he said quietly.

'What?'

'The trees to the left of the house, at the top of the drive ... there's someone behind them.'

We were nearing the driveway now. It climbed quite steeply towards the house, and at the top, between the side of the house and a narrow pathway, I could just make out a clump of tall fir trees. As I squinted through the darkness, I saw something move, but I couldn't tell what it was. It was just a vague movement. A dim shape.

'Stay on my right,' Cole told me as we started up the driveway. 'Keep your eyes on the house.'

We moved up the drive, squeezing past the parked cars, and I tried to keep my eyes on the house. A light glowed dimly in a downstairs window, but apart from that the building was dark. I couldn't see anyone watching us, but the top of my head was tingling with vulnerability[1].

I put my hand in my pocket and felt the cold steel of the pistol. It felt good now. Reassuring. Not quite so ridiculous any more.

We carried on up to the top of the driveway and stopped in front of a large wooden door set in an arched stone porch[2]. A gentle breeze was whispering through the trees in the garden, and I could smell the faint scent of pine in the air. The house was quiet. Everything was still. Somewhere in the distance a night bird screeched and, as the eerie call faded into the emptiness of the moor, I suddenly heard something else. Something closer. Rustling leaves. A footstep. Then a croaking voice.

'I been looking for you.'

I turned round and saw Big Davy coming out from behind the fir trees at the side of the house. He wasn't wearing the neck brace any more, but he sounded as if he was still suffering. He was holding his head at an awkward angle, too – walking slightly lopsided[3]. But he was just as big as before, and his eyes were just as mad.

'You got a permit for that?' he grinned, nodding at the shotgun in Cole's hand.

Cole said nothing, just watched him approach.

1 vulnerability: feeling of being unprotected **2** porch: veranda **3** lopsided: having one side lower than the other

'See, the thing is,' he started to say, then he doubled over, coughing painfully, and put his hand to his throat. 'Shit,' he wheezed, still rubbing his neck. He coughed violently again and spat on the ground, then he looked up and started lumbering towards Cole, his streaming eyes full of hate. 'I been thinking about you,' he rasped[1], 'I been thinking what I'm going to –'

Cole moved fast and hit him hard, smack in the throat, just like before. Davy went down without a sound, not even gasping for breath this time, just choking silently in the dirt.

Cole turned his back on him and stepped up to the front door. 'Get behind me, Rube,' he said. 'Watch my back.'

I did as he asked, standing behind him, facing the street. Big Davy was still writhing on the ground, his mouth wide open, begging for air. His eyes were bulging in panic and pain.

'He doesn't look too good, Cole,' I said.

'Who?'

'Davy.'

'Don't worry about him, just keep your eyes open for anyone else. You ready?'

'Yeah.'

'Cover your ears.'

I put my hands over my ears. The shotgun boomed and the air exploded in a sudden rush of splinters and smoke. When I turned round, the front door was hanging open and there was a big jagged hole where the lock used to be.

'You could have knocked,' I said.

He wasn't listening. With the shotgun at his hip, he was staring intently through the open door at the dust-filled gloom of a high-ceilinged hallway. There were no lights. No people. Just dark and dust and silence.

Cole opened the shotgun and took out the empty cartridge and dropped it to the floor. He waited a moment, then bent down quietly

1 rasp: speak with a rough voice

and picked it up again. Another moment, then he loaded the spent cartridge back in the shotgun and loudly snapped it.

I didn't get it at first, but then I realised that if anyone was listening they'd assume he'd just reloaded.

'Got your pistol?' Cole said to me.

I pulled it out of my pocket. 'Yeah.'

'I might need it. If I ask for it, just give it to me – OK?'

'Right.'

'Stay behind me.'

He stepped into the doorway and reached round the wall, searching for a light switch. After a couple of moments a pale light snapped on, revealing the gloomy interior of the hallway. It was long and high and faded with age: old walls, old carpets, old furniture. Dark portraits lined the walls – faces, figures, long-dead ancestors – the paintwork cracked and greasy. On the left of the hallway was a broad flight of stairs with scarred wooden railings and banisters[1]. There was a door at the end of the hallway, and two more along the right-hand wall. They were all closed.

'Nice,' I said, looking around. 'Very cosy.'

'Shut up, Ruben,' Cole said.

'I'm nervous.'

'I know. Just keep it to yourself, I'm trying to listen.'

I listened with him, but there wasn't much to hear – a faint sigh of wind from outside, my thumping heart, bits of wood dropping off the door.

Cole reached back and touched my arm and we stepped cautiously through the doorway together. Although the door was wide open, the outside world suddenly seemed a long way away. We were inside now. In this house. *This* was our world for now.

As we edged along the hallway, my eyes seemed to see everything. Every little detail. The patches of damp on the walls. The threadbare[2] carpet. The bare plaster[3] showing on the ceiling. I could

1 banister: handrail of a staircase **2** threadbare: shabby and old **3** plaster: *Putz*

see cracked timbers and cables and sagging lead pipes[1]. Muddy bootprints. Pinched cigarette ends. A browned apple core. There was a faint but insistent smell of gas in the air, and the air itself was like nothing I'd ever experienced before. I could taste it. It tasted of stale breath and flesh and a dearth[2] of blue sky, of inertia[3] and petrol and brick-dust.

'Wait,' said Cole, holding out his hand and stopping.

I stopped behind him. We were about halfway along the hallway, outside one of the doors. Cole was staring at it, listening hard, with the shotgun levelled at the handle.

'Pistol,' he whispered.

I passed him the gun. He took it with his left hand, keeping the shotgun aimed at the door. I heard him take a breath and steady himself, and I thought he was about to burst through the door, but the next thing I knew he was spinning round – away from the door – and aiming the pistol at the top of the stairs.

Floorboards creaked, and I saw a slight movement behind the railings on the landing. Cole pulled the trigger and the pistol cracked dully in the silence. Blue flame flashed, a railing splintered, and a man's voice yelped in pain.

'The next one goes in your head,' Cole called out.

A figure appeared slowly from the shadows. It was the Teardrop Man. A trickle of blood was running down his cheek from a splinter wound under his eye. As he raised his hands and moved cautiously down the stairs, Cole passed me the shotgun.

'Watch the door,' he said. 'If anyone comes out, shoot them.'

As I covered the door with the shotgun, Cole turned his attention to Teardrop. He was standing at the bottom of the stairs now, wiping the blood from his face.

'Come here,' Cole told him.

Teardrop hesitated. 'I was only –'

'Shut up. Come here.'

1 sagging lead pipe: *herunterhängende Rohrleitungen* **2** dearth of sth.: lack of sth. **3** inertia: laziness

He edged closer to Cole, his hands held out in surrender.

'Where's Quentin?' Cole asked him.

Teardrop glanced up the stairs, nervously licking his lips.

Cole levelled the pistol at his head. 'Don't make me ask you again.'

'Upstairs,' he said shakily. 'Back room.'

'Who's with him?'

'Red and Bowerman.'

'What about the rest of them?'

'They're all over …'

'Where? How many?'

Teardrop nodded at the door I was covering. 'There's two in there, two in the next room, two in the kitchen –'

'Where's the kitchen?'

'End of the hall.'

'Any more?'

'Upstairs – front room.'

'How many?

'Three.'

'Outside?'

'Four or five, maybe more.' He grinned, his confidence coming back. 'It's all covered. You won't get out.'

'Any weapons?'

'Henry's got his revolver. Bowerman's got a rifle. Some of the others are carrying knives. You won't –'

Cole cut him off, cracking the pistol into his head, and he slumped to the floor and lay still.

Two down, I thought to myself, only another dozen or so to go. Six downstairs, five upstairs, more out the back … I just couldn't see how we were going to make it. I looked at Cole. He had no doubts. No doubts, no thoughts, no worries. His mind was empty. He wasn't thinking at all.

'There's too many of them,' I said to him. 'You can't take them all out. What are we going to do?'

'Get Quentin,' he said simply. 'Once we've got him, the rest of them don't mean anything.'

I stared at him, wondering how he could think so clearly without having a thought in his head.

He looked back at me, his eyes strangely content. 'It's only a game, Rube. You win or you lose. It's not worth worrying about.'

As I followed Cole up the stairs, keeping the hallway covered with the shotgun, I did my best not to worry about anything. But it wasn't easy. What worried me the most was that I couldn't *stop* worrying. *What if this happens? What if that happens? What if I do something wrong?*

'If anyone opens a door,' Cole had told me, 'just shoot. Don't bother aiming at anything. Just close your eyes and pull the trigger.'

It sounded so simple, but everything about it scared me to death. What if I killed somebody? What if I froze? What if I messed everything up because I was too busy worrying about messing things up?

'All right?' Cole asked me.

'Yeah, no problem.'

We got to the top of the stairs and paused on a cramped little landing. At the far end of the landing was another closed door.

Cole turned to me. 'Can you still see the hallway from up here?'

'Just about.'

'Keep it covered. Don't move till I call you in.'

I sat down on the top of the stairs and watched the hallway. It was still empty. Still scary. I looked over my shoulder at Cole. He'd moved along the landing and was standing in front of the door, securing the pistol in the back of his belt.

'The hallway, Rube,' he said gently, without turning round. 'Just watch the hallway.'

I looked down at the hallway again. The doors were still closed, but I could feel something happening now. The silence had changed. It was a silence about to be broken. I tightened my grip on the shotgun. I felt something move. Then one of the doors slowly creaked open – and I closed my eyes and pulled the trigger.

The silence exploded as the shotgun roared, and as the deafening blast ripped through the air I was vaguely aware of another loud crash behind me – the sound of Cole smashing down the door – and then everything erupted in a hail of noise and confusion: shouting, screaming, grunting, thumping, moaning. The sound of a pistol rang out, and I was desperate to turn round and see what was happening, but I forced myself to stay where I was and keep my eyes on the hallway. Dust was rising from a crater in the wall, and the remains of an oil painting lay scattered all over the floor, but there was nothing else to see. There were no bodies. The doors were all closed. The shotgun blast had done its job.

And now, I realised, the gun was empty. Just a useless lump of metal in my hands. And that didn't feel good. I tried to convince myself that no one else knew it was empty, so it didn't really matter, but that didn't make me feel any better.

Neither did the silence behind me.

It was too still now, like the hush that falls after a battle, and suddenly I didn't want to turn round any more. I didn't want to see what was happening. I didn't want to see that Cole was hurt, or worse. Because if I didn't see it, it wouldn't be true.

'Are you going to sit there all day?'

His voice ran through me like a surge of fresh blood, and when I turned round and saw him standing in the doorway, it felt so good I wanted to cry.

'You all right?' he said.

I nodded, unable to speak for a moment. All I could do was stare at him. He was breathing heavily, and he had a slight cut over his eye, but apart from that he looked fine. The room behind him was dim and dusty, the stale air greyed with a drift of gunsmoke. A pale yellow light shone from a table lamp, showing heavy grey curtains draped over the windows, a cumbersome[1] leather settee, and lots of dark wooden furniture. One of the metal-heads was sprawled face down on the settee, the other one was curled up in a ball just beyond the door. Across the room, one of the bikers from the bar was sitting on the floor with his back against a heavy oak door. His

1 cumbersome: heavy

teeth were bared and he was clutching his leg, trying to staunch the flow of blood from a bullet wound in his thigh. From the amount of blood on the floor beneath him, I guessed he wasn't succeeding.

I looked at Cole.

'He had a knife,' he shrugged. 'I didn't have any choice.'

'What about the others?'

'They'll be all right.'

I nodded, looking over at the biker again. He didn't look good. His eyes were dull. His face was white against the dark oak door, and I wondered if he was dying. And if he died, what would that mean? Bones and dust, I thought, bits of nothing. Let the dead bury the dead ...

A floorboard creaked, ripping the thoughts from my head, and then Cole was suddenly pulling me back from the stairs and snapping a shot at someone in the hallway. Wood thwacked[1], and I heard running feet, and then Cole let off another quick shot. Something shattered and a door slammed shut, and then everything went quiet again.

'We'd better move,' Cole said, still looking downstairs. 'They're not going to run for ever.'

He turned round and helped me to my feet and told me to watch the stairs, then he crossed over to the wounded biker and dragged him away from the door. The biker moaned in agony, cursing violently under his breath, but he was too weak to resist. Cole dumped him against the wall, then turned round and picked up a flick-knife from the pool of blood on the floor. He wiped it clean, snapped it shut, and put it in his pocket.

'All clear?' he asked me.

I looked downstairs. 'Yeah.'

He beckoned me over[2]. I crossed the room and joined him by the door. He guided me to one side and we both stepped back against the wall, out of harm's way.

'All right?' he asked me.

1 thwack: bang **2** beckon sb. over: indicate to sb. to come over by making a sign

I looked at him, trying to unscramble[1] his feelings. There were shadows in his mind, echoed images of his intent: faces, figures, movements, lines, angles, actions, motions, shapes ...

None of it made any sense to me. I had no idea what he was going to do. But I knew it didn't matter; all I had to do was trust him.

I nodded at him.

He nodded back, paused a second, then stepped away from the wall and launched a kick at the door. The air shattered and the door burst open with a sudden dull crash, and then Cole was just standing there in the splintered light, waiting for the dust to clear.

1 unscramble sth.: decode sth.

Fourteen

In the steel of Cole's eyes I could see the faces of Bowerman, Quentin and Red. Quentin was at the back of the room, sitting rigidly[1] at a large oak desk, and Red was to the right of him, lurking[2] in the alcove of a high arched window. Bowerman was standing in the middle of the room, pointing a rifle at Cole. He was drunk – his body swaying from side to side, the rifle in his hands tracing circles in the air. When he spoke, his voice was slurred and ugly.

'Cole Ford,' he said, 'I'm arresting you for possession of a firearm with criminal intent. You do not have to say anything ... ah, shit. Just gimme the gun, boy. Come on ... don't be a twat[3]. I'm a police officer, for chrissake[4].' He laughed stupidly. 'You're not going to shoot *me*, are you?'

Cole raised his arm and fired the pistol. I heard a dull thwack, followed by a surprised yelp of pain, and then a metallic clatter and a heavy thump as Bowerman dropped his rifle and fell to the floor. Cole glanced down at him, then raised his eyes and stared deeper into the room. I could feel the amber eyes staring back at him through the dusted light.

'I want to talk to you,' Cole said calmly.

There was a slight pause, then Quentin said, 'You'd better come in.'

Cole waved me over and we stepped through the door together. The room was stale and dark. Heavy curtains draped the windows. The only light came from four white candles flickering palely on a dark wooden cross suspended from the ceiling.

I stood beside Cole and gazed around. Bowerman was lying on the floor just in front of us. Cole had shot him in the shoulder. There

1 rigid: stiff and upright **2** lurk: be standing somewhere as if hiding **3** twat (sl): idiot **4** for chrissakes: (swear words) for Christ's sake

wasn't much blood, but his eyes were glazed with pain and shock and he'd puked up[1] all over the carpet. His rifle was lying next to him on the floor.

'Pick it up, Rube,' Cole told me.

I picked up the rifle and passed it to Cole. He pulled back the bolt and checked the rifle was loaded, then racked it shut again and looked down at Bowerman. He was starting to struggle to his feet now. Cole watched him for a moment, then stepped forward and hit him in the head with the rifle butt. Bowerman slumped back down into a pool of beery vomit.

Cole turned his attention to Red.

'Over there,' he told him, gesturing with the rifle. 'Against the wall.'

Red smiled and moved out of the alcove. When he reached the wall, Cole told him to stop.

'Take off your jacket.'

'What?' Red grinned.

'Take it off and drop it on the floor.'

Red shrugged, but did as he was told. Still grinning.

'Now your trousers,' Cole told him.

Red's grin went cold. 'I'm not –'

'Just do it.'

Red looked at him for a moment, his jaw set tight, then he shook his head and unbuckled his belt and lowered his trousers. He started to step out of them, stooping down to his shoes, but Cole told him to stop.

'Just leave them there,' he said. 'Stand up straight. Look at me.'

Red straightened up, naked hate burning in his eyes.

'Sit down,' Cole told him.

'You just said –'

'Shut up. Sit down.'

As Red sank slowly to the floor, his eyes never moved from Cole's. 'You're a dead man, Ford,' he said quietly.

1 puke (infml): be sick, vomit

Cole looked down at him, seeming to think about it, then he shrugged to himself and looked up at Quentin. 'If he moves or makes a sound, or if anyone comes through that door, I'm going to kill you – OK?'

Quentin barely nodded his head. His face was stone-cold and his eyes showed nothing. He was dressed as before in his brass-buttoned soldier's coat, only this time the coat was undone, revealing a collarless white shirt and a carved wooden crucifix on a leather string around his neck.

'Let's see it,' Cole said to him.

Quentin raised his head a fraction[1]. 'I'm sorry?'

'Your gun. Wherever it is, take it out slowly and put it on the desk.'

Quentin blinked once – the first time I'd ever seen him blink – then he reached towards a drawer under the desk.

'Slowly,' Cole warned him.

Quentin paused, then inched the drawer open and carefully lifted out an old army revolver. Holding it by the tip of the barrel, he placed it gently on the desk in front of him.

'It's fully loaded,' he told Cole. 'I keep it for vermin[2].'

'Rube,' Cole said, without looking at me.

As I went over and picked up the revolver, Quentin turned his eyes on me. His face remained blank, but there was an ice-cold smile under his skin that sliced through my flesh and cut right down to the bone. I lowered my eyes and stepped away from the desk, feeling strangely violated.

Cole stepped up to the desk and leaned the rifle against it. He still had the pistol in his hand.

'I know what happened,' he said to Quentin.

Quentin looked at him. 'Do you?'

Cole nodded. 'The hotel complex, Abbie Gorman's house, your deal with her husband ... I know it all.' He glanced over at Red, then

1 a fraction: a little bit **2** vermin: undesirable animals e.g. rats

turned back to Quentin again. 'I don't care about any of it, I just want to know what you did with Selden's body.'

Quentin's eyes fixed on Cole. 'I'd like to help you, Mr Ford. I really would. But, as I told you before, I'm afraid I don't have the faintest idea what you're talking about. All I know about John Selden is that the police are looking for him in connection with your poor sister's death.'

Cole raised the pistol and fired a shot into the wall, missing Quentin's head by inches. Paint and plaster erupted from the wall, peppering Quentin with a fine shower of dust, but he didn't even flinch.

'Last chance,' Cole said to him. 'The next time you lie to me I'll put a hole in your head.'

Quentin calmly brushed the dust from his coat. He took his time – carefully picking out flakes of paint, scraping his cuff[1] with a horny thumbnail – then finally he rubbed his palms together and placed his hands on the desk and slowly looked up at Cole. 'Do you believe in vengeance, Mr Ford?' he said.

'I don't believe in anything.'

'How about retribution[2]?'

'I can take it or leave it.'

'Really?' said Quentin. 'And did you take it or leave it with a sinner called Billy McGinley? Or perhaps that was all your father's doing?'

Cole's face remained blank. 'What's your point?'

'Point? I have no point. I'm just trying to decide if you have what it takes to kill a man in cold blood.'

Cole just looked at him for a moment, then he raised his arm and levelled the pistol at Quentin's head. Quentin kept perfectly still, ignoring the gun and staring intently into the depths of Cole's eyes. I could feel him invading my brother's heart – searching, probing, mining his soul – and I knew he could see Cole's truth. He'd known it all along. If Cole had to kill him, he would. That was the reality, and that's how Quentin accepted it – as a plain and simple reality. It

1 cuff: end of a sleeve **2** retribution: punishment that is deserved

wasn't anything to fear, it was just something he had to deal with: a problem, an annoyance, a complication.

'Your sister's death was a mistake,' he said casually. 'She was in the wrong place at the wrong time, that's all. These things happen, unfortunately. People stumble into other people's business, a contract goes awry[1] ... I'm sure you know how it is, Mr Ford. Business is business.' He shrugged. 'Sometimes it works, sometimes it doesn't.'

'What about Selden?' Cole said. 'Was he a mistake, too?'

'Only in a genetic sense. In terms of the job, he was perfect. That's why I used him.' Quentin looked at Cole. 'Vagrant[2] instability, Mr Ford – it's cheap and expendable, it doesn't ask questions, and best of all – it's terrifying.' He paused for a moment, gazing thoughtfully at his hands, rubbing plaster dust between his fingertips. 'Of course,' he continued, 'when I first found out what Selden had done, it did occur to me that perhaps I'd underestimated his instability, but now that I've met you and your brother I'm even more convinced that my initial judgement was correct.' He looked up from his hands and fixed his eyes on Cole. 'Your sister was a fine-looking creature, Mr Ford, but I doubt if her looks alone were enough to push Selden over the edge. Physical sexuality wasn't John's thing. He just liked to look. That's why I trusted him to confront Mrs Gorman.' He smiled coldly. 'We'll never know for sure, of course, but I think the thing that pushed Selden over the edge was the fight in your sister's heart.' He cocked his head. 'She had the same spirit as you, Mr Ford. You all seem to have it – you, your father ... even your strange little brother here.' He shot me a sideways glance, then looked back at Cole again. 'If your sister had just rolled over and whimpered a little, she'd probably still be alive today.' The corner of his mouth twitched in amusement. 'What do you think, Mr Ford?'

Cole answered quietly. 'I think I'm seconds away from wasting you.'

1 go awry: go wrong **2** vagrant: person with no home who moves from place to place

'No, you're not,' Quentin said calmly. 'You need me alive. I'm the only one who knows where Selden is buried. And you're right, of course – his body would prove beyond doubt that he killed your sister. There was a lot of blood, a lot of scratching ... a lot of other things, too.' He looked at Cole to see how much he was hurting him, but Cole was past hurting now. Quentin shrugged and went on. 'That's my problem, you see? If Selden's body is found, the police won't be able to ignore it. They'll have to start looking into things. And that won't be good for anyone.'

'Especially you,' Cole said.

Quentin nodded. 'I have business commitments. People have placed a lot of trust in me. Trust and money. Important people. Connected people. I can't afford to jeopardise their trust.'

'You mean you can't afford to let them find out you've been skimming off[1] their investment.'

Quentin shrugged. 'Skimming, maximising, distributing ... it's all a matter of semantics[2].'

'Not if they find out, it's not.'

'Exactly. I'm so glad you understand. If I told you where Selden is buried, I'd be dead within weeks.'

'You'll be dead within minutes if you don't.'

Quentin shook his head. 'I don't think so. If you kill me, you'll never find Selden. I can promise you that. And, besides, if you kill me, the gentlemen downstairs will rip you and your brother to pieces.' His smile sharpened. 'I know you don't care about your own thick skin, but I'm sure you wouldn't want anything to happen to young Ruben here, would you?' He looked at me again, and this time I saw hell in his eyes. My hell, Rachel's hell ... I could feel it happening. And so could Cole. Quentin was *making* us feel it. He was making Cole see the worst things in the world happening to me. And Cole couldn't bear it any more. He was losing it. Losing control.

1 skim off sth.: take money from sth. **2** semantics: study of the meanings of words

'Imagine it, Mr Ford,' Quentin whispered. 'Imagine it happening. Imagine what *that* would do to your mother. Her only daughter's been raped and murdered, and now her strange little boy –'

Cole lunged across the desk and rammed the pistol at Quentin's mouth, aiming to stuff the words down his throat. But Quentin had seen it coming. It was just what he'd been waiting for. And when he moved, he moved like black lightning – his left hand grabbing Cole's wrist and slamming it down on the desk, his right hand clubbing Cole's head like a sledgehammer[1]. The impact shook the air. Cole went down hard, slumped over the desk, but somehow he didn't let go of the pistol. Quentin kept hammering Cole's wrist on the desk – *crack, crack, crack* – then he punched him again, a wicked short jab to the side of his head, but Cole still wouldn't let go of the pistol. With an angry shake of his head, Quentin got to his feet and raised his fist over his head and brought it down with a thundering crash on Cole's wrist. Something cracked, and the pistol finally spilled from Cole's hand.

I was trying to move now, trying to help Cole ... but the air was too thick. I couldn't get through it. Everything had slowed to dream-time. Quentin was standing slowly over Cole, slowly grabbing his hair and slowly lifting his head, then slowly smashing his face into the desk – once, twice, three times. Cole was still conscious. I could see his eyes shining black through the blood. They were looking down at my side, trying to tell me something ...

The gun, Rube ... Quentin's revolver ...

I was still holding it. Quentin's revolver ... it was in my hand ...

Use it, Rube ... shoot the bastard ...

The dream-time cracked. I dropped the empty shotgun and raised the heavy revolver in both hands, steadying the sights on Quentin's head.

Cock it, Cole told me. *It's a revolver – you have to cock it. Pull back the hammer.*

1 sledgehammer: very large and heavy hammer

I got my thumbs on the hammer and started to pull it back ... and then Quentin was suddenly gone and all I could see in the notched V of the sights was Red – bare-legged and grinning, swinging the shotgun down on my wrists. *CRACK!* A bolt of agony shot through my arms and the revolver dropped from my hands, and the next thing I knew Red was stepping up and grabbing me by the shoulders, and I was looking up into his twisted eyes, and he was smiling his smile.

'Game over,' he said.

He drew back his head and hammered it into my face.

Now I'm falling, slumping, my legs crumpling like paper tubes, and I seem to be going down sideways, and I'm thinking to myself – why am I going down *sideways?* And I know it doesn't matter. I can hear people running, shouting, kicking, punching. I hit the floor slowly and start to roll over onto my back, but my arm flops out and I push against the floor and somehow get my elbow underneath my body, and now I'm sprawled out on my side with my head half-raised, looking across the room at Cole. The air is cloudy, misformed, moving. It throbs against my eyes. Cole is a blood-drenched sack on the floor, a thousand miles away. He's surrounded by raging faces and frenzied[1] fists and hundreds of pounding legs, stomping him into nothing.

A preacher man stands back and watches.

My skull is moaning. The room is darkening. The preacher man is shining his amber eyes on me ... and now I'm following his light. I'm floating back through the light of his eyes, back through the airless black air, back into his preacher man's head, and just for a moment I can see myself through his eyes – lying on the floor, my face bloodied, my eyes half-closed, my mouth hanging open. There's a figure standing over me. A small red man. A shotgun poised over my head.

'Make sure you don't kill him,' the preacher man says.

1 frenzied: furious

And the shotgun comes down like a piston[1], and everything goes black.

1 piston: *Kolben*

Fifteen

The first thing I see when I open my eyes is a big brown rat gnawing away at the sole of my shoe. He seems quite content, for a rat. His eyes are twinkling. His nose is twitching. His teeth are yellow. I don't want to disturb him, he's only chewing my shoe, but I think I'd better. Just in case.

But when I try to flick my foot at him, nothing happens.

My foot doesn't work. My *feet* don't work. I don't know where they are. I know *where* they are – they're right there, at the end of my legs, where they usually are – but my legs don't seem to recognise them.

I don't get it.

I don't *get* it.

I'm closing my eyes now, trying to work out what's going on. But I can't seem to think straight. My head hurts. My wrists hurt. I feel sick. My shoulders are aching. My arms are paralysed.

Maybe I'm dreaming.

But I know I'm not. And when I open my eyes again, the rat's still there. I watch him for a while, intrigued by his chewing action, then I turn my attention to my legs. They seem to be stretched out in front of me. I think about that for a while – *why are my legs stretched out in front of me?* – and eventually I come to the conclusion that I must be sitting down. And that makes me think – *if I'm sitting down, I must be sitting* on *something*. So then I turn my mind to the hard brown stuff I can see either side of my legs, and it doesn't take too long for me to realise what it is: it's wood. A wooden floor. Floorboards.

Now I'm getting somewhere.

Summary: I'm sitting on a wooden floor with my legs stretched out in front of me, and a rat is chewing my shoe.

I still don't want to disturb him, but they're old shoes, and the soles aren't all that thick, and if I leave him chewing much longer he'll be through the shoe and into my socks and then he'll start on my feet, and I don't want that. So I think I'd better try flicking my foot again ...

And this time it works. My foot moves. Not very far, and not very fast, but it's enough. Ratty jumps back and scurries away, leaving a small cloud of dusty air in his wake. And now I'm just staring at the dust. It's fine and old, like the dust of an unused room. There are bits of straw in it, too.

Straw?

I seem to remember seeing bits of straw somewhere before. Somewhere? Where? On the floor? I look down at the floorboards again. Bare wood. Dusted wood. Flecks of yellow on faded brown.

Floor.

OK, so that's the floor. What about the ceiling?

And then I'm throwing my head back to look up at the ceiling, but before I get to see anything a roar of thunder rips through my skull and the veil of blackness comes down again.

I only passed out for a second or two, but when I opened my eyes this time, everything had suddenly become clear. I knew what had happened. I still didn't know where I was, or how I'd got there, but at least I could remember what had happened. I remembered being in Quentin's house, and Cole getting beaten up, and Red hitting me with the shotgun. I could feel the blunt gash[1] on the back of my head. It was bleeding again. Fresh blood. Fresh pain. It hurt like hell, but that was OK, because now I knew what had happened.

When I'd looked up at the ceiling, I'd cracked the gash on my head against the thick wooden post[2] behind my back, the post I was sitting against ...

The post I was tied to.

My arms weren't paralysed. They were just tied so tightly behind my back I couldn't feel them any more.

1 gash: injury **2** post: pole fixed to the ground

I sat there for a while, staring at nothing, just slowing my heart and trying not to panic. It wasn't easy. I *wanted* to panic. I was tied to a post, my head felt weird, I couldn't move my arms, I didn't know where I was, I didn't know where my brother was, or even if he was still alive ...

God, I wanted to see him. I'd never wanted anything so much in my life. I wanted to scream and shout and cry like a baby. I wanted him to be here. I wanted to know he was all right. I wanted him to tell me that *I* was all right, that everything was going to *be* all right ...

I *wanted* him.

I *needed* him.

But he wasn't here. And I couldn't feel him. And crying like a baby wasn't going to help, was it? So I didn't. I just sat there for a while, staring at nothing. And when I was sure I wasn't going to cry, I started looking around again.

And this time I kept the back of my head well away from the wooden post.

I took my time, letting my senses soak up everything around me – the floor, the walls, the roof, the air, the light, the emptiness, the silence – and when I was done I was pretty sure I knew where I was.

I was in a large wooden building with a timbered roof. The roof was cracked. The walls were cracked too, and painted black. There were no windows or lights, but a pale dawn light was seeping in through the cracks, and I could just about make out the shapes of things: a hatchway in the floor on the far side of the building, discarded sacks, loose piles of straw.

I was in a barn.

The air was calmed with a cool height of silence, and when I thumped my foot on the floorboards, the sound echoed emptily beneath me.

I was in the loft[1] of a barn.

I knew it.

1 loft: space under a roof

And I knew there had to be dozens of barns around Lychcombe, and they probably all looked the same, but there was something about this one that told me I'd been here before. I could feel the memory of myself in the air, smiling stupidly in the emptiness beneath me. I could see myself standing at the foot of a ladder, looking up at the hatchway, guessing that there probably wasn't anything up there, and deciding not to bother.

I'd been here before ...

I knew it.

I was in the barn at Abbie and Vince's place.

I *knew* it.

Not that it made much difference; I'd known where I was all along. I was tied to a post – *that's* where I was. And after I'd spent the next ten minutes twisting my arms and flexing my fingers and gouging the skin off my aching wrists, I knew I wasn't going anywhere, either. The wooden post was bolted to the floor. It reached all the way up to the roof. It was at least six inches square, and as tough as a cast-iron girder[1]. I couldn't see my hands, but I was guessing they were bound with plastic handcuffs. Police-issue[2], probably, courtesy of Mr Bowerman.

Trying to escape was a waste of time and energy.

So I didn't bother.

Instead, I closed my eyes and shut down my mind and put all my energy into opening up every cell in my body. I might not know if Cole was still alive or not, but if he was, I'd find him. Wherever he was, I'd find him.

I had to.

It was all I could do.

I don't know how long it took – I wasn't aware of the passing time – but when I finally felt Cole stirring within me, the sun had risen and the dusty air inside the barn was dappled with the light of a golden morning.

1 cast-iron girder: *Stahlträger* **2** police-issue: specially made for the police

Sixteen

Cole is just waking up. He's been unconscious for a long time, and it's taking him a while to come to his senses. He knows he's outside, he can feel the open air on his skin. It's cold. Very cold. Cold and damp and earthy. His body is stiff and racked with pain and he can feel a sickness that he knows as fear, and it's the only fear he knows – his fear for me.

'Ruben?' he says weakly, 'Ruben ... where are you?'

I'm here, I tell him. *I'm here ...*

But he can't hear me. He's miles away. He can't feel me. All he can feel is the pain and the cold and the fear. He can deal with the first two, but the fear is something else. He can't stand it. He doesn't want it. It doesn't do him any good.

So he closes his eyes and snuffs it out.

He lies still for a while, taking stock[1] of himself, checking the damage. His pockets have been emptied. No guns, no flick-knife, no wallet, no nothing. His clothing is muddy and torn. He has a broken finger on his right hand, a hairline fracture in his right wrist. His left hand is OK. Badly bruised[2] legs. Feet OK. Two, maybe three, cracked ribs. Twisted shoulder. Broken nose, couple of busted teeth, split lip. Nasty gash over the right eye. Swollen cheek, swollen eyes, swollen head. Lumps[3], scratches, bruises, more cuts ...

He'll live.

He cracks open his eyes and winces at the pale morning sunlight. He's lying on his back, looking up at the sky. He can see grass, red earth, a woodlouse[4]. The back of his head is damp.

He's lying in a ditch.

He's alive.

1 take stock of sth.: think carefully about sth. (e.g. a situation) and form an opinion about it **2** bruised: hurt **3** lump: swelling **4** woodlouse: *Kellerassel*

I try calling out to him again – *Cole ... Cole ... can you hear me?* – but he still doesn't answer. He's feeling the cold now, the stagnant moisture seeping into his pain-racked bones, and he can feel something pressing against his chest ... and then suddenly all he can feel is the race of blood in his heart as a looming grey shadow falls over him.

There's someone at the side of the ditch, someone standing over him, someone crouching down ...

Cole tries to sit up, straining against the pain in his ribs, but it's just too much. The pain cuts through him like a knife, pushing him back down into the dirt, and all he can do is look up into the crouching face and take whatever is coming.

'Are you all right?' the face says. 'Christ, look at you. Shit.'

The sun's in Cole's eyes, so he can't see who it is, but I recognise the voice straightaway.

It's all right, Cole, I tell him, breathing a sigh of relief, *there's nothing to worry about. It's Jess.*

But he can't hear me. He's straining to see her face now, trying to shield his eyes from the sun, but one of his arms is trapped under his body and the other one is squashed up against the wall of the ditch.

'Stay there,' Jess tells him, 'don't move.'

'Who are you?' he says, still struggling. 'What do you want?'

'Just keep *still* a minute.'

'I don't *want* to keep still,' he snaps. 'I want to get out of this stinking ditch.'

'You'll hurt yourself if you carry on like that.'

'I'm already *hurt*,' he says, squinting angrily into the sun. 'If I stay here much longer I'll freeze to death.'

'I'm only trying to help,' Jess says huffily[1].

'Well, do something then.'

'What?'

'I don't know ... anything. Just get me out of here.'

1 huffy: offended

Jess hesitates for a moment, then she shuffles forward and reaches down into the ditch. As she does so, her head moves to one side and blocks out the glare of the sun, giving Cole his first look at her face.

'Jess,' he mutters, softly surprised. 'Jess Delaney.'

She smiles, tugging gently at his trapped arm. As Cole looks up into her eyes, I can feel that strange movement inside him again – the tingling movement he'd felt when he'd first laid eyes on her. It still doesn't feel quite right to share it, but this time I just can't help myself.

It feels too good.

'I'm Cole Ford,' he tells her, 'Ruben's brother. I met your uncle –'

'Yeah, I know,' she says, trying again to free his arm. 'Do you think you could give me some help here? My back's getting stiff.'

After a lot more careful tugging – and rolling and pulling and lifting – Jess finally manages to help Cole out of the ditch and they both sink down to the ground – breathing hard, damp and muddied, exhausted. As Jess does her best to clean herself up, Cole looks around to see where he is. There's a thorn hedge in front of him, then a strip of scrubby grass and a low stone wall, and beyond the wall is the road that leads down from the bus stop to the village. The village is off to his left, slumbering quietly at the bottom of the hill, and away to his right he can see the flat grey roof of the petrol station glimmering dully in the morning light.

'Who did this to you?' Jess asks him.

'Who do you think?'

She nods. 'You need to get to a hospital. You're all broken up –'

'Have you seen Ruben?' he interrupts her.

She shakes her head, looking puzzled. 'Why – what happened? Did Quentin –?'

'I've got to get back to the village,' Cole says, starting to get up. He stumbles, his head still dizzy. Jess reaches out and steadies him.

'You can't go anywhere in that state,' she says. 'You need ... what's that?'

'What?'

She reaches down and picks something up from the ground. 'This … it just fell out of your shirt.'

She passes Cole a plain white envelope spattered with mud. He looks at it, opens it up, and removes a single sheet of paper, folded in two. He unfolds the paper and starts to read. The words are written in fine black ink:

Dear Mr Ford, he reads, Your brother is safe and well. In order for him to remain so, you will leave the village and return to London today. A bus leaves for Plymouth at 14.32, arriving at the railway station at 15.21. The train to Paddington departs at 15.40. Your journey will be monitored. On confirmation of your arrival in London, your brother will be released without harm and no further action will be taken.

I trust you understand that the consequences of any refusal will be final.

Sincerely yours

The message is signed with the mark of a crucifix.

I left Cole and Jess alone for a while and returned in my head to the solitude of the barn. I wanted to be on my own. I wanted to think. I wanted to get the facts straight in my mind and weigh up the options.

Facts: It was early Sunday morning. I was tied up in a barn and I couldn't get out. Cole didn't know where I was. If he didn't go back to London today, I was dead.

Options?

I couldn't think of any.

I thought long and hard, looking at the situation from every possible angle, but no matter how many times I looked at it, the position remained the same: there was nothing I could do. It was all down to Cole. Either he went back to London, or he didn't. If he did, Quentin would probably let me go. There was no guarantee, of course, but he had nothing to gain by *not* letting me go, and gain was all that mattered to him. As long as Cole did what he was told, I was pretty sure that nothing would happen to me, and by the end of the day I'd be on my way home too, and that would be that. No further action. Quentin would get on with his business, Selden's body would never be found, and no one would ever be charged with Rachel's murder.

Would that be so bad? I asked myself. *Who cares what Quentin does? Who cares about murder charges? Justice doesn't change anything. And Selden's dead anyway. The only thing that matters is getting Rachel's body back, and that'll happen eventually. We'll just have to wait a bit longer.*

Would that be so bad?

No more hurt. No more death. No more Quentin ...

No more Rachel.

No more Rachel.

No more Rachel.

It kept coming back to me now – Rachel was dead. The reality kept welling up inside me, floating up from the depths like a great black cloud, filling my heart with darkness and my eyes with tears.

There was nothing I could do. I just sat there crying in the golden light, watching my tears turn to dust in the dirt.

Drifting ...

Floating ...

Feeling ...

The heat in the trailer is blue and sleepy. I can hear the gas fire hissing. The air is scented with cigar smoke and coffee and freshly washed sheets drying on a clothes rack. I can see Cole sitting in an armchair in front of the fire and Jess kneeling on the floor at his feet. She's cleaning and bandaging his hand. Her uncle is making coffee in a kitchen area at the back, and her little sister, Freya, is sitting on a foldaway bed in the corner, dandling[1] a baby in her lap. The baby is silent, sucking its thumb. Freya is staring mutely at Cole.

A clock on the wall shows nine o'clock.

Everything is quiet.

Cole looks away from the fire and glances slowly around the trailer. He likes what he sees. Fine-china plates on the wall, fancy carpets, framed photographs of smiling children. Potted plants, ornate mirrors, glass ornaments on a delicate table ...

'Keep your hand still,' Jess tells him.

Cole looks down at her. He feels slightly embarrassed – being nursed, being looked after, being pampered[2] – but it's not too hard to put up with.

'You want sugar, boy?' Reason asks him.

Cole smiles and nods. Through a small window behind the old man, he can see a white BMW and a jet-black Shogun parked beside a pale-blue trailer. The trailer is trimmed with silver and gold and decorated with baskets of flowers. To its right, a straw-haired man in a greased coat and boots is lumping broken pallets into an oil-drum fire. Wood smoke twists into the morning sky. Cole smiles quietly to himself. He can see dogs lying at the base of an angle-iron stake[3], two piebald ponies tethered to a pole, metal pails[4], wheels, a washtub on a table, rabbit skins, gas cylinders, a red plastic truck lying in the mud ...

'Take your shirt off,' Jess says.

Cole looks at her, his eyes flicking awkwardly at Reason and Freya.

'Don't be stupid,' Jess tells him. 'They're not nuns. Just take off your shirt. I need to tape up your ribs.'

As Cole begins to unbutton his shirt, Reason comes over and places a mug of coffee on a small wooden table beside him. The message from Quentin is lying face up on the table. Reason glances at

1 dandle sb.: hold sb. (esp. a baby) and move it up and down **2** pamper sb.: treat sb. with much kindness and give him special treatment **3** angle-iron stake: strong post made of iron **4** pail: bucket

it, then looks at Cole. He's taken his shirt off now, revealing a lurid[1] mess of welts[2] and bruises.

'I seen your old man battered like that one time,' Reason says. 'Big showman from Truro, 'twas. Fists like cannonballs.'

Cole smiles. 'Who won?'

'Who d'you think? Baby-John soaked him up[3] for an hour then opened up one of his eyes and switched him off.' The old man grins and takes two small cigars from his coat pocket. He lights them both with a match and passes one to Cole, then nods at the message on the table. 'What you doing about that, then?' he says.

Cole puffs on his cigar. 'What would you do?'

Reason shrugs. 'Ain't my brother.'

'What would you do if he was?'

'Probably the same as you.' He looks down at Jess, scratching thoughtfully at his grizzled chin, then turns back to Cole again. 'You need any help, just say it.'

Cole nods. He likes the old man now. He likes his simplicity. He likes his cheap cigars. And he likes his niece, too – if that's what she is. Cole somehow doubts it. Not that it matters. He doesn't care who or what she is – he just likes her. I can feel the attraction tingling in his veins like electric blood.

I can feel his uncertainty, too. He isn't used to liking things, and he isn't sure what to do about it.

'I need some air,' he says to Jess. 'Can we go for a walk or something?'

The long white grass is still moist with dew. I can feel the heavy moisture under Cole's feet as he walks with Jess around the field at the edge of the camp. They walk slowly, not speaking for a while – just walking together, alone with their thoughts. Leaving me on my own with mine.

1 lurid: (here) terrible **2** welt: red skin caused by beatings or cuts **3** soak sb. up: (here) receive the blows from sb.

Drifting ...

Floating ...

Feeling ...

In the middle of the field, a small grey horse is drinking from a trough. Dark eyes, strong head, ragged tail flicking at a storm of flies. And I wonder for a moment if it's the horse from my dad's first memory. I know it's not, of course – it couldn't be – but there's something there ... something ... I don't know what it is. I can feel Dad's presence somewhere, but I don't know where it's coming from. It could be something to do with his memory, mixed up with the feelings I'm getting from Cole, or it could be something to do with Cole, mixed up with his memories of Dad. Or maybe it's something else altogether ...

I just can't tell.

Whatever it is, though, it's taking me to Dad.

I can feel his memories and his long-held sadness, and I can see his face – worn and hard – and his troubled eyes, staring coldly at the whitewashed walls of his cell, and for a fraction of a second I can hear his voice – *let it come, Rube, just let it come* – and then he's gone again.

And so is the small grey horse.

The field is empty. No trough, no horse. Just Cole and Jess, still walking slowly, and Finn the lurcher, moping along in front of them. I wonder why it doesn't feel strange – the sudden disappearance of a small grey horse. But I don't think about it for long. It *doesn't* feel strange. And it doesn't bother me at all.

Finn the lurcher doesn't look well. His eyes are glazed. His coat is dull. He has no sense of purpose to his movement any more. He just slouches along in front of them, mournfully scanning the distant hills, waiting – as animals wait – for Tripe to come home. Jess is thinking about Tripe, too. I can feel the black cloud rising inside her. It's all she can do to force it back down and bring her attention back to Cole.

'Are you all right?' she asks him.

'Yeah,' he lies.

I can feel him suffering. His broken bones ache. His head throbs. His mouth hurts. His ribs are screaming with every breath and every step he takes. He's trying to ignore it all. Not out of any sense of bravado, but simply because that's what he does.

'Come here,' Jess says, taking his arm.

She leads him over to a large granite boulder half-buried in the earth at the edge of the field, then helps him to sit down. He lights a cigarette. She sits down beside him. He gazes around. The early brightness of the morning sky has faded to a raw grey dullness. Rain clouds are scudding[1] over the distant hills, darkening the moor with their shadows. I can hear the whisper of a coming wind in the air. Cole shivers. The fields of white grass are beginning to stir.

'He meant what he said, you know,' Jess says quietly.

'Who?'

'My uncle. If you need any help –'

'Why would you want to help me?' Cole says suddenly. 'What have I ever done for you?'

'It's not a question of *debt*,' Jess says. 'We're not saying we *owe* you anything. We're just offering to help.'

'Why?'

She shrugs. 'Does it matter?'

'Are you going after Red for killing your dog? Is that it?'

Her voice goes cold. 'That one's had it coming for a long time. Killing Tripe was just the last straw. Red was always going to get it before we left, dog or no dog.'

Cole looks at her. 'You're leaving?'

She nods. 'Tomorrow.'

'Where are you going?'

'Somewhere ... anywhere ...' She shrugs again. 'As long as it's away from here, I don't really care.'

'Don't you like it here?'

1 scud: move quickly

'What's to like?'

Cole nods his head. 'I did wonder ...'

'What?'

'Nothing ... it's none of my business.'

'You wondered what we were doing here?'

'Well, yeah ...' He looks around at the emptiness. 'I mean, it hasn't got much to offer, has it?'

Jess smiles at him. 'No work, nowhere to sell anything. No fairs. It's not even much of a site.'

Cole stares at her, his mouth half-open.

Jess laughs quietly. 'To tell you the truth, I really don't know what we're doing here. It was Uncle's idea. He saw this place in a dream.'

'A dream?'

'Yeah, he gets them sometimes – dreams of journeys, dreams of places. He doesn't know what they mean, but he thinks they mean something.'

'And do they?'

'Who knows?' She shrugs. 'They probably mean as much as anything else.'

Cole shakes his head. 'And you actually *follow* these dreams? You go to places that your uncle *dreams* about?'

'Sometimes – if we're bored, or if we don't have anything better to do. It doesn't happen often, but if there's no work around, or if we don't need any work ...' Her voice trails off and she gazes around at the surrounding moor. 'I know it's not much of a place,' she says, 'but it makes a change from living in the gutters of a shit-hole town that looks and smells like every other shit-hole you've ever been to.'

Cole nods again. 'The people are just the same, though.'

'People are always the same.'

They sit in silence for a while: Cole looking around, breathing the air, thinking about dreams and possibilities; Jess gazing sadly at Finn. He's lying in the grass at her feet now – his head on the ground, his soft brown eyes fixed on nothing. Jess wants to comfort him, but she knows it isn't possible – you can't comfort those who don't understand. She sighs heavily and looks up at the sun. It's sinking rapidly behind the closing clouds, filling the sky with a smouldering black light that turns the world to ashes.

'Do you think Ruben's all right?' Jess says quietly to Cole.

'He'd better be.'

She looks at him. 'What are you going to do?'

'Find him.'

'How?'

'He's my brother ... I'll find him.'

'But what about Quentin? He's not bluffing, Cole. If you stay here and go looking for Ruben, Quentin will kill him.'

'So I'll leave.'

'But you just said –'

'I'll find him.'

'You can't do both.'

Cole looks at her. 'He's my brother, Jess. I can do anything.'

Seventeen

I was tired now. My head was pounding. I was hungry and thirsty and cold. Black lights were flashing behind my eyes, and the numbing agony in my arms had spread up into my shoulders, across my neck, down into my chest, making me whimper like a wounded animal. My backside ached from sitting on the hard wooden floor, and the bloated pain in my bladder had got so bad I'd had to let go and pee in my trousers.

I didn't know what I was doing.

As the light faded to a senseless dusk, I let myself drift away again.

It's raining when he comes out of the trailer, a fine cold rain that colours the air with a dimming silvery-black. Faces and forms are indistinct. He's wearing a dark coat, a hat, a rucksack on his back. His right hand is bandaged. He moves cautiously, painfully, his head bowed down against the rain. As he leaves the trailer he half-raises his hand and nods his head to someone inside, then he shuts the door and pulls up his collar and shuffles away across the rain-sodden campsite.

I can feel the reddened clay clinging to the soles of his shoes.

The cold mist of rain.

The smell of damp cloth.

He keeps his head down, his eyes fixed to the ground. He walks with the weight of surrender on his mind. Along the rutted track, past the trunks of stunted trees, ghosting through the rain towards the village road. An unseen figure in a parked car watches him. He doesn't have to see the car to know it's there – edged in behind a storm-blackened oak at the side of the road, some way down the hill – he knows it's there.

He pauses at the end of the track, shrugs his shoulders, adjusts the rucksack on his back, then turns to his left and begins trudging up the hill.

The rain is falling harder now, dragging the black clouds down to the ground. The moor is melting into the storm-black sky, becoming one great mass of darkness. Granite, stone, earth, time. Thorn trees, flesh, dust and bones. Everything is black.

He keeps moving, climbing the hill. Past the petrol station, where another figure in another parked car watches him slowly, then flicks a switch[1] and grunts a few words into the crackle of a CB radio. Someone, somewhere else, says *copy that*[2], and the radio goes quiet.

He's soaked now, soaked to the bone. His feet wet inside his shoes. He carries on up the hill, uncaring of the things around him: the dry-stone walls, the stricken trees, the jutting tors on the distant hills …

I can smell the memories of ponies, their horse-sweet breath in the air. I can smell dark earth and wood smoke and gorse, and I can see what I saw once before: stone walls encrusted with lichen scabs, little white fingers dipped in blood. Devil's Matchsticks.

He's stopped.

We've reached the bus stop.

And I'm mesmerised again by the unholy silence of the moor. No human noises. No traffic. No voices.

The silence of another age.

Another time.

Another bus stop. Another day. Another night.

Nothing changes.

The sky is always black with rain. Rachel is always getting off the bus, trying her mobile, hurrying across to the telephone box, trying to call Abbie. The phone is always out of order. Broken, busted,

1 flick a switch: push a switch on a two-way radio **2** copy that (infml): I understand

jammed. No signal. No answer. Rachel is always alone. It's always cold and it's always wet and it's always dark and windy, and there's always something out there, something that shouldn't be there ...

Don't think about it.

He's standing beside me, his hand on my shoulder.

I can't help it, I tell him.

I know.

He gives my shoulder a squeeze, then looks over at Rachel. She's waiting for us at the side of the road.

What are you doing here, Rach? I thought you were dead.

She looks at the figure beside me – the lowered head, the dark coat, the hat. *Is that really Cole?*

Sometimes, I tell her. *Other times I'm not so sure. His face keeps shifting. Sometimes I think he's an* anti-*Cole.*

He looks at me.

I shrug.

Headlights appear in the gloom, the rattle and judder of an approaching bus. He holds out his hand. The bus pulls up, the doors open. He gets on, pays the driver, walks down the aisle, sits at the back. The only other passenger is a lank-haired man in a long waxed coat, pretending to read a newspaper.

I watch the bus as it clunks into gear and pulls away with a tired groan, and I can see the faceless figure with the bandaged hand in the rain-swept window at the back, but I can't feel anything from him. He's just a shade, a shadow, an anti-brother ... going home ...

And now he's gone, and all I can see are the rain-blurred stars of the bus's rear lights, fading dimly into the senseless dark.

'Wake up,' the voice said.

I felt something nudge my foot, and for a moment I thought the rat had come back again. I couldn't understand why he was telling me to wake up.

'Hey, shit-head,' the voice said. 'Wake *up*.'

I felt someone kicking me, and now I knew it wasn't the rat. Rats don't kick. They don't talk, either. Rats have twinkling eyes and twitching noses and yellow teeth. Rats are quite content to leave me sleeping.

'Maybe he's dead,' another voice said.

'He'd better not be. Quentin'd kill us. Kick him again.'

I really felt it this time, a full-blooded boot in the thigh, but I was too numb and tired to react. All I could do was open my eyes and stare at the boot – a scuffed[1] old Timberland with worn leather laces – then slowly look up to see who it belonged to. Careless eyes looked back at me, a pinched face, sour and hard … I didn't know who it was. It was just a man. A boy. A humanimal thing in a brown Diesel top.

'You alive?' he grinned.

His streaky blond hair was gelled into a fashionable mess that didn't seem to belong to him. It looked like someone else's hair. A small silver crucifix hung from his ear. His lip was pierced with a tarnished gold stud.

'Nice,' I mumbled.

He jerked his head at me like a curious chicken. 'You *what?*'

His breath was sweet with marijuana.

'What'd you say?' he hissed at me.

I couldn't speak, I just looked at him. A thin string of spit bubbled in a gap in his teeth. I knew he was going to kick me again, but I didn't really care. I was too tired to care. I lowered my head and waited for the blunt crack of his boot, but then the other voice spoke up again.

'Leave it, Sim – just get his hands.'

'Uh?'

'His hands … just do what Henry said.'

I lifted my head again and saw Vince standing at my feet with a bottle of water and a scrunched-up Tesco carrier bag in his hands. His hair was moist with rain, shining greasily in the broken light, and his skin was pale and tight. He didn't look very comfortable. His eyes were troubled with the fear you feel when you know you've

1 scuffed: worn out

gone too far. He wanted out, but he knew it was too late for that now. He was in too deep.

'Enjoying yourself?' I heard myself say to him.

He stared at me for a moment, then turned to Sim. 'Come on,' he said, 'let's just do it and get out of here.'

I heard a sharp metallic snap, then Sim was stooping down beside me with a bone-handled flick-knife balanced in his hand. An instinctive breath of emptiness caught in my throat, but before I had time to think about it, Sim had ducked around behind me and was cutting through the ties on my hands. He wasn't too careful about it, and even though my arms were numb I could still feel the blade nicking and slicing my skin. But that was nothing compared to the pain I felt when he finally cut through the ties and my hands were suddenly freed and the blood started flowing again. That was almost unbearable – my shoulders ripping apart, my flesh burning up, my skin stripped raw with a thousand burning needles.

As the tears streamed down my face, Vince stepped forward and placed the bottle of water on the floor beside me.

'You all right?' he asked.

'Yeah, great.'

He nodded at the bottle. 'Have a drink.'

'Where's Cole?' I said.

Instead of answering me, he opened up the carrier bag and pulled out a couple of slices of dry white bread and a small chunk of cheese.

'Here,' he said, offering me the food.

When I didn't move to take it from him, he dropped it on the floor and looked at his watch.

'You've got five minutes,' he said. 'Eat it now or go hungry. It's up to you.'

'Where's Cole?' I asked him again. 'When are you going to –?'

'Five minutes,' he repeated, then he turned his back on me and walked away to the other side of the barn.

Sim followed him.

I didn't move for a while, I just watched them. They sat down on a bale of straw. They lit cigarettes. They talked quietly. I couldn't hear what they were saying. They didn't seem to be watching me though, and for a fleeting moment I thought about making a run for it.

I looked over at the hatchway. It was propped open with a wooden pole. No more than ten metres away from me. I glanced over at Vince and Sim. They were still talking, still smoking. I wondered if I could get to the hatchway before they spotted me. They were closer to it than me ... but maybe if I surprised them ... maybe if I moved really fast ... maybe if I ...

Maybe nothing.

It was pointless. I couldn't move fast. I couldn't move at all. I couldn't even get to my feet.

I reached for the water bottle and took a long slow drink, then I put the bottle down and started ripping into the sliced bread and cheese. It was wonderful – the freedom, the water, the taste of the food. The bread was dry and the cheese was stale, and all of it was humiliatingly hard to swallow ... but it was still wonderful.

I was just swallowing the last mouthful of bread and washing it down with another long drink, when Vince and Sim came back. Sim was chewing gum, pulling a strip of blue plastic from his pocket, whipping it against his leg to straighten it. Plastic handcuffs. I could already feel them cutting into my wrists.

'You done?' Vince asked me.

'Looks like it,' I said. 'What's for afters? You got any cake?'

Vince nodded at Sim. Sim got his knife out and moved round behind me.

'Give him your hands,' Vince told me.

'How much longer—?'

'Just put your hands behind your back.'

I looked at him, wondering if there was anything I could say, anything to persuade him to help me ... but then Sim grabbed my hands and yanked my arms back around the wooden post, and the burning pain shot through me again, making me feel sick, and I couldn't think of anything. I felt the cuffs cutting into my wrists, then Sim pulled them tight and locked them off, and I was right back where I'd started from – absolutely nowhere.

Vince was picking up the empty bottle now, getting ready to go, and I could feel Sim standing up behind me, folding his flick-knife away, and I knew that in a moment I'd be on my own again – hurting, aching, shaking, crying – and it was all I could do to stop myself crying now. I *wanted* to cry. I wanted to break down in tears and beg for mercy. I wanted to *plead* with them to let me go ...

And I don't know why I didn't.

But I didn't.

After they'd gone, I felt a little ashamed of myself for a while. I knew I shouldn't. I hadn't done anything shameful. I hadn't done anything wrong. There's nothing wrong with being afraid. Nothing wrong with wanting to cry, wanting to beg, wanting to plead. There's nothing wrong with anything. I just didn't like the idea of my faith in Cole being shaken, that was all. I knew there was nothing wrong with that, either, but I still couldn't help feeling bad about it.

And I didn't want to feel bad.

Never feel guilty about anything, my dad once told me. *Shame and guilt are a waste of time. Just do what you do – and deal with it.*

So that's what I did.

I dealt with it.

Then I closed my eyes and released myself and drifted back to the moor.

It's early evening now. The rain has stopped but the sky is still heavy and dark. Although the sun won't go down for at least another hour or so, there's already a feeling of night to the air – the hills are slumbering, the rooks[1] are starting to roost[2], the colours of the moor are fading to a cold and shapeless grey. And as I drift down over the village, I see no lights, no people, no movement. The hotel is shut. The houses are dark. The streets are empty and still. Even the river is quiet, its bronze-black waters gliding in silence beneath the old stone bridge.

1 rook: *Krähe* **2** roost: rest

I drift on, following the rise of the hill, riding the rain-scented air over fields of greyed grass and granite, and in the distance I can see the lights of the gypsy camp. A faint blue glow in the half-light, a shimmering crescent[1] of warmth. The trailers are haloed[2] in the dusk. I can see pale lights burning behind curtained windows, vent pipes[3] misting, blue flames dying in the embers[4] of a fire. The camp is shrouded in its own sapphire night.

Moving closer, I can feel things beginning to stir. Inside the trailers, shadows are moving behind the curtains. Dogs are unsettled – whining, pacing. A pony snickers and stomps. It's a quiet stirring – intermittent[5]. A door opens. Voices murmur. The door shuts. A man in a greased coat and boots comes out carrying something wrapped in an oil-stained cloth. He crosses the yard, gets into a Shogun, lays the cloth on the passenger seat, quietly drives away – along the rutted track, then left, up the hill.

Some time later, another door opens and more voices murmur. This time two younger men come out, both carrying small canvas bags on their shoulders. The bags look heavy. The two men drive away in a white BMW – along the rutted track, then right, down the hill.

This goes on for a while – people leaving, driving away – until eventually there's only one car left: a red Mercedes.

The gas fire is still burning in the Delaneys' trailer. The windows are fogged. Reason is sitting at a fold-out table, smoking one of his cheap cigars and sipping from a tumbler of brandy and port. His face is flushed with the mix of heat and alcohol. A sawn-off shotgun[6] lies on the table in front of him.

'I ain't saying you *can't* go,' he says to Jess, who's over at the sink filling a glass of water. 'I'm just saying ...'

1 crescent: *Halbmond* **2** be haloed: look like sth. has a ring of light **3** vent pipe: *Lüftungsrohr* **4** ember: wood or coal that is still burning after a fire has no more flames **5** intermittent: happening occasionally **6** sawn-off shotgun: shotgun with a very short barrel

'What?' she asks him. 'You're just saying what?'

Reason smiles and glances at Cole. 'What d'you think, boy?'

Cole shrugs. He's sitting in the armchair, legs crossed, smoking a cigarette. He's dressed in someone else's clothes – jeans, a faded check shirt, an old black jacket. His eyes are tired and the bruises on his face are darkening to the colours of a storm: blue-black, yellow, the purple of thunder.

I never doubted him.

My faith in him might have stumbled for a moment, but I never doubted his presence. I knew he wouldn't leave me. But even so ... the sight of him, the *feel* of him ... it's still the most uplifting thing I've ever felt. It gives me energy. It powers me. It gives me life.

I can feel his heart now. He's ready to go. Impatient. Calm. Steady. Patient. He doesn't like having to rely on others, but he knows he has to do it. Whatever it takes – waiting, tolerating, small talk, trust – whatever it takes to get things done.

'What's the time?' he says.

Reason reaches into his pocket and pulls out a dull brass watch on a chain. 'Just gone seven,' he says. 'Jake'll be in London in an hour.'

Cole nods.

I can see how it went now. I can see the switch: Cole swapping clothes with the gypsy called Jake; Jess bandaging Jake's hand; Cole giving him his rucksack; then Jake getting into his dark coat and hat and leaving the trailer ... half-raising his hand, nodding his head, shutting the door, pulling up his collar, shuffling away across the rain-sodden campsite.

I could feel the reddened clay clinging to the soles of his shoes.

The cold mist of rain.

The smell of damp cloth.

'We'd better get going,' says Cole.

Reason nods, drains the last few drops of his drink, stubs out his cigar, starts buttoning his coat. Jess has moved away from the sink and is perched[1] on the edge of a mauve settee, sipping from a glass of water. Hot and cool in black jeans and a thin black cardigan, her shadowed eyes are quietly angry.

'What am I?' she says. 'Invisible?'

'Who said that?' Reason grins.

'It's not *funny*. You're totally ignoring me here.' She glances at Cole. 'Both of you. You're treating me like I don't exist.'

Cole doesn't know what to say. It's not his business. It's not up to him whether Jess comes with them or not. It's between her and Reason. But then again ... it *is* his business. He wants to be with her, but he doesn't want her getting hurt. He wants her to come, but he doesn't know if he needs her or not. She might be useful; she might be a liability[2]. He needs all the help he can get, but he can't afford to take any risks.

He doesn't know what to say.

'It's not my business,' he says.

Jess looks at him for a moment, then turns to her uncle. 'I've got a *right* to be there,' she tells him. 'Red killed my dog. It's my right to see him pay for it.'

Reason doesn't answer immediately. He carries on buttoning his coat, staring thoughtfully at the floor, his steady old eyes showing nothing. Then he looks up, suddenly sombre, a sad smile weighing down his face. He gazes fondly at Jess for a while, then turns to Cole again.

'What d'you think, boy?'

'I think she's right,' says Cole, staring openly at Jess. 'She's as much a part of this as anyone.'

Jess looks back at him, and the heat of the trailer moves in the silence between them. They have a yearning[3] to be somewhere else, somewhere alone, somewhere together. They can both see it – a place of soft grass and whispers and wide-open skies – but they

1 be perched on sth.: (here) sit on the edge of sth. **2** liability: burden
3 yearning: strong desire

both know it's not going to happen. It's another place, another time, another life.

'Come on,' says Reason, breaking into the moment. 'If we don't go now, the two of you'll be crying at the moon for ever.' He picks up the sawn-off shotgun and throws it across to Cole. Cole catches it, glad to have something to distract him from his embarrassment. 'You all right with that?' Reason asks him.

Cole hefts[1] the ugly-looking gun in his hand. 'Yeah,' he says. 'It'll do.'

Minutes later, the trailer is empty and the red Mercedes is coasting down the dark moorland road towards the village. As the car glides slowly into the valley, the shimmering blue light of the gypsy camp fades into the background, and the horizon up ahead begins to glow with a blood-red flicker of heat.

1 heft: hold and weigh

Eighteen

I've never been so far outside myself as I was that night. It was almost as if my physical self had ceased to exist. It was still *there*, still tied to a post in an empty barn, still hurting, still scared, still tired, but it wasn't really me any more. I'd become something else. I'd risen from the flesh of my body, up through the timbered roof, up into the boundless skies, rising higher and higher and higher, until eventually my other self was nothing more than a scrape[1] in the ground below.

I'm floating. Drifting. Riding the air like a spiderling borne on the wind. I have no control over anything. I have no say in where I'm going, or what I can see, or what I can feel, but it doesn't seem to matter. Wherever I am, whatever I'm seeing and feeling, that's it: that *is* the world.

There simply isn't anything else.

There's Quentin's house, cold and grey and glowering in the dusk. The stone walls seem to grow from the ground, the lightless black windows scowling down at the village like the sockets of staring dead eyes. There's the splintered front door, hastily boarded up. There's a growing whisper of wind in the trees, the electric scent of a coming storm. There are vehicles in the driveway – the petrol tanker, the Toyota pick-up, motorcycles parked in the shadows – and away from the house, away from the lights, there are gypsies waiting in cars. There's the Shogun, the BMW ... there's a Renault, a Jeep, an Audi estate. There are others, too. And back at the house, there's the straw-haired man in the greased coat and boots and the two younger men from the gypsy camp.

The straw-haired man is leading the others around the side of the house, keeping in close to the walls, moving slowly, cautiously,

1 scrape: mark

quietly. The Straw Man has a pair of bolt-cutters[1] in his hand. The other two have lengths of lead piping[2] tucked in their belts.

At the corner of the house, the Straw Man pauses and turns round. 'Stay here and wait for the call,' he whispers to one of his companions. 'Watch the door and the windows.' He touches the other one on the arm and gestures towards the top of the house. The other one looks up and nods. The Straw Man pats his shoulder and they both move off around the corner into the cold stone shadows.

Inside the house, a room downstairs has been turned into a makeshift hospital. The curtains are closed and the lights burn brightly. The air smells of whisky and blood. The wounded are lying wherever they can – on dining tables, on settees, on blankets on the floor. There's Ron Bowerman with his gunshot shoulder. Big Davy – crushed windpipe[3]. The metal-heads and Teardrop – three broken skulls.

It was Quentin's idea to keep them all here. 'There's too many for hospital,' he'd told Red earlier this morning. 'If we take them all in, there's going to be questions. Get Jim Lilley out here.'

And now Jim Lilley is here, in this room, dressed in a long white doctor's coat, drinking whisky and tending to the biker with the gunshot leg. He knows the biker might die, and he knows there's nothing he can do about it. If he was a doctor, there might be a chance. But he's not a doctor – he's a vet. And for the last five years he's been using and illegally selling a drug called ketamine, an animal anaesthetic. And Henry Quentin knows that. Which is why he's got Jim Lilley out here. Because he knows there's nothing he can do about it.

Quentin himself is sitting at his desk in the room upstairs, waiting for the phone to ring. Red is watching him from a leather armchair across the room. The two heavy bikers standing guard at the door are part of a gang that Quentin has called in from Plymouth. There

1 bolt-cutters: *Bolzenschneider* **2** lead piping: *Bleirohr* **3** windpipe: passage for air between mouth and lungs

are two more downstairs, another two in the garden. Red doesn't rate them. They're mercenaries[1], only in it for the money. Not that he cares. As far as he's concerned, the whole thing's gone to shit anyway. Henry's lost it. Gone too far. Too complicated. Too soft. He should've just whacked the breeds and buried them on the moor.

'What are you looking at?' Quentin says to him.

'Nothing,' Red grins. 'I was just wondering ...'

'What?'

'Nothing. I was just wondering.'

Quentin glares at him, sick of his dumb smiling face, then he turns his attention back to the phone.

'He won't be there yet,' Red says.

'I know.'

'The train's not due in for another ten minutes.'

'I know.'

'It's not going to be early.'

Quentin looks up. 'Don't you have anything better to do?'

Red just grins again. 'You really think Ford's gone?'

'He's gone.'

'You sure?'

Quentin's face remains blank, his voice stone cold. 'He got on the train. He hasn't got off. We've had him watched all the way. He's gonc.'

'What if he comes back?'

'He won't come back.'

Red jerks his head at the bikers by the door. 'So what are they for? If Ford's not coming back, why do we need them?'

Quentin says nothing. His resinous[2] eyes are burning hard into Red now, warning him not to go any further, but either Red is too stupid to notice or he just doesn't care any more.

'And another thing,' Red says, 'what are you going to do with the kid? You can't just let him go –'

1 mercenary: *Soldner* **2** resinous: (here) amber-coloured

The telephone rings, cutting him off. Quentin looks at it for a moment, then calmly picks it up.

'Yes?'

The room is quiet. I can hear everything: the faint tinny voice coming from the telephone; Quentin breathing, listening to the voice; Red sniffing, wiping his nose ... and then a strange muffled click from outside, and suddenly the tinny voice has gone.

'Hello?' Quentin says into the phone. 'Hello?'

His eyes narrow at the silence.

He frowns. 'Hello?'

'What's up?' says Red.

Quentin carries on staring at the receiver for a while, then a slow realisation comes over his face and he carefully puts down the phone and turns towards the window.

The Straw Man pauses halfway down the drainpipe[1] and glances back up at the top of the house. The rain has started, filling the air with silver-black needles. The thickly painted drainpipe is slick and greasy, getting harder to grip. But it doesn't matter. The job is done. The severed telephone cable is flapping loosely in the wind, tapping lightly against the guttering[2].

The Straw Man looks down and drops his bolt-cutters to his waiting companion, then he turns back to the drainpipe and clambers down the last few metres to the ground.

'You see anything?' he says, drying his hands on his coat.

His companion shakes his head.

The Straw Man nods and looks at his watch. 'Two minutes,' he says. 'Let's go.'

His companion tosses the bolt-cutters into some bushes and passes the Straw Man a sawn-off rifle. The Straw Man checks it, glances up at the window again, then they both move off around the back of the house.

1 drainpipe: pipe that carries water from the roof to the ground **2** guttering: pipe that carries water on the roof

'Has Vince got a radio?' Quentin asks Red.

'Why?'

Quentin carries on looking through the open window for a moment, gazing down into the rain-swept dusk, then he leans forward and glances up at the severed telephone cable. There's no anger or surprise in his face, just sheer calculation. He steps back from the window and turns to face Red.

'Has Vince got a radio? Yes or no?'

'No.'

'What about Sim?'

Red shakes his head. 'What's going on?'

'The phone's dead. Someone just cut the line.'

'Shit,' says Red, getting to his feet and moving over to the window. 'Did you see who it was?'

Quentin says nothing. He sits down at his desk and stares straight ahead, thinking hard. Red pulls back the curtain and checks the telephone wire, then glares down through the window, searching the ground below. His mouth is tight, his eyes wired. He can't see anything through the rain.

'Shit,' he says again, closing the curtains and turning back to Quentin. 'It's Ford, isn't it?'

'Get out to Vince's place,' Quentin tells him. 'Get the boy and take him down to the Bridge.'

Red stares at him. 'Is Ford back in London or not?'

'It doesn't matter where he is – just go. Use the basement door. Leave your car out the front and take the Transit.' He throws Red some keys. 'It's parked in the road round the back. I'll meet you at the hotel in a couple of hours.'

The basement door leads Red out into a narrow alleyway at the far side of the house. Hidden from view behind a thick growth of bramble[1] and knotweed[2], he moves briskly through the teeming

1 bramble: *Brombeere* **2** knotweed: *Knöterich*

rain[1] towards a wrought-iron[2] gate at the end of the alleyway. The gate is bolted and topped with barbed wire. As Red unlocks it and steps through into a moorland wasteground, a high-pitched whistle suddenly pierces the air. Red pauses, looking back at the house. He hears muffled thumps, running feet, shouting voices. He carries on listening for a moment, then he grins to himself and moves off into the wasteground, heading for the road at the back of the house.

I'm lost for a while. Drifting out of control. I'm everywhere and nowhere, and everything is tumbling around me. I'm in Quentin's house. Upstairs, downstairs. Upstairs, in his room, looped in the moment of his ancient voice – *get out to Vince's place ... get the boy and take him down to the Bridge ... get the boy and take him down to the Bridge ... take him down to the Bridge.* I'm downstairs, floating through chaos, through bedlam[3], through a frenzied clamour of violence and hatred, through savagery and pain, through lead pipes and knives and clashing heads. *Gypsy men are born to fight.* I'm the Straw Man, beating on a biker in the kitchen. I'm a black-haired gypsy kid, cracking a hood with a rock. I'm Teardrop, lunging for the kid with a scalpel. I'm the fight in their hearts. I'm lost in it. I'm drifting out of control ...

I'm in the barn, cowering in the crash of the storm. I'm cold. I'm shivering. It's dark. I'm scared.

Red is coming to get me.

I'm broken.

Red is coming.

I'm seeing dead rabbits and dogs and thorn trees and stones and twitching rats with sharp yellow teeth ...

And then suddenly they're gone. All my pictures, all my places, all my different worlds ... everything has fused into one. One place, one time; right here, right now.

I'm back in my brother's heart.

1 teeming rain: pouring rain **2** wrought-iron: iron that is formed into shapes
3 bedlam: confusion

The chaos has stilled and the house is quiet. The fight is over. All that's left is the murmuring sound of the aftermath – groaning bodies, scuffling feet, sniffs and coughs, lowered voices. The house is gradually emptying. Most of Quentin's men have already gone, scattered into the night, and now the gypsies are leaving too. There's nothing left for them to do. They've fought Quentin's men, they've run them off, they've locked the wounded in the room downstairs and posted a guard outside. They've searched the house from top to bottom, looking everywhere for me, and they've kept Henry Quentin in the room upstairs, waiting for Cole to arrive.

And now he's here.

With me in his heart.

He's standing in front of Henry Quentin with the sawn-off shotgun levelled at his head. Reason is on his right, smoking a cigar, and Jess is on his left. Quentin is still sitting at his desk. Still calm, still upright, still smiling under his skin. Right now he's studying Reason and Jess – looking them over, weighing them up – like a farmer examining livestock[1]. His eyes wander up and down Jess, then he nods to himself and focuses on Reason.

'You surprise me, Mr Delaney,' he says. 'I expected a lot less of you.'

Reason says nothing, just stares at Quentin and spits a shred of tobacco from his tongue.

Quentin turns to Jess. 'If it's Red you're after, my dear, I'm afraid you're too late – you just missed him. I'm sure he'll catch up with you soon, though.'

Jess looks back at him for a moment, then turns to Cole. 'Red's car is still here, but there's no sign of him anywhere. He must have got out through the basement.'

Cole nods.

Reason says, 'He'll have gone for your brother.'

1 livestock: farm animals, e.g. horses, cattle

Cole nods again. All this time he hasn't taken his eyes off Quentin. I can feel his finger on the trigger of the shotgun, and I know he wants to pull it. He wants Quentin's blood. He wants him dead.

But he wants me more.

'Where is he?' he says, raising the shotgun to his shoulder.

Quentin stares past the barrels at Cole, his eyes as steady as ever. 'I believe we've been though this before.'

'My brother – where is he?'

'Oh, your *brother*,' says Quentin. 'I'm sorry, I thought you meant John Selden. Are you not looking for Selden any more?'

This is it for Cole. This is enough. Enough games, enough words, enough holding back. Enough of everything. No more. It's time to finish it.

He says to Reason, 'Go downstairs and see if you can find out where Red went. I don't expect anyone knows, but ask them anyway. Let me know if you get anything – OK?'

Reason nods.

Cole looks at Jess. 'Go with him.'

'What about you?' she says. 'What are you going to do?'

Cole holds her gaze for a moment, then looks away without answering. She carries on staring at him for a while, then Reason takes her gently by the arm and guides her towards the door. As they leave the room, she glances back at Cole again – her eyes full of feelings I don't understand – and then she's gone, her footsteps fading down the stairs.

Cole feels nothing. As he backs across the room and locks the door – keeping the shotgun on Quentin – I can feel his heart turning black. He's emptying himself, voiding himself of everything, including me. And by the time he's walked back over and stopped in front of the desk, I can barely feel him at all.

Quentin just sits there, looking up at him, totally unmoved.

'You're not going to kill me,' he says, almost smiling.

'No,' Cole tells him. 'I'm not going to kill you. But you're going to wish that I had.'

The feelings died completely then. I floated with Cole for a few more moments, time enough to see him taking hold of the desk and pulling it away from Quentin, but I wasn't *with* him any more. I wasn't feeling anything. I was just floating, just looking down, just watching things happen. And then that died, too, and Cole was gone, and I wasn't floating any more, and I wasn't looking down – I was tied up in a rain-soaked barn, looking out through the cracked black walls at the headlights of a Transit van bursting into the yard outside.

Nineteen

I could hear the van lurching and skidding[1] across the yard, bouncing up and down in the rain-sodden mud, and I could see the glare of its headlights strobing[2] through the cracks in the barn wall, illuminating the loft in a blaze of flashing white lights, and just for a moment I was floating again ... floating back through the lights ... through the cracks in the wall ... out into the airless black air of the yard. And in that moment I could see everything. I could see Red in the windscreen of the Transit van – his grinning face, his grubby red suit, his wrong eyes glazed in mad concentration. I could see the headlights sweeping around the yard, lighting up flashes of static rain. I could see the barn, the outhouses, the mutant shack. Bins and boxes and empty sacks. I could see the storm-drenched moorland beyond the yard, the wind-whipped trees, the ash-black fields, the hills in the distance rising from a plain of darkness ...

And then suddenly the lights were gone and the barn was black again, and I was back in the flesh of my body, and my lungs were filled with the gaseous stink of decay. The smell was so thick I could taste it. It was vile[3], sickening, like a poisonous cloud in my belly. It was the smell of dead things, rotting things ... the smell of terrible dreams. I knew it didn't *mean* anything – it was only the stink of choking exhaust fumes and the churned-up mud[4] in the yard – but knowing that didn't make me feel any better. My belly wasn't rational.

I breathed steadily, trying to keep calm, but it didn't work. My stomach gave a sudden heave and I threw up all over myself.

The van pulled up outside the farmhouse. I couldn't see it, and it was hard to hear anything above the steady roar of the rain, but

1 skid: slide **2** strobe: (here) make a long beam of light **3** vile (infml): disgusting **4** churned-up mud: mud that has been heavily moved

my senses were pumped up with blind sight and fear, and I could hear what I needed to hear: the engine idling, the wind howling, the engine dying. The rain intensified for a moment, drowning out everything but the beat of my heart, and then a gust of wind swept over the yard and the rain slackened off again.

I closed my eyes and listened to the unseen sounds from the yard: a horn beeping, long and loud; the van door sliding open, slamming shut; another door opening – the farmhouse door – then voices calling out through the rain. Ugly voices, blunt and sour.

'Who's that?'

'Red. Where is he?'

'Uh?'

'The *kid,* chrissake. Henry wants the kid. Where is he?'

'In the barn.'

'Get out here. Bring some rope and a torch.'

For the next couple of minutes I just sat there in the darkness, listening to the sound of the falling rain – the roaring on the roof, the quiet drip-dripping on the dusty floor, the heavy splattering in the mud outside. It wasn't the same as listening to the rain at home. It didn't make me feel happy any more.

I wanted it to stop.

I wanted everything to stop: the noise, the fear, the stink, the pain, the sickening ache in my belly. I didn't want to feel anything any more. I didn't want to do anything. I didn't want to be here. I didn't want to be scared. I didn't want to be brave. I didn't want to be strong or weak or smart or stupid or precious or careless or dead ...

I didn't want to *be* anything.

I was exhausted.

Empty.

Cramped and cold.

My arms ached.

My eyes hurt.

I smelled bad – vomit and piss, the stink of my fear ...

They were coming now. I could hear them outside, trudging across the yard. Opening the barn door. Crossing the floor. Voices. A ladder rattling against the hatchway. The hatchway opening. The flash of a torch.

My insides were twitching like electric soup.

'Christ, you stink.'

I kept my eyes fixed firmly on the floor and said nothing. Red was standing over me, shining a torch in my face, and Sim and Vince were waiting in the shadows behind him. I wasn't going to look at them. I wasn't going to speak. I wasn't going to be anything.

'Hey,' said Red, jabbing me with his boot. 'What's the matter with you? Look at me.' He kicked me again. 'I said *look* at me.'

When I still didn't move, he leaned down and cracked me across the face with his torch. My head jerked back, and I felt a numbing shock in my jaw, but it didn't seem to hurt. I swallowed a trickle of blood and let my eyes roll back to the floor.

There was a knot-hole[1] in one of the floorboards – an odd little oval shape with intriguingly slanted sides – and that was my sanctuary[2]. That was where I was nothing. Deep in the hole. Lost in the dark. Being nothing. Riding the pain.

When Red grabbed my hair and slammed my head back against the post, I still didn't feel anything, but this time – when my head rolled back – I couldn't get back to my hole. Red was keeping hold of my hair, forcing my head back, shoving his face into mine. Making me look at him. I closed my eyes. I could feel his sour breath scouring[3] my skin.

'Open your eyes,' he hissed. 'Look at me.'

I imagined my hole. My sanctuary.

A flick-knife snapped. Cold steel pricked the skin of my eyelid.

'Open them or lose them,' Red said.

My sanctuary shimmered, the hole closed up, and I opened my eyes to Red's wired face. He was so close I could see myself in his

1 knot-hole: *Astloch* **2** sanctuary: place of safety **3** scour: rub demented eyes. I was distorted, convexed, like a looming face in the back of a silver spoon. I was monstrous.

Red breathed on me again, his breath like rotting silence. I closed my mouth and stared at myself in his eyes. My monster-self. My monster-face. My monster-eyes. Two new holes. My monster-sanctuary. I held it for a while, but then Red blinked and his grin twitched and I felt the knife blade stroking my cheek, and then suddenly everything was gone – the knife, the face, the monstered eyes – and I was watching Red as he moved away and straightened up, folding the flick-knife shut.

'That's better,' he said, still staring at me. 'When I tell you to look at me, you look at me – understand?'

I nodded.

'Answer me.'

'What?' I said.

'Answer me. Don't just nod your head – *answer* me.'

'Right ...'

'Yeah, right.' He leaned his head to one side and scratched his neck. He sniffed, wrinkling his nose, and I saw his eyes flick down at my legs. He sniffed again, shaking his head. 'You always piss yourself?'

'What?'

'You stink of piss. Every time I seen you, you stink of piss. Now you've gone and puked all over yourself too. What's the matter with you?'

It was one of those answerless questions again, a fear-sucker's question – *what are you looking at? what's your problem?* – and as I thought about it, my mind flashed back to the ring of stones and the stunted thorn tree, to Jess and Tripe and Skinny and Nate, and Red in his red suit, standing there smiling, just as he was now – nodding his head, twitching his shoulders, wiping his nose on the sleeve of his jacket, waiting for my reaction ...

I wondered what he'd say if I asked him why he did it. *What do you get out of it, Red? I mean, all this nasty stuff – the vicious*[1] *games, the taunts, the threats ... this dance of violence – why do you do it?*

But it was pointless asking. I knew why he did it. He did it for the same reason that any of us do anything. He did it because he liked it.

'D'you miss your daddy?' he sneered at me. 'Is that it? D'you piss yourself cos you miss your daddy?'

I didn't say anything.

He laughed – a thin little snigger. 'Shit,' he said, spitting on the floor. 'What d'you do for them Delaneys anyway? How d'you get them on your side?' He grinned his grin at me. 'You pay them? You get the girl a new *dog* or something? Is that it? Get a dawg for the dawg?' He drew back his lips and barked. His eyes were crazy. 'Dawg for a dawg,' he started hooting[2], 'dawg for a dawg, bitch for a bitch ...' Then suddenly he stopped, jerking his face at me, and his voice went cold. 'What d'you do?'

'Nothing,' I said.

He stepped closer, shining the torch into my face. I turned away and closed my eyes.

'Look at me,' he said.

I didn't move. I'd had enough.

'Open your *eyes*.'

I held my breath.

I heard the knife flicking open, and I could sense the blade inching towards my face, and I knew it was too late to do anything now. My eyes were staying closed whether I liked it or not. I shut myself down, getting ready to ride the pain, but as the tip of the blade touched my skin, and I reached out for the darkness inside my head, a voice from the shadows said, 'Come on, Red – this is stupid,' and suddenly everything went still.

The knife stopped moving.

Red sighed.

I pulled myself back from the darkness.

1 vicious: nasty **2** hoot: (here) howl like an animal

The voice was Vince's.

I kept my eyes closed and listened hard to the stillness.

'What?' said Red, his voice a bare whisper.

'There isn't time –'

'*What* did you say?'

'We haven't –'

'You calling me *stupid?'*

'No, I was just trying to –'

'What? You were just trying to *what?'*

Another short silence.

Then Sim spoke up. 'He's right, Red. We ought to get going. Get the kid out of here. If Henry wants –'

'I *know* what Henry wants.' Red's voice was calmer now, less manic. 'What d'you think I'm doing?'

'Yeah, I know,' said Vince. 'But if Ford finds out where we are –'

'He won't.'

'He might. And if he does –'

'What? You think I can't handle him? You think I'm running from a *gypsy?'*

'No –'

'I ain't running from *shit*.'

'No one's running from anything, Red – we're just taking care of business, that's all.'

Silence again. The torchlight was out of my face now. I raised my head slightly and half-opened my eyes. Red was standing with his back to me; the other two were facing him. Vince looked tired and worried. Sim had a length of rope in his hands. Vince glanced over at me. Our eyes met for a moment, but his face showed nothing. He turned back to Red again.

'If we don't go soon, the lane's going to be flooded. You know what it's like –'

'Yeah, all *right*,' Red said irritably. 'We're going – OK?' He sniffed hard and spat on the floor. 'Come on, then – what are you waiting for? Let's get the little shit out of here.'

As Sim got to work on the handcuffs again, hacking them off with his usual vigour, Vince stooped down beside me and looped the length of rope around my neck. I didn't try to stop him. I didn't do anything. I just stared at nothing and tried to think. It wasn't easy. I wanted to close my eyes and open my heart and float away to find Cole, but I knew that I couldn't. There wasn't time. Things were happening. Here and now. I had to be *here*. I had to be me.

I had to do something now ...

I had to *think*.

Think, look around, think: *Red's over there, on the other side of the barn, smoking a cigarette; Sim's behind you, still hacking your wrists to shreds; Vince is adjusting the rope round your neck, leaning in close to tighten the knot ...*

'Just keep your mouth shut and you'll be all right – OK?'

The whisper came from the back of his throat. It was so quiet I could barely hear it. I looked at him. His head was lowered in front of my face, his eyes fixed intently on the knotted rope.

'Don't do anything,' he breathed. 'You won't get hurt.'

'What?' I said, not bothering to whisper. 'You mean like Rachel didn't get hurt?'

Vince froze for an instant, then suddenly jerked the rope tight as Sim spoke up from behind us.

'What's he saying?'

'Nothing,' Vince said, standing up quickly. He glared at Sim. 'You ready yet?'

'Yeah, hold on.'

I felt a sharp tug on my wrists, then Sim grabbed my arms and pulled me up to my feet. Vince stepped back, uncoiled the rope, and gave it a spiteful yank. My head nearly jerked off my shoulders. I would have fallen over if Sim hadn't been holding me up. He spun me round and shoved me up against the wooden post.

'Put your hands behind your back,' he said.

I did as I was told, but as he let go of me and reached into his pocket for another pair of cuffs, my dead legs buckled and I slumped to the floor.

'Shit,' hissed Sim. 'What you doing? Get up.'

He kicked me in the ribs. I struggled up off the floor, got to my knees, but that was it – I couldn't get any further. My legs were numbed from sitting on the floor for hours.

'Get *up*,' Sim said, kicking me again.

'I can't,' I said. 'My legs –'

Sim kicked me down to the floor, then knelt on my back and grabbed my arms and snapped a new pair of cuffs on my wrists. He stood up, grabbed the rope round my neck, and yanked me up to my feet.

'Stay there,' he spat, pushing me against the post. 'You go down again and I'll stomp the shit out of you.'

He let go of me and stepped back. My legs started going again, and I saw his face tighten, but I managed to keep myself up by leaning back against the post and gripping it between my arms.

He stood there staring at me, breathing hard. I looked back at him – his dumb streaky hair, his dumb streaky eyes. There wasn't anything there. Vince was standing next to him, the rope in his hand, looking at me as if I was his dog and I'd just jumped up and bitten his hand.

I was still trying to be here. Still trying to do something. Still trying to think. But I still hadn't thought of anything.

Red was coming over now, walking tough, his cigarette gripped tightly between forefinger and thumb. He raised his hand and flicked the burning cigarette at me. It hit me in the chest and bounced to the floor in a hail of sparks.

'What's going on?' he said, stopping in front of me.

'Nothing,' Vince told him. 'He fell over.'

'His legs are gone,' Sim added. 'He can't walk. We were just –'

'Carry him,' said Red.

'What?'

Red stepped up and sank his fist into my belly. The pain groaned out of me and I sank to the floor in a heap.

'Carry him,' said Red.

They picked me up and carried me across to the hatchway. Vince was at my shoulders, Sim had hold of my legs. The rope was still attached to my neck. My belly was still moaning with pain. I didn't like the sounds I was making – sad little groans, like a dying animal – but I just couldn't help it. The pain was everywhere – tearing me apart, eating right down into me. Sim didn't like the sounds I was making, either. I could see the growing irritation in his face, and when we got to the hatchway and they dropped me to the floor, he let out his anger with a sharp little kick to my head.

'Christ,' he spat. 'Will you stop that bloody *moaning*.'

I swallowed the pain and lay still, staring up at the roof.

'Shit,' Sim muttered to himself.

Vince was keeping quiet, keeping out of it. He'd do what he had to do, but no more. No cruelty, no kindness. No guilt, no risk. No faith in himself. I hated him for that. I hated them all, of course, but at least Red and Sim were true to themselves. They didn't try to right their wrongs by feeding me crumbs of false pity – they just did what they did, and that was that. It wasn't much to be admired, but at least it was honest.

Red had opened the hatchway now and was climbing down the ladder, leaving Vince and Sim to work out how they were going to get me down. I rolled my head back and looked down through the hatchway. I could see some of the barn below, flickering in the glow of Red's torch – the dirt floor, the big double doors at the front, clouds of straw-dust drifting in the torchlight.

'You go down,' Sim said to Vince. 'I'll pass you the rope.'

Vince nodded. He passed the end of my leash to Sim, then stepped through the hatchway and started climbing down the ladder. Sim watched him go. The torchlight was fading now, so I guessed Red had moved away from the foot of the ladder. In the dimming light, Sim crouched down beside me and held his knife to my face. I looked at him. He twitched his neck, jerking his head like a lunatic bird.

'All alone now,' he whispered, 'Just you and me.'

'Great,' I said.

He grinned. 'You think Vince is going to help you?'

'Vince is full of shit.'

'You got that right.' He blinked hard, then tapped the flat of the knife blade against my nose. 'You scared?'

'What do you think?'

He grinned again, then gave me another tap with the knife and stood up as Vince called out from below.

'All right, Sim – you ready?'

Sim picked up the end of the rope and dropped it through the hatchway. 'You got it?' he called down.

'Yeah.'

Sim turned to me and nodded at the hatchway. 'Go on, then,' he said. 'Move yourself.'

I looked at him, waiting for him to take the cuffs off my wrists, but he didn't move.

'I can't climb down with my hands tied,' I said. 'I'll break my neck.'

'I'll break it for you if you don't.'

'Yeah, but –'

'Just *move*,' he snapped, kicking me in the leg. 'You want me to *throw* you down?'

I rolled over onto my front, then slithered around and lowered my legs through the hatchway. I somehow managed to get my feet on the ladder, but then I just hung there, half in and half out of the hatchway, too scared to go any further. I was going to fall. I knew it. My legs weren't numb any more, they were shaking. I had no hands. You can't climb down a ladder with shaking legs and no hands.

But Sim was standing over me now, nudging me with his foot, and I knew that if I didn't start moving he'd carry on kicking me until I did. So I just closed my eyes and pressed myself into the ladder and started climbing down. Very slowly, one step at a time, resting my chin against the rungs[1] ...

'Mind how you go,' Sim called down.

1 rung: step on a ladder

… leaning forward, feeling my way down, inch by inch, until finally I'd made it. My feet were on the ground. My neck was still in one piece. I'd done it.

I breathed out and leaned back, straightening the stiffness from my back, and just for a moment I felt so pleased with myself that I almost forgot about everything else. But then Vince gave the rope a hard yank, jerking me off my feet, and everything else came back again: the pain, the hate, the anger, the fear … my inability to think.

I was no closer to doing anything now than I had been ten minutes ago. I was still here. Things were still happening. Time was running out.

I had to do something.

I had to stop thinking and do something.

Look, don't think, just look around: *Red's over there, sitting on the wheel guard of the old Fordson tractor, idly shining the torch at the roof; Sim's coming down the ladder; Vince has got the rope in his hand, leading you across the barn towards Red. No one's watching you.*

Do something.

Now.

I started running towards Vince. I didn't know what I was doing, I just fixed my eyes on his back and ran at him like a madman. I had no idea what I was going to do when I got there – jump on him? bite him? kick him to death? – but it didn't matter anyway, because I never got near him. As soon as the rope went slack in his hands, he spun round and skipped to one side, tightening the rope as he moved, then he yanked down hard on it, jerking my head to my knees, and the next thing I knew I was sprawling on my face in the dirt.

I couldn't breathe for a moment, couldn't get any air into my lungs. I just lay there, shocked and breathless, dazed and useless …

I couldn't do it. I'd tried. But I just couldn't do it.

I couldn't do anything.

Someone was hauling me back to my feet now. I guessed it was Sim. He wrenched me up off the ground, then Vince started reeling me in[1], and the two of them shoved and dragged me across the barn towards Red and kicked me to the ground in front of him. As I slowly got to my knees, Red picked up the end of the rope and shone the torch in my face.

'Is that it?' he grinned. 'Is that the best you can do?'

I looked at him and shrugged. I was so tired of it all now. I just didn't care. Red carried on staring at me for a moment, then shook his head and turned to Vince. 'Bring the van up,' he told him. 'Leave the engine running.'

Vince hesitated. 'You want me to drive?'

'Did I say that?'

Vince frowned at him. 'I don't understand.'

Red sighed. 'Just bring the van up to the barn doors and leave it there, then go back to the house. D'you think you can manage that?'

Vince nodded silently, then turned round and walked away. As he opened one of the barn doors, the rain blasted in and the howl of the storm filled the air. A gust of wind caught the door, ripping it out of Vince's hand and slamming it back against the wall. Vince pulled up his collar and stepped out into the rain, and the door slammed shut behind him.

After a moment's silence, Sim said to Red, 'Vince is staying here then, is he?'

Red nodded. 'You both are.'

Sim looked surprised. 'I thought you said we were taking the kid to the Bridge?'

'Change of plan,' Red said simply, looking at me. 'I'm taking him somewhere else. Somewhere quieter.' He turned back to Sim. 'All right?'

'But Henry said –'

'Henry's not here, is he?' Red looked slowly at Sim. 'You're staying here. I'm taking the boy. You got a problem with that?'

1 reel sb. in (infml): pull sb. over

No one said anything for a while. We all just waited. Red was sitting there, idly flicking the knife open and shut … open and shut … open and shut. *Snick snick snick.* Sim couldn't look at him. He couldn't look at me, either. He just stood there leaning against the barn wall, staring moodily at the ground. I didn't know if he *did* have a problem with Red's change of plan, or if he was just pissed off because it didn't involve him. Not that it made any difference to me. Even if he didn't agree with what Red was doing, he wasn't going to do anything about it.

No … the problem was all mine.

And I couldn't see any way out of it.

Once I was in the back of the van, that was it. If I'd been going to the Bridge, I might have had a chance, but I wasn't going to the Bridge any more. I was going somewhere quieter. And that could only mean one thing: Red wanted me dead.

I didn't know if it was a personal thing – just something he wanted to do – or if he was simply being practical – tidying things up, getting rid of the evidence. I didn't know, and I didn't care. Reasons didn't matter. All that mattered was that Red was going to take me out on the moor somewhere, probably back to the stone circle, and I couldn't see any way back from there.

'What the hell's he doing?' Red said suddenly.

I could hear the van's engine whining and spluttering outside.

'Won't start,' Sim muttered. 'It's the rain.'

I listened harder, energised with a faint glimmer of hope. Vince let the motor rest for a moment, then tried it again. The engine whined and whirred, roared for a moment, nearly got going … then coughed and spluttered and died.

'Shit,' said Red.

But he needn't have worried. Sim was right – there was nothing wrong with the van. The engine was wet, that was all. I could tell by the sound. It was probably going to start next time …

Before I had time to think any more, I lunged at Red and kicked the knife from his hands. He was too shocked to move for a moment, and that was all I needed. I brought my head down into his face, felt his nose cracking, then butted him[1] again. The rope fell from his hands and I started for the door. Sim was after me in a flash, but I was running for my life now – he *couldn't* catch me. Even with my arms tied behind my back, he couldn't catch me. I was running faster than I'd ever run before. Fast and hard, pounding across the ground towards the door. Nothing could stop me. I was running so fast I was going to smash through the door without stopping – through the door, out into the yard, up the lane, away into the darkness ...

No one could stop me now.

No one ...

I was almost there ... the door was just a few metres away. I was already imagining myself crashing through it – the sudden cold rush of the rain and wind in my face, the squelch of the mud beneath my feet as I raced away across the yard ...

And then it all disappeared in a blur of shock as Sim caught up with me and hacked at my legs and bowled me down to the ground. I hit the dirt face-first again, rolled over a couple of times, and then Sim was jumping on my back and thumping me in the head.

I just about gave up on myself then. I didn't have anything left. I couldn't be me any more. There wasn't any point. As Sim's fists kept raining down on the back of my head, I closed my eyes and shut myself down. There was nowhere else to go. *Thump.* Nowhere. *Thump.* Nothing. *Thump.* Floating. *Thump.*

'Bring him over here.'

The voice was empty and distant, a long way away. I was floating now, not quite seeing myself, but vaguely aware that the thumping had stopped and I was being dragged across the floor again. Lifted to my feet again. Propped up against a wall.

'Hold him there.'

The voice was closer, but still just as empty.

I could see Red now. I could see both of us. I was pale and dead-looking, my head hanging down, nothing there. Red was standing in

1 butt sb.: strike sb. with your head

front of me, blood streaming from his broken nose, his wrong eyes crazed. Twitching like a madman.

The rain was screaming, the wind was shaking the barn. I could hear the van starting up in the yard, the engine roaring into life. I could feel Red spitting blood into my face. I could feel him pounding me in the belly again.

Thump.

'Hold him up.'

Thump.

It didn't hurt.

Thump.

I wasn't there. I was drifting over him, watching as he stooped down and picked up an old piston-rod[1] from the ground, watching as he hefted it in his hands, watching as he swung it back and aimed it at my head ...

A stillness came down.

Sound, silence, light, dark ... everything slowed to a moment of nothing. I was there, body and heart. Sim was there, his chicken eyes staring. Red was killing me. The piston-rod was coming down. I could hear its whisper in the silence. The rain had stopped. The wind had dropped. I could hear the Transit van rumbling across the yard ...

It didn't matter any more.

I wasn't going anywhere.

Red was killing me.

The piston-rod was coming down.

The van was getting closer, getting louder ... the engine roaring in the silence. I could see the headlights strobing through the cracks in the wall ...

It didn't matter any more ...

The piston-rod was coming down ...

It didn't matter.

But I could see the lights ...

1 piston-rod: *Kolbenstange*

Getting closer …

And I could feel the roar …

Getting louder …

And suddenly I knew what it was. The lights, the roar … it wasn't the Transit van. I knew what it was. I could feel it coming. I could *feel* it. I was floating again … following the lights, following the roar … following my heart as it carried me out into the cold black night. And now I could see everything. I could see the Transit van parked at the house, dark and still. I could see the lights of the petrol tanker hurtling down the lane and roaring into the yard. And I could see the devil's angel in the windscreen – his killing face, his hell-bent heart, his black eyes burning in the darkness.

I opened my eyes and smiled …

The roar thundered, the barn doors exploded, and the petrol tanker came crashing through in a blaze of screeching metal and steaming white light.

Twenty

The tanker was still moving as Cole flung open the door and threw himself out of the cab. The wheels were screeching to a halt, the brakes were hissing, and I could see Jess in the passenger seat, leaning over and grabbing the steering wheel, swinging the tanker away from Cole as he flew through the air and smashed into Red, slamming him down to the ground. The back of Red's head cracked dully in the dirt and the piston-rod flew from his hand, and then Cole was just pounding him, hammering his fist into his face – *bam, bam, bam* – like a man possessed.

Sim was still holding me up, too shocked to let go. He was staring wide-eyed at Cole, watching him beat the shit out of Red, and I knew he didn't want anything to do with it. He wanted to run. I could feel him twitching, getting ready to move, but then he realised that I was his only protection. If he let go of me and just ran, Cole might come after him. But if he took me with him …

He yanked me away from the wall and started backing away towards the barn doors, holding me in front of him. I was trying to stop him, trying to hold him back, trying to struggle free. And he was cursing me and dragging me and twisting my arms behind my back, and then – *BOOM!* – the blast of a shotgun rang out, and we both stopped dead in our tracks. I looked over and saw Jess walking towards us with a sawn-off shotgun in her hands.

'Let him go,' she told Sim.

He looked at her for a moment, then took his hands off me.

'Move away,' she told him, gesturing with the gun. 'Over there. Turn round and face the wall.'

'I wasn't—' he started to say.

'Shut up. Move.'

He walked over to the wall and slowly turned round.

'Put your hands on your head,' Jess told him.

She watched him raise his hands and place them on top of his head, then she slipped a penknife from her pocket and came over to me. I turned round and held out my hands. She gently cut the cuffs off my wrists, then steadied me as I turned to face her.

'Are you OK?' she said, loosening the rope and lifting it carefully over my head.

I nodded.

We both looked over at Cole. The sudden blast of the shotgun had broken into his void, and he was just sitting there now – crouched over Red, breathing hard, staring into the battered face beneath him. Red wasn't moving. His eyes were closed and his face was a mess. I kept my eyes on him until I saw his chest rise and fall, then I turned my attention to Cole. His bandaged hand was red with blood, and his heart was black and empty. I couldn't feel anything. He was gone, somewhere else, beyond feeling.

'Cole?' I said softly.

His head turned, but he didn't seem to recognise me. His glazed eyes focused on the gun in Jess's hand.

'Give it to me,' he told her, his voice a dead-cold whisper. 'Give me the gun.'

Jess looked hesitantly at me. For a fraction of a second I was tempted to tell her to give it to him. *Why not?* I thought. *Just shoot the bastard. Put him out of his misery.*

Why not?

I gazed back at Jess for a moment, then I looked back over at Cole. He was staring at Red again now, gazing blindly into his bloodied face, his eyes as empty as two black holes.

Why not? I didn't *know* why not, all I knew was what I felt.

'Come on, Cole,' I said quietly. 'Let's go.'

His head turned again, and this time he saw me.

'Ruben?' he said.

I smiled at him.

He glanced at Jess, blinked lazily, then looked back at me again. 'Are you all right?'

'Yeah,' I said. 'How about you?'

'I'm OK.' He blinked again. 'What's going on?'

'We've got to get out of here,' I told him.

He didn't move for a moment, just sat there staring at me. Then all at once something seemed to lift from his face, like an invisible shroud, and he just nodded his head and got to his feet and walked away from Red without so much as a glance.

I didn't know what to make of it, and I didn't care. Cole was alive. He was here. He was crossing the barn towards me. Nothing else mattered.

'Here,' said Jess, nudging me in the arm and passing me a white silk scarf. 'You're bleeding.'

I looked at her. She was covering Sim with the sawn-off shotgun. I looked down at my hands. My wrists were red with blood from Sim's clumsy hacking.

'Thanks,' I said, taking the scarf from her.

As I started cleaning the blood from my wrists, Cole came up and stopped in front me. We stared at each other for a second or two, making sure we were both still there, then Cole reached out gently and cradled my face in his bloodstained hand.

'Christ, Ruben,' he whispered, 'look at you ...'

I could feel the tears burning my eyes.

'You don't look so great yourself,' I said, trying to smile at Cole's beaten-up face.

'It shouldn't have happened,' he muttered sadly. 'Not to you. It shouldn't have happened ...'

I couldn't say anything. I just looked at him – my brother.

He was my *brother*.

I think we could have stayed there for ever, just being together without any words, but when the silence was suddenly broken by the sound of the Transit van turning around in the yard, we both came back to our senses and rejoined the rest of the world.

'It's Vince,' I said quickly, looking out through the hole in the barn wall where the tanker had crashed through the doors. 'I forgot about him. He's in the van.' The Transit was racing out of the yard now, heading towards the lane. I turned to Cole, expecting him to do something, but he didn't seem to care. He just watched the van as it screamed away up the lane, crunching wildly through the gears, then he looked down at me and smiled.

'You ready to go?' he said.

'What about Vince?'

'What about him?'

'He's getting away ...'

'Let him go,' Cole shrugged. 'He's nothing.' He turned to Jess. 'You OK?'

She smiled at him. He smiled back at her, then glanced over her shoulder at Sim. He was still standing against the wall with his hands on his head, but he'd turned his neck slightly to see what was going on. When he saw Cole looking at him, he quickly turned back to the wall.

Cole said to Jess, 'Get the tanker started.'

She nodded at him, then came over to me, took me by the arm and started leading me over to the tanker. I glanced over my shoulder. Cole was walking up behind Sim. I could hear Sim talking to him, his voice in a panic, but Cole wasn't listening. He stepped up and flat-handed him hard in the back of his head, slamming his face into the wall. Timber cracked and Sim went down without a sound, dropping to the floor like a bag of cement. Cole looked down at him for a second, then went over to Red.

Red hadn't moved. He was still splayed out on the ground, his body limp, his mouth hanging open, his swollen eyes shut. It didn't look as if he'd be moving for a long time. I was half-expecting Cole to give him a final whack in the head or something, but he didn't. He just looked at him for a moment, his face blank, then he turned round and started following Jess and me across the barn to the petrol tanker.

Jess had let go of my arm now. We'd reached the tanker and she was clambering up to the cab to open the door on the driver's side. Steam was rising from the heat of the engine, and the air was thick with petrol fumes. I could smell the fetid stench of the mud again, too – only now it seemed even worse. Like the stink of a dead animal. I looked up at the tanker. It was a wreck: old, rusty, scratched and dented[1], its greasy white paintwork spattered with mud.

Jess opened the door and laid the shotgun on the seat, then she turned round and called down to me.

'Wait there, Ruben,' she said. 'I'm just going to –'

She stopped abruptly, her eyes suddenly drawn to something behind me. I turned round to see a figure emerging from around the other side of the cab, pointing a rifle at Jess. It took me a moment to realise it was Abbie. Her face had aged, the life drained out of it. Her skin was empty and grey, her eyes unfocused, her movements stiff and cold.

'Get down,' she told Jess. 'Leave the gun in the cab.' Her voice was flat and dull, almost trance-like. 'Down,' she repeated. 'Now.'

Jess moved slowly, backing down the steps of the cab, keeping her eyes fixed steadily on Abbie.

'It's all right,' Jess said calmly, showing her hands. 'I'm not going to do anything.' She flicked a quick glance at the rifle. Abbie's finger was resting on the trigger. Jess smiled at her. 'Why don't you put that down? We've got a tanker full of petrol here –'

'Shut up,' Abbie said, gripping the rifle tighter. She blinked a couple of times, looking around the barn, then her eyes suddenly fixed on Cole. As he walked up quietly and stopped beside us, Abbie levelled the rifle at him.

'Stay there,' she said.

Cole just looked at her.

'Don't move,' she told him.

He stared at her. 'What do you want?'

'It wasn't Vince's fault ...' she muttered. 'He didn't mean anything ... it was a mistake –'

'No, it wasn't,' Cole said. 'You know that.'

She shook her head. 'He didn't mean any harm.'

1 dented: with many bumps

'He gave you up. He used you. He got Rachel killed. He kept my brother tied up like a dog –'

'No,' Abbie whispered, beginning to cry, 'that wasn't him –'

'– and now he's run out on you. You don't owe him anything.'

'He's my husband,' she said, trembling with tears. 'He's all I've got …' She lowered her eyes for a moment, lost in her sadness, then she sniffed back her tears and lifted her head again, jerking the rifle at Cole. 'You're not taking him away from me,' she said. 'I can't let you do that.'

'I'm not taking him anywhere,' Cole told her. 'He's already gone.'

She shook her head. 'You'll talk to the police. You'll tell them what he did. They'll take him away. I can't let you do that.'

Cole looked at her, and I could feel him struggling to understand himself. He hated her, despised her, reviled[1] her … he didn't want to feel anything but disgust for her. But he did. He couldn't help it. Despite all her faults – her cowardice, her selfishness, her self-delusion – she was doing something for someone she loved. And that meant something to Cole.

'I'll talk to him,' he said to her.

'Who?'

'Vince.' He looked over her shoulder, nodding towards the lane. 'He's coming back, look.'

As Abbie's eyes lit up and she turned to look at the lane, Cole stepped forward and snatched the rifle from her hands. Realising she'd been tricked, she spun round and lunged at him, clawing wildly at his eyes, but before she could reach him, Jess stepped up and grabbed her from behind and quickly pulled her away. As she struggled and screamed, spitting and cursing like a crazy woman, Cole unloaded the gun, threw away the round[2], then raised the rifle over his head and smashed it into the ground.

Abbie's screams had turned to sobs now. Her madness had burned itself out. She was slumped in Jess's arms, her head bowed down, her body heaving with moans and tears.

1 revile sb.: dislike sb. strongly **2** round: ammunition

'We'd better get her back to the house,' Cole said to Jess.

Jess looked at him, quietly surprised at his concern. 'Do you think that's a good idea? I mean, we shouldn't hang around here much longer.'

'She needs help,' he said simply, stepping up and taking Abbie's arm. 'Come on, I'll give you a hand.'

I followed them out of the barn and across the yard to the house. Abbie wasn't crying any more ... she wasn't *anything* any more. Her face was blank and her eyes were white and she didn't seem to know where she was going. I don't think she cared, either. If Cole and Jess hadn't been there, guiding her along by her arms, I think she would have wandered off into the moorland night and carried on walking for ever.

We got her inside the house and took her into the front room. While Jess helped her over to the settee and covered her up with a blanket, Cole went over to a cupboard by the phone and started searching through the drawers.

'What are you looking for?' I asked him.

'Her mother-in-law's phone number.'

'Why?'

'Who else is going to look after her?'

I watched him rummaging through the drawers, leafing through address books and odd scraps of paper – cool and calm and steady – and I knew he wasn't struggling any more. He'd given up trying to understand himself. Something was telling him to do what he was doing, and that was enough for him. He didn't need to know why.

I glanced over at Jess. She was watching Cole, too. Her eyes were still, seeing nothing but him, and I could feel the silent contentment inside her. She was *with* him now, feeling what he was feeling, and as he flipped through the pages of a small tattered notebook and found the number he was looking for, she could sense his uncertainty.

'Do you want me to do it?' she asked him.

He looked at her.

She smiled at him, then came over and picked up the phone. 'What's the number?'

Cole showed her the notebook and she dialled the number. It was late now – the early hours of Monday morning – and the phone rang for a long time before it was answered.

'Mrs Gorman?' Jess said eventually. 'Sorry to wake you. I'm at your daughter-in-law's house. Vince isn't here and Abbie needs someone to look after her ... no, she isn't hurt, but she shouldn't be on her own right now.' She stopped talking and listened for a moment, and I could hear a distant voice barking out questions down the phone – *Who are you? What's the matter? What's going on?* Jess said nothing. She looked at Cole, he nodded quietly, and she put the phone down.

She smiled at Cole again. 'All right?'

He nodded. 'Thanks.'

They gazed at each other for a second or two, and as I watched them I could feel all the stuff I'd felt before – the good stuff, the tingling stuff, the stuff that didn't feel right to share – only now it felt different. It was deeper now. More than I could understand.

Cole looked over at Abbie. She was still lying on the settee, not moving, just staring blindly at the ceiling. Her lips were fluttering, but she wasn't making a sound.

Cole turned back to Jess. 'Do you think she'll be all right on her own for a while?'

Jess shrugged. 'I don't think there's much else we can do for her.' She looked at Cole. 'What about the others in the barn?'

'What about them?'

'Maybe we should call an ambulance?'

Cole looked puzzled. 'Why?'

Jess shrugged again.

Cole looked at her for a moment, then he dropped the notebook back in the drawer and started moving towards the door. 'Come on,' he said, 'let's get out of here.'

I didn't notice the smell inside the tanker cab until we were halfway up the lane. Cole was driving, Jess was in the passenger seat, and I was sitting on a narrow little armrest between them. The rain had stopped and Cole had his window open, letting in a cold draught of stormy air, but the stench was so thick that the breeze didn't make any difference. The smell clung to everything. I thought it was me at first – my filthy clothes, my blood and sweat – but it didn't seem to be coming from me. It smelled like the mud from the yard – rotten, sick, gaseous, nauseating. I started sniffing and looking around – at Cole's shoes, Jess's shoes, my shoes, the floor of the cab – but I couldn't see anything. I was beginning to feel something, though. It was the memory of a dream – a dream of death. A feeling of skin and blood and purpled hands ... of cold earth and crawling things. A dream of a dead man dreaming of me ...

I could feel him.

He was here.

I could smell him.

I couldn't breathe now. I couldn't move. I didn't *want* to move. But slowly my head began to turn, and then my shoulders, and as I leaned back and looked behind the seat, my skin went cold and the air in my throat turned to ice. There he was: the Dead Man.

'Shit,' I whispered. '*Shit.*'

He was wrapped up tightly in binliners[1] and tape, entombed in a roll of old carpet. The carpet was damp, caked with patches of thick dark soil. Small pink worms were wriggling in the soil, some of them white with rain, and the yellowed tape on the binliners was dotted with hundreds of tiny black flies.

I turned away, gagging[2] slightly, and stared at Cole.

'Sorry,' he said. 'I forgot to tell you.'

'You *forgot*?'

He nodded, keeping his eyes on the road. We'd turned off the lane now and were heading towards the village.

'Shit,' I muttered again.

Cole looked at me, but didn't say anything. He glanced briefly at Jess, then turned back to the road and carried on driving, his battered hands effortlessly working the tanker's heavy steering wheel. I turned away from him and gazed out through the windscreen. Away

1 binliner: rubbish bag **2** gag: (here) nearly be sick

in the distance, the dark horizon was beginning to glow with the first faint light of day. The sun was rising, reddening the sky, and as I looked out over the dawning moor I could see that nothing had changed – the desolate fields, the bone-white grasses, the hills and the forests and the distant tors ...

It was all still there.

Still empty. Still dead.

'It's what we came for,' Cole said.

I looked at him. 'What?'

'The body ... it's what we came for.'

'I know.'

'It's only a body.'

'I know.'

'We can go home now. We can bring Rachel home.'

'Yeah, I *know*.'

'So what's bothering you?'

I didn't know what to say. I didn't *know* what was bothering me. Cole was right – he was right about everything. We'd set out to find the Dead Man, and now we'd found him. Now we could go home. Now we could bring Rachel home.

Did it matter how Cole had found Selden's body? Or where? Did it matter how he'd got Quentin to tell him? Did it matter where Quentin was now?

I looked through the windscreen again. We were entering the village, passing the ancient stone house where so much had happened, so much I didn't know about. The driveway was empty, the lights were all out. The house was dark and silent.

Did any of it matter?

I looked at Cole. He was exhausted – his face drained, his eyes heavy, his body weighed down with pain.

'Is it over now?' I asked him.

'Yeah,' he said quietly, 'it's over.'

I smiled to myself and settled back in the seat. I knew it wasn't over, and I knew it never would be. There were still things to do, things to take care of, and home was still a long way away. Everything was a long way away – where we'd been, where we were, where we were going.

It was a long road.

But we were on it together.

And that was enough for me.

As we drove off into the blood-red dawn, and the hills behind us faded into the crimson sky, I closed my eyes and said goodbye to Rachel's ghost, then I closed my mind and let myself drift away.

ADDITIONAL MATERIAL

1. The gypsies and travellers of Britain

Gypsies and travellers are people who belong to ethnic groups that used to lead and in some cases still do lead a nomadic lifestyle.

The term 'gypsy' refers to a Romani ethnic group whose ancestors migrated from India to Europe from the 10th century onwards and there mixed with different people. 'Travellers' is often used to mean Romanis but can be used to refer to English people who live a nomadic lifestyle.

Living in Britain, gypsies, of course, speak English and have adapted to the British culture but they still have their own language and customs, which they keep alive and pass on down the generations. There are between 50,000 and 300,000 gypsies in Britain. There are no official statistics for gypsies in the UK, and it is unknown how many migrants from the Balkans are actually gypsies, hence the rough estimation.

Family and children are very important for travellers. Looking after and caring for each other, even for members of extended families, is typical for their culture. Older family members are much respected and their opinion and advice is valued.

In the past gypsies traditionally travelled around using caravans and horses, but now they usually live in mobile trailers and motorized caravans. As nomadic people, they tend to look for flexible jobs, e.g. doing seasonal work, making and selling goods and attending fairs. But travelling around has led to difficulties, too. Continuous schooling for children is difficult for people on the move and when they do attend school, they are often regarded with suspicion, prejudice and hostility.

The question where to stay became a problem in the late 20th century, as Britain became a modern state in which people's lives were regulated by laws covering all aspects of life. With most land being privately or communally owned, gypsies found it difficult to stay where they wanted. Their presence was not desired by the local people, and they had to deal with racism, verbal abuse or physical assault. Staying without permission on land that was not theirs meant they could easily be driven off by the police. There are now, however, authorized sites for gypsy caravans but there is often fear that the existence of a gypsy site may lead to increased crime in the area. The media is very quick at reporting criminal activity and thus reinforces the general prejudice that gypsies are anti-social and criminal.

While some gypsies do still travel around the country, others have decided to live permanently on caravan sites, while others have decided to give up their nomadic lifestyle and settle in permanent housing.

2. I couldn't do everything, could I?

I sat down, cross-legged[1], on the very edge of the roof.

In the darkness below, Crow Town was getting ready for the night. Groups of kids were hanging around – on street corners, in the shadows of the towers, at the side of the road – and others were cruising the estate in cars or on bikes. Faint sounds drifted up into the night – shouting, dogs barking, cars, music – but up here, high above the rest of the world, everything was quiet.

I gazed up into the starless night, and all I could see was a boundless[2] world of darkness and emptiness ... but I knew it wasn't empty. The sky, the atmosphere, the air, the night ... the whole world was alive with radio waves. They were everywhere, all around me, all the time – TV signals, radio signals, mobile-phone signals ... WiFi, microwaves, VHF[3], UHF[4] ... electromagnetic waves.

They were everywhere.

And although I couldn't see them, I could sense them. I could connect to them. I knew them.

I closed my eyes and tuned in, at random, to a mobile-phone call: ... it's just past the post office in the High Street, someone was saying. You go past the post office and there's a pub, and it's just there.

1 cross-legged: *im Schneidersitz* **2** boundless: infinite; with no end **3** VHF: very high frequency (used for radio) **4** UHF: ultra-high frequency (used for TV)

What pub? someone else said. The George?

No, that's on the other side of the road ...

And another random conversation: ... why not? You said it'd be all right if I didn't do it again.

Yeah, I know, but you did ...

And another: ... *take the fucker down, innit*[1]*? He can't fucking do that, I'll fucking pop*[2] *the fucker ...*

Someone, somewhere, was sending an email to someone called Sheila, telling her that unless she sorted herself out, she wouldn't be seeing her baby again. Someone else was emailing someone in Coventry from a supposedly untraceable[3] email address ... but I could trace it. *the bio*[4] *is easy, it read. anyone can make a germ*[5] *bottle and drop it in the water supply and kill 100000. the martyr would commit*[6] *himself leaving no trace of j involvement.*

And someone else was texting a really obnoxious[7] message to a girl called Andrea, saying all kinds of nasty things to her ...

And on the web ... God, there was a whole *world* on the web. A world of so many things – good things, bad things, dull things, mad things – it was just like the real world. Just as wonderful, just as beautiful ... but also just as vile and sick and heart-breaking.

I stopped scanning.

There was too much going on out there, too much bad stuff, and I didn't know how to cope with it all. All the stuff I knew, but didn't *want* to know ... everything that wasn't good, that wasn't right, that wasn't fair ... I knew it. And I *knew* that I could do something about it ... or, at least, I *could* do something about *some* of it. I mean, for example, I could find out who'd sent that obnoxious text message to Andrea, and why they'd sent it, and I *could* find out where they lived, and I *could* go and see them and try to persuade them that sending obnoxious text messages is a really shitty thing to do. But then what about the millions of other bad things, the things that are a

1 innit (sl): isn't it **2** pop sb. (infml.): kill sb. **3** untraceable: unable to be found **4** bio: biology **5** germ: seed; microorganism **6** commit yourself: (here) kill yourself **7** obnoxious: horrible

million times worse than sending shitty text messages – the abuses, the terrors, the sick things that people do to each other – the things that I wouldn't be able to do anything about because I'd be too busy trying to help Andrea, like terrorist plots to kill 100,000 people with a biological weapon ...?

What was I supposed to do about them?

I couldn't do *everything*, could I?

I wasn't God.

I was just a kid ...

(From: Kevin Brooks, iBoy, *2010)*

The Author

Best known for his novels *Lucas* (winner of the North East Book Award 2004), *Martyn Pig* (winner of the Branford Boase Award 2003) and *iBoy* (winner of the North East Book Award 2004), Kevin Brooks grew up in Exeter, England and studied Psychology and Philosophy at Birmingham, Aston University in 1980 and Cultural Studies in London in 1983. He has had a variety of jobs including: musician, gasoline station attendant, crematorium handyman, civil service clerk, hot dog vendor at the London Zoo, post office clerk, and railway ticket office clerk.